Mixed Race Students in College

SUNY series, Frontiers in Education

Philip G. Altbach, editor

MIXED RACE STUDENTS
IN COLLEGE

The Ecology of Race, Identity,
and Community on Campus

Kristen A. Renn

STATE UNIVERSITY OF NEW YORK PRESS

Published by

STATE UNIVERSITY OF NEW YORK PRESS, ALBANY

© 2004 State University of New York

For information, address
State University of New York Press,
90 State Street, Suite 700, Albany, NY 12207

Production, Laurie Searl
Marketing, Anne M. Valentine

Library of Congress Cataloging-in-Publication Data

Renn, Kristen A.
  Mixed race students in college : the ecology of race, identity, and community on campus /
Kristen A. Renn.
    p. cm. — (SUNY series, frontiers in education)
  Includes bibliographical references and index.
  ISBN 0-7914-6163-7 (alk. paper) — ISBN 0-7914-6164-5 (pbk. : alk. paper)
    1. College students—United States—Attitudes. 2. College environment—United States. 3.
Racially mixed people— United States. 4. Race awareness—United States. 5. Education,
Higher—Social aspects—United States. 6. Educational surveys—United States. 7. United
States—Race relations. I. Title. II. Series.

LA229.R45 2004
378.1'9829'073—dc22
                                                                                        2004045290

10   9   8   7   6   5   4   3   2   1

To N.T., R.L., J.S., and E.L.,

who were there at the beginning.

CHECK IT,
OR THE ANGRY MUTT'S MANIFESTO

Jason Sperber

Don't tell me that everybody fits into neat little categories.
       Don't say that to me, cause I don't buy it, won't ever,
I know better.

Don't tell me that how you look is who you are
       That what others think is always truth
Don't tell me lies like that.
       Eyes don't know everything yet.

Don't tell me that you can define me, outline my life from
       someplace away from me cause
you think you know who I am.
       You don't. Can't if you don't try.

Don't tell me to check off one little box on some damn piece
       of paper to tell you who I am.
Won't fit in one box.
       Cause you don't think enough.
Not enough boxes.

Don't tell me that, don't even try.
       You tell me to check one little box?
Check this!

Why don't I make the boxes?
       Let's put you in one. Try it on for size, see.
Make my own box that never closes.
       Then I'll check it, see.

Contents

Preface

I had the unusual opportunity to be working at a university that attracted some of the nation's most gifted undergraduates while I was in my doctoral program at another fine university. One of my responsibilities was to direct a women's residential peer counseling program, which placed upper-class students as advisors in first-year student living areas. At one winter retreat, we took up the topic of the so-called Wall of Shame that had become a matter of intense campus scrutiny the previous semester. The incident revolved around the posting in the university's African American studies interest housing unit of a list of names of black men who were dating white women on campus; the list was posted in plain view on a black female student's door. Controversy within the black community spilled into the community of students of color, women's communities, and the queer student community as issues of race, identity, racism, sexism, and heterosexism were brought into the debate.

At the retreat for women peer counselors, we were discussing the situation and its fallout with an eye toward helping first-year students of all identities learn what they could from the incident about individual rights, community standards, and identity politics. During the retreat, one woman asked the other peer counselors how many of *them* would consider marrying or partnering outside their race. Of the thirty-six women present, a racially and ethnically diverse group, all but two said they would. Those two were a black woman and a white Jewish woman; the two spoke eloquently and vehemently about their desire to raise children in a culturally congruent household, passing on identity pride and cultural knowledge to them. The group was respectful, attentive, quiet.

And then someone broke the quiet—one of the student coordinators of the group, a woman well respected for her leadership in the black women's community on campus. "I understand why that's important to you. I really do. And when you talk about why it's so important to you to have children who are 'whole' black or 'whole' Jewish, you need to know that I'm not. My father is black, and my mother is white. This is *my family* we're talking about here."

I remember the women's peer counselor retreat as a rare moment in my professional life as a dean, when I was aware of the privilege of being in the presence of a genuine community of learners. I also remember it as the genesis of my strongest research interest. From the ensuing conversation grew my interest in learning more about the experiences of students who, like the woman who broke the silence, live as mixed race individuals on campuses where monoraciality is the norm and race is highly salient.

This book is the result of research that continued for several years after the retreat. In it I attempt to present the voices of fifty-six mixed race students from six campuses, arrayed across five patterns of mixed race identity. I do not imagine or pretend that these students represent the full range of experiences of mixed race students in the United States, but I do believe that their stories have much to tell us about living in, on, and between the borders of the highly racialized landscape of modern higher education.

I write elsewhere (Renn, forthcoming) about my concerns with reifying racial categories by doing work on "mixed race." Indeed, it seems a paradox to argue against the validity of racial categories using the terms *multiracial* and *mixed race*, but that is what I attempt to do. I attempt to illustrate through the experiences of mixed race college students the futility of insisting on the permanence and stability of artificial racial constructions. One way in which I attempt to challenge the easy acceptance of racial categories is through linguistic choices. Throughout the book, I use the words *biracial, multiracial, mixed race*, and *multiple heritage* interchangeably. In an attempt to create parity between mono- and multiracial descriptors, I have decided not to capitalize the names of racial categories (i.e., black, white, asian, latino) except when a word relates specifically to a nation of origin (e.g., Samoan, Chinese, Hungarian). There is no general agreement in the multiracial literature as to terminology or conventions of capitalizing racial designators; my choices represent my interest in minimizing racial categories as immutable entities without being distractingly disruptive to the reader. When I quote from another source (including student writing), I use the original capitalization.

This book would not have come about without substantial participation, assistance, and support on the part of others. My intellectual and professional mentors Karen Arnold, Philip Altbach, and Polly Ulichny were critical in my original thinking about this project and in the many years since it began. I am especially grateful to Philip for his encouragement and assistance in getting the project into print in book form and to Priscilla Ross and Laurie Searl of the State University of New York Press for embracing the project and sheparding me through the publication process. Student affairs colleagues, including Robin Rose, Kisa Takesue, Kevin Duffy, Bob Sherwood, Sue Alexander, Jack Kuszaj, Larry Dietz, Larry Chapman, and Nikki O'Brien, who facilitated access to students on their respective campuses, have been an essential link for me between higher education research and practice. An AERA/Spencer Doctoral Research Fellowship supported Phase II of the study, and a Faculty Research Grant from Southern Illinois University partially supported Phase III.

Faculty colleagues, those at my present and former institutions and those around the country, have been enormously supportive of my scholarship in this area, asking important questions and pressing me to think in new ways about race and identity; Kathy Hytten, Anna Ortiz, Patrick Dilley, Ana Martínez Alemán, Susan Pliner, and Kendra Wallace deserve special acknowledgment. Kerry Ann Rockquemore assisted me with technical questions about data she and David Brunsma present in their book about biracial identity. Jason Sperber granted permission to include his poem "Check It" in the book. Two research assistants, Christine Pereira and Christy Lunceford, contributed to the later processes of this project. Their identities as mixed race women in higher education provided important perspectives; their good humor and hard work were equally important to the success of this research. Other graduate students who have helped me to consider issues of identity include Brent Bilodeau, Jane Pizzolato, and Connie Tingson. Three anonymous reviewers of the manuscript provided additional criticism and insight. Of course, the interpretations and presentation of this study are mine, and any fault to be found rests with me and not with anyone whose contributions are acknowledged here.

My family has learned to live with me and The Mixed Race Study since its inception. They have supported and encouraged me, helping me to keep a healthy outlook on the process. My partner, Melissa, has lived in particularly close proximity to this project for many years; I am deeply grateful for her commitment and support, patience and perspective, insights and insightful questions.

Finally, the fifty-six students who participated in this project deserve special acknowledgment for sharing their experiences and identities with me and, by extension, with unknown readers. I was and am constantly aware of the trust they placed in me to treat them and their stories with integrity and respect. I hope that they will find that their faith was well placed and that other mixed race college students will see something of themselves reflected in the book.

chapter one

The Context of Mixed Race Students in American Higher Education

It's kind of an odd thing, really, because it's not like I'm one or the other, or like I fit here or there, but I kind of also fit everywhere. And nowhere. All at once. You know?

—Florence

IN OCTOBER 1997, the United States Office of Management and Budget (OMB) issued revisions to its Directive 15, changing the federal racial identification process to expand the number of racial categories and to include the option for respondents to indicate more than one category (OMB, 1997). The 2000 census marked the first time in U.S. history that individuals had the option to self-identify in more than one of five designated racial categories (American Indian or Alaska Native, Asian, Black or African American, Native Hawaiian or Other Pacific Islander, White) in addition to indicating Hispanic or Latino ethnicity (see appendix A for more detailed information on OMB categories). Of all census 2000 respondents, 2.7 percent indicated more than one racial category; while these respondents represent a small minority of the total population, it is important for higher education that *4.0 percent of those under age eighteen and 7.7 percent of those under age eighteen reporting Hispanic or Latino ethnicity* indicated more than one category (U.S. Census Bureau, 2001).

In the next two decades, the population eligible to enter postsecondary education will shift noticeably away from a monoracial norm to a more racially mixed cultural context. Mixed race students, who in 2000 represented a very small fraction of the student body, will be about as common in 2020 as asian undergraduates were in 2000 (National Center for Education

Statistics, 2001). To be sure, the distribution of mixed students will not be even across geography and regional cultures, but they will be a significantly stronger presence on campus than they have ever been.

Do these students bring experiences, interests, and needs different from those of monoracial white students or students of color? Will curricula, policies, programs, and services designed under the assumption of racially distinct student identities satisfy the learning and personal development objectives of mixed race students? And how will campus peer cultures, known to be critical factors in student learning and development change and be changed by these students?

The answers to these questions would be important even if mixed race students remained a small fraction of the student body; better understanding the experiences and needs of students from diverse backgrounds is an important prerequisite for planning and creating campus environments that maximize student learning and development. But the outcome of the 2000 census lends urgency to the task of learning about the experiences and identities of mixed race students, who will comprise an increasing percentage of the undergraduate population. Little is known about how they negotiate the racialized landscape of higher education and how that landscape will be altered by the imminent influx of students who do not identify in only one racial category. If indeed a growing portion of the student population in the next two decades will have more than one racial heritage, then postsecondary educators, administrators, and policy makers must begin now to learn about mixed race students' experiences in order to plan effectively for this demographic—and cultural—shift.

Concerned about preparing for this shift, I conducted a study of mixed race college students with the goal of learning more about how they identified, what those identities meant to them, and what they might mean for higher education policy and practice. In this book I describe the findings of a study of fifty-six mixed race students at six colleges and universities, positing five identity patterns exhibited by the participants. I utilize a developmental ecology framework to understand students' experiences in the context of campus peer culture, as well as in the context of individual background, experiences, and personal traits. I suggest that the findings could have bearing on policy, practice, theory, and research.

To set the stage for interpreting study findings, in this chapter I situate the study in the literature on race, mixed race, and racial identity development. In chapter 2, I provide a description of the developmental ecology model used to analyze data and a description of the research design. Readers who are most interested in the identity patterns and student experiences are encouraged to go directly to chapter 3 and proceed from there through the five identity patterns. Those readers interested in a deeper understanding of the scholarly context, the analytic framework, and the research design will find chapters 1 and 2 useful in contextualizing the presentation of identity patterns and student voices.

gay men who do queer theory (Shrage, 1995). Work from women's studies and queer studies informs theories of how compulsory heterosexuality (Rich, 1986) constructs and reproduces racial boundaries. Cerulo (1997, pp. 387–88) summarized additional work in these areas.

Race, gender, and sexuality form an "unstable triad" in which "shifts in one create disturbances in the other two" (Allman, 1996, p. 279). According to Allman, the "cult of true womanhood" in late nineteenth-century America created an image of white female purity that needed to be defended against the ravages of black men, and thus rich, white male identity was based in part on providing that protection. Racial group membership requires women to relinquish their sexuality to the men of that group in a sort of "sexual pledge of allegiance" (Twine, 1996, p. 303). Because women's bodies are the sites of racial reproduction, Streeter (1996) considered biracial black-white women the "symbolically charged gatekeepers" of the boundary between whiteness and blackness. Root (1997) proposed, "Race and gender co-construct each other in this country" (p. 157), and Rockquemore (2002) examined the specific co-construction of race and gender identities in biracial black-white women. Race, gender, and sexuality reinforce and re-create one another, and people on the margins of each category have unique perspectives from which to observe the process.

THE STUDY OF MULTIRACIALITY

The literature on multiraciality divides roughly into four categories: the history of mixed race people in the United States, theories about biracial identity and biracial individuals, popular literature about multiracial individuals, and models of bi/multiracial identity development, which I discuss in this section. The majority of writing comes from the disciplines of psychology, sociology, and anthropology and the interdisciplinary fields of education and ethnic studies. With the exception of writings about the history of mixed race people, the research is mainly empirical, with a shift from quantitative to ethnographic studies over the last ten to fifteen years. Recently, popular media has taken up the issue of multiraciality in drawing attention to the ancestry of sports and entertainment personalities such as Tiger Woods, Derek Jeter, Keanu Reeves, and Vanessa Williams. The following brief review provides a backdrop against which to examine evolving ideas about the study of race and mixed race.

Histories of Mixed Race People in the United States

There are a number of excellent histories of mixed race people in the United States. These histories are proof that the myth of racial purity is false. Briefly, blacks and whites in the seventeenth and early eighteenth centuries engaged in sexual unions that produced the first "mulattoes" in the British colonies

(Daniel, 1992; Williamson, 1995). Despite stern action to prohibit such behavior, a small but steady mixed race population persisted. By the 1850 census, a distinction was made between whites, blacks, and nonwhites, with clear instructions that census takers should "take special care in reporting 'Mulatto (including quadroons, octoroons, and all persons having any perceptible trace of African blood)' because *Important scientific results depend upon the correct determination of this class*'" (italics in original, Goldberg, 1995, p. 240). By 1880 a category for "Indians" was refined to account for various mixtures of white, black, and mulatto within the indigenous population.

In 1930, the census had shifted to the racial categories of white, Negro, Indian, Mexican, Chinese, and Japanese. The "mulatto" category, and all of its accompanying designations of smaller and smaller proportions of black ancestry, had disappeared, and any "racially mixed person" with a white parent was designated by the race of the nonwhite parent (Goldberg, 1995, pp. 241–42). Not until the 1970s did citizens self-identify on the census, but at that time they could not refuse to identify in one of the designated racial categories; if they did so they would be automatically assigned "Other" (Farley, 2001). Following a political movement that included such unlikely participants as then House Speaker Newt Gingrich, in October 1997 the federal government changed its regulations to allow individuals to check more than one race from among the five official categories: American Indian or Alaska Native, Asian, Black or African American, Native Hawaiian or Other Pacific Islander, and White (for a description of the events leading to the revisions, see Farley, 2001, or Renn & Lunceford, 2002). According to the 1997 revisions, "respondents shall be offered the option of selecting one or more racial designations. Recommended forms for the instruction accompanying the multiple response questions are 'Mark one or more' and 'Select one or more'" (OMB, 1997, p. 2).

The census has not been the only bureaucratic mechanism concerned with interracial unions and their offspring; laws proscribing miscegenation originated in the 1630s colonies and persisted in several states until struck down by a Supreme Court ruling in 1967. After *Loving v. Commonwealth of Virginia* (commonly abbreviated as *Loving*), the number of interracial marriages increased from 651,000 in 1980 to 1,464,000 in 2000 or 2.9 percent of all marriages (U.S. Census Bureau, 2002). People under age eighteen reporting two or more races in census 2000, the majority of whom are children resulting from these interracial marriages, numbered 2,856,886 (or 42 percent of all "two or more race" respondents) (Jones & Smith, 2001).

As multiraciality gained momentum as a legitimate social identity, a political movement made up of people who identify as multiracial evolved (see Farley, 2001). Though multiraciality is still a contested identity—both outside and inside the movement—theory has emerged to describe the growing movement. One theory proposes three major approaches within multiracial politics (Nakashima, 1996). The first approach is *the struggle for inclusion in traditional racial/ethnic communities*. Multiracial people can work to have all of their (mono)racial parent communities accept them in their multiraciality or can work to be accepted as full members of these communities (Nakashima, 1996). The second approach seeks to create *a new agenda for a movement of multiracial people*. This approach assumes that the experience of being of mixed heritage has enough common themes to constitute a meaningful reference group. The third approach seeks to *dismantle dominant racial ideology and group boundaries to create connections across communities into a community of humanity*. The central thinking of this approach is that binary thinking and the boundaries it facilitates must be destroyed in order to end oppression based on race, gender, class, and so on (Nakashima, 1996). Owning multiple positionalities and transgressing boundaries places multiracial people not as marginal but as liminal and advantaged, as in Anzaldùa's (1987) construction of *mestiza* identity. In her final analysis, Nakashima (1996) moved from historical and theoretical analysis to call for the construction of a multiracial identity that reflects the diversity of voices in the multiracial movement.

Theories about Mixed Race People

The second category of literature on multiracialty concerns theories about mixed race people. This area of research falls into four categories; the first three were identified by Thornton and Wason (1995) and augmented by Renn (1998) with the fourth. They are the problem approach, the equivalent approach, the variant approach, and the advantaged approach. Each approach casts mixed race people differently in relation to self, family, and society.

The problem approach encompasses much of the pre-Poston writing on mixed race people in the United States. It assumes that monoracial identity is preferable and that multiracial people experience problems because they are "between" races. Moving back and forth across color lines is viewed as maladaptive. Stonequist's (1937) *Marginal Man* was the foundation for this mode of research, though it continued into the last decade of the twentieth century primarily through psychological studies of clinical populations (see Brown, 1990; Gibbs, 1989; Herschel, 1995).

Proponents of the equivalent approach conclude that mixed race people and monoracial people (generally assumed in the research to be people of color) undergo similar identity development and assimilation processes with similar outcomes. This research appears to be in reaction to the problem approach and includes several studies designed to test whether biracial individuals were as well-adjusted in general as their peers (see Cauce, Hiraga, Mason, Aguilar, Ordonez, & Gonzales, 1992; Gibbs & Hines, 1992; Hall, 1992; Kerwin, Ponterotto, Jackson, & Harris, 1993). In the area of ethnic identity in particular, a number of studies showed that multiracial people are equally well adjusted as their monoracial peers of color (see Field, 1996; Grove, 1991; Pinderhughes, 1995; Sodowsky, Kwan, & Pannu, 1995).

Departing from the equivalent approach, some researchers argue that taking a variant approach to mixed race identity allows for the uniqueness of the multiracial experience and the possibility of situational identity patterns. The concern of these researchers is how multiracial individuals live in a society predicated on monoracial definitions. Brown (1995) and Stephan (1992) contributed to this approach, finding that the majority of mixed race individuals do not consider themselves to be of a single heritage. Standen (1996) noted that new research on biracial identity development has led to a kind of "forced choice" dilemma. Whereas biracial people are now more free than ever to claim biracial identity rather than choose between their dual heritages, they are "put into a position where they are accused of being in denial for not accepting biracial identity" (p. 247). He advocated for the creation of models of identity development that account for various factors of development rather than prescribe a singular identity resolution. Bradshaw (1992) explored the role of physical appearance in the life of the mixed race person, arguing that a sense of "specialness," involving highlighted self-awareness or self-consciousness, is an issue for biracial people.

Finally, the advantaged approach proposes not only that mixed race people are a separate, equivalent group but also that the experience of this separateness confers advantages to them. In discussing resolution of "other" status and four types of "border crossings" mixed race people encounter, Root (1990, 1996b) alluded to the increased cognitive flexibility prompted by and required by these situations. Kich (1992) emphasized cognitive flexibility required to transcend external definition and move toward self-definition, and Weisman (1996) acknowledged the reflexivity required to achieve a sense of "positive alterity." Daniel (1996), in an apparent reference back to Stonequist (1937), used the term "positive marginality" to describe the situation of mixed race individuals.

Popular Literature about Multiracial Individuals

Popular literature—in magazines, books, and newspapers—makes up the third major area of what might be called the "multiracial literature." From the mid-1990s, a growing literature of personal narratives and other nonacademic writing has augmented the empirical and theoretical work on the lives of mixed race people (e.g., Azoulay, 1997; Baron, 1998; Barrath, 1995; Camper, 1994; Chao, 1996; Jones, 1994; Minerbrook, 1996; Moraga, 1993; Williams, 1995). Authored almost exclusively by mixed race people, these essays, autobiographies, poems, and novels help create a multiracial culture. In contrast to the "tragic mulatto" stories prevalent until around the middle of the twentieth century (see Streeter, 1996, for an analysis of this literature), recent work gives voice directly to multiracial people. Together with book-length reports of journalistic and ethnographic studies of biracial people (see Funderberg, 1994; Kilson, 2001; Rockquemore & Brunsma, 2002; Tizard & Phoenix, 1993; Wallace, 2001) and growing attention in the popular media, personal narratives provide access to information on how multiracial people understand and represent their lives. The success of mixed race individuals in public arenas (sports, entertainment, news media) has spawned near-weekly articles in newspapers and magazines (from *Time* to *People* to *Glamour*) about multiraciality and mixed race identity.

Viewed against this backdrop of history, theory, and narratives about the multiracial experience, the study of mixed race college students fits in a national, transhistorical context. It is necessary also to understand something about their identity development in a specific setting—higher education institutions—to contextualize the findings of my study. I turn now to an introduction of multiracial identity formation and college student development theory.

BI- AND MULTIRACIAL IDENTITY FORMATION

Erikson (1968) believed that the development of a positive racial identity was critical to the establishment of a healthy identity. He pinpointed adolescence as the time when this work on identity occurred. Chickering and Reisser (1993) concurred, including racial identity development in the "Establishing Identity" vector of their student development schema. Stephan (1992) proposed, "Identities are meaning that the self acquires through social interaction, and as such are crucial to an understanding of an individual's sense of himself or herself" (p. 51). Further, ethnic identity is particularly important because it is a "master status, an identity that overrides all others in others' judgments of the self" (p. 51). Atkinson, Morten, and Sue (1993) focused on the individual's feelings about her or his race, defining racial identity development as pride in one's racial and cultural identity. The underlying premise of these theories is that people cannot develop a healthy sense of identity if they lack a positive racial identity.

THEORIES OF RACIAL IDENTITY DEVELOPMENT

A number of theories attempt to describe how an individual achieves such a positive racial identity, and most of them focus on how people of color accomplish this developmental task (e.g., Cross, 1995; Atkinson, Morten, & Sue, 1993). Exceptions include Helms (1990, 1995), who has proposed models for both blacks and whites, and Tatum (1995) whose theory of white identity development closely parallels Helms's theory. Virtually all of the theories are based on a psychosocial or social interactionist paradigm in which an individual comes to understand him- or herself through a series of racialized encounters with family, friends, and others. These models follow a general format of increasing sophistication from a stage of no awareness of race or racial difference to a stage of integration of race as an aspect of a complete adult identity. Kich (1992), Kilson (2001) King and DaCosta (1996), Poston (1990), Renn (2000), Rockquemore and Brunsma (2002), Root (1990, 1992b), Wallace (2001), Williams (1996), and others have found that while the psychosocial assumption holds up when translating monoracial models to multiracial situations, the traditional stage models pose problems in exploring healthy biracial identity formation. In order to create models of mixed race identity, we need to reconsider existing theories about racial identity development.

There is general agreement that development of racial self-identity occurs within the context of social encounters. Helms (1995) posited that development occurs as needed by an individual to cope effectively with "personally meaningful racial material in her or his environments" (p. 186). Cross (1995) revised his 1978 theory of Nigrescence to accommodate the notion that it describes the resocializing experience in which a black person is transformed from a non-Afrocentric preexisting identity into one that is Afrocentric. Similarly, Atkinson, Morten, and Sue (1993) outlined how a lifetime of social encounters propels individuals from one stage to the next, and King and DaCosta's (1996) four-fold theory of the construction of race relies on self-other interactions to stimulate identity development.

While there is agreement that race is socially constructed at both macro and micro levels, there is a diversity of opinion about the pattern of racial identity development at the individual level. Stage and typology theories predominate among the traditional models, but research with multiracial people shows that these models do not necessarily translate well from monoracial populations. According to the stage theories, an individual moves from "preencounter" (Cross, 1995; Helms, 1990, 1995) to "internalization-commitment" (Cross) or "integrative awareness" (Helms, 1995) through a process of rejecting majority (white) culture and embracing minority culture. There is not consensus on the immutability of the stages or the possibility of regression from a "higher" stage to a "lower" one. Helms (1995) changed her 1990 theory from "stages" to "statuses" to imply permeability in the model. In the revision, she intended to clarify that an individual may exhibit traits reflective of more than one status, that the statuses are dynamic interactions between cognitive and emotional processes, and that "neither theory nor measurement supports the notion of the various stages as mutually exclusive or 'pure' constructs" (p. 183). Phinney's (1990) model allows for an individual to return to a foreclosed state of disinterest in ethnic issues from a moratorium state of ethnic identity search. Cross's (1995) model is more rigid, implying development from one stage to the next in irreversible order, though he accounts for individuals who may choose not to progress through to the highest stage. See table 1.1 for a summary of the minority identity development models.

Since multiracial people have historically been declared people of color (and not white), theory predicts that they follow the same stages as their monoracial peers of color. In any of the models, rigid or permeable, the middle stages of questioning identity, rejecting majority culture, and immersing in minority culture could prove problematic for individuals of mixed heritage. It was this phenomenon that led numerous researchers over the years to deem biracial people poorly adjusted. Pinderhughes (1995) cited a number of such studies, and Root (1992a) described how the methodological difficulty of doing research with multiracial people yielded biased results. A number of recent studies found that mixed race people were as well adjusted as their monoracial peers (e.g., Brown, 1995; Cauce et al., 1992; Field, 1996; Gibbs & Hines, 1992; Hall, 1992, 1996), and these studies supported the creation of models of biracial identity formation that accounted for these findings (e.g., Kerwin & Ponterotto, 1995; Kich, 1992; Root, 1996b).

MODELS OF BIRACIAL IDENTITY DEVELOPMENT

In attempts to describe biracial identity formation, traditional stage models of minority identity development have been criticized for being too linear (Miller, 1992; Root, 1992a, 1992b, Wallace, 2001), for paying inadequate attention to the socioecology of race (Clancy, 1995), for relying on rejection of white culture as a necessary middle stage (Kerwin & Ponterotto, 1995; Kich, 1992; Poston, 1990; Root, 1990), and for lacking adequate empirical support (Rockquemore & Brunsma, 2002). Multiracial identity formation is generally believed to be personal and multidimensional, though stage-based models predominate (e.g., Kich, 1992; Poston, 1990).

There is disagreement among theorists over the goal of biracial identity formation. Achievement of an integrated identity similar to that achieved at the highest levels of the traditional minority identity development models is the goal of one family of theories, while a second group of theories holds that development of a distinct biracial/bicultural, mixed race, interracial or multiracial identity is the goal. In this second group, there is a subset of theories that holds that an individual will not just achieve an identity as a multiracial person, but she will also achieve a sense of "positive alterity" (Weisman, 1996) or specialness in her "otherness" (Root, 1990). Finally, emerging theories propose that the goal of multiracial identity development is an individual's ability to engage in a variety of "border crossings" between and among social contexts defined by race and ethnicity (Root, 1996a; Wallace, 2001). In this section I discuss theories in each of these three categories.

TABLE 1.1
Racial and Ethnic Identity Development Models

Atkinson, Morten & Sue (1993)	Conformity	Dissonance	Resistance/ Immersion	Introspection	Synergetic articulation and awareness
Cross (1995)	Preencounter	Encounter	Immersion/ Emersion	Internalization	Internalization/ Commitment
Helms (1995)	Conformity (Preencounter)	Dissonance (Encounter)	Immersion/ Emersion	Internalization	Integrative Awareness
Phinney (1990) [uses Marcia's Ego Identity Statuses]	Unexamined ethnic identity, diffused: lack of interest in or concern with ethnicity	Unexamined ethnic identity, foreclosed: views of ethnicity based on opinions of others	Ethnic identity search		Achieved ethnic identity

Toward an Integrated Identity

Poston's (1990) pioneering work on biracial identity development was based on Cross's (1987) work on personal identity (PI) and reference group orientation (RGO). In Cross's model, PI included constructs independent of racial categorization such as self-esteem and interpersonal competence, whereas RGO included racial identity, racial esteem, and racial ideology. Poston designed his theory for black-white biracial people, but it may be generalized to incorporate other mixed race people as well. Poston was concerned that existing models of minority identity formation and theories about the social marginality of mixed race people implied that biracial people must choose one group's culture and values over another in order to achieve racial group pride, and that whereas monoracial people might reject first minority then majority culture, biracial people come from both cultures. Consequently, Poston believed that existing theories did not allow for the integration of several group identities. He also noted that minority identity development theories relied on some acceptance of an individual into the minority culture of origin, but that biracial people might never gain this acceptance.

Poston proposed a five-stage theory of biracial identity development. Stage one is *Personal Identity*. Children who are just becoming aware of membership in any particular ethnic group are in this stage. Their sense of self is independent of ethnic background and their RGO attitudes have not yet developed, thus their identity is primarily based on PI. Stage two is *Choice of Group Categorization*. Individuals are pushed by family, peers, or other social groups to choose a racial identity, usually of one ethnic group. This stage can be a time of crisis and isolation. While individuals might choose to identify multiracially at this point, they are more likely to choose one ethnicity over another. This decision often leads to feelings of confusion and guilt at having to choose one identity that is not fully expressive of an individual's heritage. These feelings signal entrance to the third stage, *Enmeshment/Denial*. Typically an adolescent stage, it is characterized by feelings of disloyalty at choosing one parent's background and not the other's (Sebring, 1985 in Poston, 1990). Prompted by these feelings, a biracial person might begin to learn about her various ethnic heritages, to appreciate her multiple identity, and to broaden her RGO. She has entered the fourth stage, *Appreciation*. When she is ready to recognize and value all of her ethnic identities, she moves to the final stage, *Integration*. According to Poston (1990), here she develops a secure, integrated, and multicultural identity. The majority of biracial people will achieve this stage.

Whereas the middle stages of the Helms (1990, 1995); Cross (1991, 1995); and Atkinson, Morten, and Sue (1993) models are characterized by enthusiastic immersion in a minority culture, Poston (1990) identified stages two (choice) and three (enmeshment/denial) as the most difficult times of adjustment for biracial people. That they fall during late childhood and adolescence when factors of personal identity might be most affected by the attitudes of members of one's reference group does little to facilitate the overall development and adjustment of mixed race youth. Poston acknowledged the additional potential burden of an individual's internalizing societal prejudice and negative reference group values. However, he believed that positive resolution of feelings of guilt and disloyalty could lead to full exploration of an individual's identity and was therefore associated with positive indicators of mental health.

The Kerwin-Ponterotto (1995) model also follows a stage pattern and leads to an integrated multiethnic identity. According to this model, identity formation depends on a number of psychosocial factors and is an individual process. The Kerwin-Ponterotto model contains six stages, beginning with *Preschool*, when racial awareness emerges. *Entry to school* is the second stage, in which "What are you?" questions and a need to categorize people and objects prompt children to reassess their self-concept. *Preadolescence* is marked by increased awareness that physical appearance represents group membership and awareness that parents are from different racial groups. Awareness of living in an interracial family may not occur until triggered by such an event or environmental circumstances.

Stage four is *Adolescence,* and like Poston (1990), Kerwin and Ponterotto (1995) marked this stage as the most challenging one for biracial youth, both because of the developmental issues characteristic of adolescents and the particular challenges society presents to biracial people. Kerwin and Ponterotto noted that dating during adolescence may bring racial issues to the surface, and Twine (1996) examined the role of heterosexual romance in transforming racial identities. Kerwin (1991) found significant peer pressure for biracial teens to identify with only one racial group but also found that these pressures could be neutralized by nonrace-related RGO factors such as sports teams, school or church groups, or other interests (pp. 212–13). Still, individuals in this stage are likely to identify with one aspect of their heritage over others.

College/young adulthood may bring continued immersion in one culture (and rejection of others), but as young people develop a more secure personal identity, they are more likely to reject others' expectations and to accept their biracial heritage. Often, they begin to see advantages as well as disadvantages of being biracial. College affords particular opportunities to explore racial identity. As they move into the sixth stage, *Adulthood,* they seek a continuing integration of the different facets of their racial identity. They may experience an enhanced sense of self as they function effectively in varying situations and understand different communities. This final stage represents an integration of racial self/selves and other aspects of identity.

Toward a Multiracial Identity

While Poston (1990) and Kerwin and Ponterotto (1995) saw integration of ethnic/racial identities as the endpoint of multiracial identity development, other theorists saw the claiming of a distinct multiracial identity as the endpoint of this process. From an ethnographic study of fifteen biracial adults of white and Japanese heritage, Kich (1992) concluded, "For a person who is biracial, a positive expression of that reality is the integration and assertion of a biracial identity" (p. 304). He proposed a three-stage model of biracial/bicultural identity development. Stage 1 generally occurs from ages three through ten and is characterized by "an *initial awareness of differentness* and dissonance between self-perceptions and others' perceptions" (p. 305). Kich found that this awareness and dissonance often occurred during the transition from home to early peer group when individuals found themselves not fitting into any reference group outside the family.

Stage two occurs through grade school and into late adolescence or young adulthood. During this stage, the biracial person engages in a *struggle for acceptance by others*. Most people in this stage will either claim one heritage or will simply list their different heritages, though some will claim an interracial identity. Kich (1992) believed that this stage enables biracial people to learn how to negotiate racial boundaries in society. Late in this stage, individuals will begin to examine their own stereotypes about multiracial people and will begin to take on an independent identity, apart from parental expectations.

When an individual accepts herself as a person with *a biracial and bicultural identity*, she has entered stage three. In this stage, identity is influenced by but different from the quest for acceptance by others. Individuals come to form congruent, positive self-definitions that reverse negative social constructions of mixed race people. They explore aspects of ethnic heritage and culture and use terms such as *interracial* to describe themselves. These individuals are less defensive toward those who are confused by multiraciality and understand identity as "something constructed out of the relationship between personal experience and social meanings of ethnicity, race, and group membership" (Kich, 1992, p. 316). People in stage three are able to educate others about multiraciality and to recognize parameters of group roles and rules and are accepted into different groups.

Kich's model relies on the agency of the individual to overcome external restrictions imposed by societal ideas about biraciality. This model requires reflexivity; in order to achieve the final stage an individual must develop the cognitive flexibility to view race as a social construction and multiraciality as one construct among many. Further, a person must learn to "take the self as an object" (Mead, in King & DaCosta, 1996) and apply that construct to it. Kegan (1982, 1994) would describe such a phenomenon as a "subject-object shift," involving "self-authorship," and use it as evidence of cognitive growth. See table 1.2 for a summary of the lifespan models of multiracial identity development.

Toward a Positive Alterity

A subset of the group of theories that holds formation of a multiracial identity as the desired goal is the set that features a theme of "positive marginality" (Daniel, 1996) as the endpoint of healthy development. In these theories, an individual comes not only to see himself as biracial, but also to understand biraciality as a privileged position from which to experience social interactions. Daniel's contribution was not a stage model but rather a theory that healthy biracial identity lends itself to a sense of "positive marginality" characterized by "a style of self-consciousness that involves a continuous process of 'incorporating here, discarding there, responding situationally'" (Adler in Daniel, 1996, p. 134). People living in this state experience an increased tolerance for difference and appreciation of commonalities, as well as multiple points of reference.

Daniel (1996) outlined four ways of being in positive marginality that correspond roughly to Root's (1996a) types of border crossings. Daniel described *integrative identity* as a simultaneous referencing in black and white communities. *Synthesized integrative identity* occurs when individuals identify equally and comfortably in the two communities and shuttle between both (like Root's "both feet in both camps" border crossing). *Functional integrative identity* occurs when an individual identifies with and functions within both communities but feels a greater acceptance from and comfort in one or the other community. A functional integrative/black individual, for example, would feel more accepted in the black community and would have a strong commitment to issues within that community. Functional integrative identity corresponds to Root's idea of shifting foreground and background according to context.

Pluralistic identity, on the other hand, blends aspects of both parent groups, but these individuals consider themselves part of neither (Daniel, 1996). They create instead a new primary reference group of mixed heritage individuals. *Synthesized pluralistic identity* occurs when people reference themselves equally in black, white, and multiracial communities (again, like Root's feet in both groups border crossing, but with feet in an additional, mixed race group). The *functional pluralistic identity* group identifies variously with black, white, and racially mixed people, but feels more comfortable in and accepted by one reference group or another. These people might be seen as shifting foreground and background or as setting up a home base in one group and venturing periodically into others (see Root, 1996a). Daniel's description of life on the racial boundary accounted for a variety of outcomes

TABLE 1.2
Lifespan Models of Biracial Identity Development

Kich (1992)	Initial awareness of difference		Struggle for acceptance by others		Biracial/bicultural identity	
Poston (1990)	Personal identity, no racial RGO	Choice of group categorization, forced to choose one category		Enmeshment/denial, choice of one category leads to confusion and guilt	Appreciation, learn more about various ethnic heritages and consider broadening RGO	Integration, recognize and value all ethnic identities
Kerwin-Ponterotto (1995)	Preschool, racial awareness emerges	Entry to school, reassess racial self-concept	Preadolescence, awareness that phenotype represents group membership and that parents are not from same group	Adolescence, pressure to identify with one racial group	College/young adulthood, immersion in one culture with beginning to reject others' expectations	Adulthood, continuing integration of different facets of racial identity

and relied on the development of the cognitive and emotional flexibility Kich (1996) said accompanies a marginal existence.

Weisman (1996) employed a similar theory that incorporated the development of a "positive alterity" or positive reference group. Since identity maintenance is not posited as possible without a reference group (Stuart & Abt, 1973), and society does not provide a multiracial reference group, a self-proclaimed alterity provides mixed race people such a group. Weisman argued that societal recognition of a reference group is not as important as recognition of that group by those who define it and seek to belong (p. 157). She also pointed out that although development of a positive alterity is important, insistence on a separate multiracial reference group reifies the existing structure of race in the United States. Nevertheless, incorporation of positive marginality or positive alterity into the final stage of racial identity development requires the kind of cognitive ability necessary for Kich's (1992) final stage, and moving beyond the concept of race altogether requires a level of cognitive ability along the lines of Kegan's (1994) subject-object shift.

Root (1990) presented a model for how individuals might develop and manage positive marginality or alterity. In remarking on studies that attest to the adjustment difficulties of biracial people, she claimed that *"it is the marginal status imposed by society rather than the objective mixed race of biracial individuals which poses a severe stress to positive identity development"* (p. 188, italics in original). Like Kich (1992), Root emphasized the importance of shifting from seeking approval from others to defining oneself. She proposed that healthy development for biracial children must include learning strategies for coping with the "otherness" forced on them by a dichotomous, black-white society but noted that these children have few models available in this attempt to resolve "other" status.

Root (1990) proposed four strategies for this resolution. These strategies are not mutually exclusive or progressive, and they may exist simultaneously. They share a number of themes. In each, the biracial person accepts both sides of her heritage, she has the right to declare how she chooses to self-identify, she develops personal strategies for coping with social resistance, and she no longer internalizes questions about her identity as inferences that there is something wrong with her (pp. 201–02). The strategies echo Nakashima's (1996) "voices" from the multiracial movement.

In the first strategy biracial people can *accept the identity society assigns*. Root (1990) called this strategy the most tenuous, as it depends on external forces, which may change depending on time and place. The second strategy involves *identification with both racial groups*. This solution can be a positive one if an individual's personality remains stable across groups and if she is accepted in both groups. Root notes that this strategy does not change other people's behavior and that the biracial person may need to develop strategies to cope with social resistance in both groups. The third strategy is *identification with a single racial group*. This strategy might look identical to the first one, but Root calls it active rather than passive. The individual is choosing to identify in this way. A major obstacle to this strategy may occur if an individual does not fit the phenotype of the group with which they identify, in which case he will need to develop strategies to manage questions by members of the chosen reference group. The fourth strategy for resolution of "other" status is *identification as a new racial group*. These individuals feel a strong relationship to other biracial people because of their mutual struggle with marginal status. They may move fluidly between racial groups but view themselves apart from these reference groups without feeling marginal, because they have developed their own reference group. Root calls this resolution positive if the person is not choosing it in order to hide or reject any aspect of his racial heritage. She notes, though, that the greatest challenge to those who choose it is that society is just beginning to recognize multiracial status as a viable identity alternative.

In this model, Root (1990) did not propose a series of stages but rather suggested a number of possible developmental outcomes. The Kerwin and Ponterotto (1995), Kich (1992), or Poston (1990) models could lead to any of these outcomes, though some strategies for resolving "other" status seem more likely for some models than for others. For example, Carter's theory relied heavily on conforming to external pressures and might therefore be more closely aligned with the first solution (acceptance of the identity society assigns) than with the fourth (identification as a new racial group). Poston and Kich implied that healthy resolution of biracial identity would not result in identification with only one racial group, but rather a more fluid identity claiming either both racial groups or a multiracial reference group. Daniel (1996) and Weisman (1996), with their reliance on positive marginality or alterity, suggested that individuals would identify as members of a new racial group.

Root (1996a) further developed the idea of resolving "other" status, describing multiracial families and individuals as occupying the "borderlands of the 1970's five-race framework" (p. xx) and identified four types of border crossings that subvert this construction. The border crossings do not exactly match the strategies for resolving marginal status but view them through a postmodern lens. In the first type of border crossing an individual has "*both* feet in *both* groups" (p. xxi, italics in original). Unlike someone who has a foot in two worlds, but both in none, this person is able to hold and merge multiple perspectives simultaneously. A second type of border crossing requires situational ethnicity and situational race, with a conscious shifting of foreground and background as the individual moves across social group boundaries maintained by race and ethnicity. Root calls this not "switching loyalties" but a "natural response to race as socially co-constructed by economics, by gender, and by sexual orientation" (p. xxi).

The third border crossing is actually not a crossing but rather a decision to sit on the border and to make it the central reference point. These individuals may claim a multiracial label or a "mestiza" consciousness (Anzalduà, 1987). In the final type of border crossing, an individual creates a home base in one identity and makes occasional forays into other identities, possibly even settling into a new home base. Root (1996a) stated that this apparent transiency is not racial disloyalty but rather a strategy to meet psychological, emotional, social, or political needs (p. xxii). As in her earlier model of strategies to resolve "other" status, this final method of border crossing allows for individuals to change their way of identifying over their lifetime. Though not an explicit developmental model, Root's (1996) border-crossing paradigm suggests that healthy resolution of multiracial identity in a postmodern world allows an individual consciously to choose a manner of negotiating life in the borderlands of our constructed racial ecology.

Compared to the identity development models for monoracial individuals, the models for bi- or multiracial identity development lack consensus on ideal outcomes as well as developmental processes. While this variation is inconvenient for educators seeking a tidy model on which to base programs and interventions, it is an intriguing challenge to researchers seeking to understand better the experiences of mixed race people. If the endpoint of multiracial identity development is not unitary ("integrated" or "synthesized" identity), what might it look like? How could an individual hold multiple, perhaps even contradictory, identities? And what might educators do to promote healthy identity formation? In the next section, I discuss these questions in the context of higher education and college student development, completing the theoretical context for understanding this study of mixed race college students.

COLLEGE STUDENT DEVELOPMENT

College student development theory aims to predict patterns of growth and change in students along a number of dimensions: cognitive, intellectual, moral, social, and personal identity (see Evans, Forney, & Guido-DiBrito, 1998). Like its parent field, psychology, this body of theory and research is deeply ingrained in a tradition of modernism. Assuming the universality of students' experiences, stage theories predominate (e.g., Erikson, 1968; Fowler, 1976; Gilligan, 1981; Heath, 1978; King & Kitchener, 1994; Kohlberg, 1976; Perry, 1968, 1981). Stage theories rely not only on traditional social science research to evaluate individuals and delineate discreet levels of development but also on the modernist values that "progress is possible and good, and that the way to move in that direction is through education" (Bloland, 1995, p. 3).

Student development theory assumes that given adequate levels of involvement (Astin, 1984) and appropriate challenges and supports (Sanford, 1960) all students will move up through a series of stages in a more or less orderly fashion, unless or until they achieve a developmental moratorium or foreclosure (Marcia, 1966, 1980). Students' developmental trajectories can therefore be predicted, and the impact of college on students can be dissected and measured in fine detail (see Pascarella & Terenzini, 1991). As in the vast majority of higher education scholarship, the modernist notions of rationality, reason, and discoverable truth pervade the student development literature. I do not believe that this perspective is necessarily wrong or yields incorrect conclusions, but rather that the area of student development theory should be examined for the underlying modernist biases it may contain.

Identity development is a central tenet in many of the student development theories (see Evans, Forney, & Guido-DiBrito), and both lifespan and student development theory generally include identity development as a central task of traditional age (eighteen through twenty-two years old) collegians (e.g., Chickering & Reisser, 1993; Erikson, 1968). The concept of 'identity development' is understood generally to be achieving "that solid sense of self that assumes form as [other] developmental tasks . . . are undertaken with some success, and which . . . provides a framework for interpersonal relationships, purposes, and integrity" (Chickering & Reisser, 1993, p. 80). College students engage in a process of examining the systems of values and ethics taught to them by family and peers, creating new systems of beliefs and behaviors to match their self-definitions and lifestyles. They emerge from college with an identity forged in the academic and peer culture of the campus. This sense of self includes conceptions of body and appearance, as well as clarification of gender, sexual, and racial identity.

As postmodernism increasingly influences curricula and campus culture, the notion of identity development becomes more complicated. Indeed, William Tierney (1993) has written that a postmodern society will not even have a unitary, consensual definition of identity or identity formation. Kenneth Gergen proposed, "As belief in essential selves erodes, awareness expands of the ways in which personal identity can be created and re-created in relationships" (1991, p. 146). His scheme of development traced an individual from a modern self-conception of essential individual identity through a series of changes in self-perspective, ending with the postmodern "relational self . . . in which it is relationship that constructs the self" (p. 147).

When we challenge traditional definitions of the self as something that can be discovered and identified, rather than continually constructed in relationships, existing theories of student development are inadequate to describe what is happening while young people are at college. Chickering and Reisser's (1993) assertion that identity formation precedes the development of mature interpersonal relationships makes little sense if identity formation occurs through engagement in those very relationships, as Gergen (1991) and Tierney (1993) believed. Astin's (1984) theory of involvement and Sanford's

(1960) notion of challenge and support hold true in a postmodern view of student development but require a shift in emphasis from the individuals operating in a college environment to their relationships within that setting. Although there are promising efforts underway (see Jones & McEwen, 2000), the field of student development lacks an overarching theory that can account for the construction of various aspects of identity in the college context. In 1979, Urie Bronfenbrenner created such a unifying theory for the field of cognitive development, and his ecology model formed a basis for organizing data and findings from this study. In chapter 2, I outline Bronfenbrenner's model and lay the foundation for transferring it to student development theory.

Whatever perspective student development theorists adopt, we live in a modernist society where race is considered a "master status, an identity that overrides all others in others' judgments of the self" (Stephan, 1992, p. 51). Since identity is either formed through or literally created in social interactions (the modern and postmodern theories, respectively), a sense of racial identity is part of understanding oneself on campus and in society as a whole (Chickering & Reisser, 1993; Stephan, 1992; Williams, 1996). Therefore, in either a traditional or postmodern view of student development, racial identity formation is an important element of identity development.

The models of racial identity formation described in the previous section have been broadly applied to college students. These models rely on a progression from conformity with majority (white) culture through stages of dissonance and resistance to an immersion in minority culture, ending with an integration of racial identity with other aspects of the person's self-definition (Atkinson, Morten, & Sue, 1993; Cross, 1991; Helms, 1990). In each model, the opportunity to immerse oneself in minority culture is a critical element in developing self-confidence and pride (see table 1.1). For monoracial students of color these models seem to work well, describing familiar situations on college campuses, where self-defined groups of black, asian, native american, and latina/o students create communities that support students through the first several stages of racial identity formation, though not always to the endpoint of integration of racial identity (see Tatum, 1995, for a discussion of this phenomenon).

As already discussed, the racial identity models do not necessarily address the needs of mixed race students, who cannot engage entirely in an immersion in one of their component cultures without putting aside, at least for that time, other aspects of their heritage (Kerwin & Ponterotto, 1995; Kich, 1992; Poston, 1990). Furthermore, even when these students do choose to affiliate with monoracial student cultures, they are often rejected if they express their multiraciality (Daniel, 1992; Renn, 1998, 2000; Yemma, 1997). The communities of like-others that support the development of many students of color are not generally available to assist multiracial students in exploring their racial identities (Renn, 1998, 2000, 2003; Williams, Nakashima, Kich,

& Daniel, 1996). Accordingly, models of multiracial identity formation generally do not include a stage of immersion in a monoracial minority culture.

Early models of biracial identity development (Kich, 1992; Poston, 1990) were stage-based and modernist in orientation, but more recent theories take a postmodern approach. Multiraciality is seen as a state of "positive alterity" (Weisman, 1996) or "positive marginality" (Daniel, 1996) in which the goal of multiracial identity formation is an individual's ability to engage in a variety of "border crossings" (Giroux, 1992) between and among social contexts defined by race and ethnicity (Root, 1990, 1996a). Maria Root (1996a) proposed a theory of identity formation that does not depend on an orderly progression through developmental stages but rather relies on an individual's ability to be comfortable with self-definition in, across, and/or in between categories. The notion of racial borderlands or border zones (Anzalduà, 1987; Giroux, 1992; Root, 1990, 1992b, 1995, 1996a; Zack 1995) sets the stage for the dissolution of race as an impermeable, essential category. If mixed race students straddle the border between races, live their lives in one ostensibly monoracial student community and then another, or feel comfortable with a flexible, situational self-definition, then they are evidence that the myth of fixed, genetically pure races is untrue (see Nakashima, 1992; Zack, 1995).

Neither student development theory nor multiracial identity development theory addresses how multiracial young people make sense of their identity in the context of the college environment. Early in my research, I learned that mixed race students faced the paradox of acknowledging the social construction of race (and wished to dismantle it as such) while also acknowledging the need to create and maintain a self-identified multiracial community on campus. Armed with postmodern theory, but living in a modernist, racialized society, they simultaneously rejected race as a valid construction and valorized it through their campus involvement, academic work, and personal identification. Based on that work, I wanted to explore the experiences of mixed race students to learn more about how they understood and described their multiracial identities in the context of higher education.

The results of that work are presented here as an introduction to theories about race, mixed race, and college student development (chapter 1); an introduction to an ecology model of development and to my research design (chapter 2); and an overview and detailed discussion of five patterns of mixed race identity in college students (chapters 3 and 4 through 8). An exposition of implications for higher education practice, policy, theory, and research completes the text (chapter 9).

chapter two

The Ecology of Multiracial Identity on Campus—An Analytic Framework and Research Design

---

> So I've got these different groups of people and different places on campus. And I get different things from them, like different ideas about school and stuff. I feel like I can fit in lots of places, and I'm glad about that, 'cause I learn different things in different places.
>
> —May

COLLEGE CAMPUSES REPRESENT unique developmental environments. Ostensibly dedicated to the improvement of the mind, they are also settings for psychological, physical, personal, and interpersonal development. Indeed, the professional field of college student affairs—and the student development theories on which the field relies for its intellectual foundation—is premised on the notion that higher education institutions can be seamless learning environments (Kuh, 1996) dedicated to the development of the whole person (see American College Personnel Association, 1994).

Seamlessness, however, has not been a hallmark of student development literature,[1] which with few exceptions measures narrowly defined outcome variables (e.g., Pascarella & Terenzini, 1991) or divides student development into discrete elements, such as racial identity (e.g., Cross, 1995; Helms, 1995; Tatum, 1995), sexual orientation identity (e.g., Cass, 1979; D'Augelli, 1994), and cognitive and ethical development (e.g., King & Kitchener, 1984; Perry, 1968, 1981). While useful unto themselves in higher education practice and research, taken alone most student development theories fail to capture the richness and complexity of the college student's developmental experience. More important, while many describe very well the stages and outcomes of development, few provide clues as to the process of development. What prompts an individual to move from one point to another? What environmental presses promote development, and which inhibit it? What does the whole of a student's developmental environment entail, and how does he or she interact with it? What might a more seamless approach to student development look like? And specifically, what might such an environment look like for a mixed race college student?

For answers to these questions, I turn to an ecology model of human development, first introduced by Urie Bronfenbrenner (1977, 1979, 1989, 1993, 1995). In this chapter, I describe Bronfenbrenner's model and its elements, propose ecology theory as an alternative to stage-based theories of identity development, and use the model to discuss the influence of college peer cultures on individual identity. Although I use a few examples from other areas of identity development, I focus the majority of my discussion on issues of race and racial identity. I complete the chapter with a description of my study design and how I came to understand the data in the context of the ecology model.

BRONFENBRENNER'S ECOLOGY MODEL AS A FRAMEWORK FOR UNDERSTANDING THE PERSON-ENVIRONMENT INTERACTIONS THAT INFLUENCE IDENTITY

Because racial identity is constructed in the context of social relations, in the ongoing interactions between individuals and their environments, a theoretical model that shines light clearly on those interactions is useful in exploring racial identities and multiracial identification. A model that also accounts for interactions among and between the various subenvironments an individual encounters is even more useful, as it provides a means to examine the dynamic, fluid nature of college life, where students move from one setting to another, constructing and reconstructing identities in relationship with others and in reaction to the messages they receive from interacting environments. Importantly, the Bronfenbrenner model accounts for both the individual and his or her interactions within this dynamic environment. Bronfenbrenner built his theory around two central axioms: (a) "development is an evolving function of person-environment interaction" and (b) "ultimately, this interaction must take place in the immediate, face-to-face setting in which the person exists" (1993, p. 10). In the following sections, I describe these axioms as applied to Bronfenbrenner's ecology model of human development.

MAJOR CONSTRUCTS OF BRONFENBRENNER'S ECOLOGY THEORY

In 1935, developmental psychologist Kurt Lewin posed the classic equation: $B = f(PE)$ to represent behavior (B) as a function (f) of the interaction of person *(P)* and environment *(E)* (p. 73). Later in the century another developmental psychologist, Urie Bronfenbrenner, translated the equation to $D = f(PE)$ to indicate that *development*, too, was the outcome of interactions of person and environment. Assessing the state of research on psychological development, Bronfenbrenner pointed to the "hypertrophy of theory and research focusing on the properties of the person and only the most rudimentary conception and characterization of the environment in which the person is found" (1979, p. 16). To remedy this imbalance, Bronfenbrenner proposed an "ecology of human development" as a framework for research and theorizing about developmental environments. Specifically, he proposed,

> The ecology of human development involves the scientific study of the progressive, mutual accommodation between an active, growing human being and the changing properties of the immediate settings in which the developing person lives, as this process is affected by relations between these settings, and by the larger contexts in which the settings are embedded. (Bronfenbrenner, 1979, p. 21)

In this model, the environment and the individual shape—and are shaped by—one another; the model represents a dynamic, shifting relationship of reciprocal influence.

Bronfenbrenner (1979) highlighted three aspects of the model that differentiate it from others. First, the ecology model posits the individual as a "growing, dynamic entity that progressively moves into and restructures the milieu in which it resides" (p. 21). Second, "the interaction between person and environment is viewed as two-directional," characterized by mutual accommodation and reciprocity (p. 22). Third, the environment is not limited to the immediate setting containing the growing individual, but includes "interconnections between such settings, as well as to external influences emanating from the larger surroundings" (p. 22). The ecology model therefore captures the ever-changing world of the developing person as he or she moves from home to school, then school to work or college, and so on, seeking and shaping environments just as he or she is attracted to and shaped by them.

In 1977 and in subsequent writing, Bronfenbrenner laid out the basic concepts of his model, the key elements of which are person, process, context, and time (PPCT). *Person* refers to the individual, her current state of development, and the characteristics that lead her to engage in particular ways with particular environments. *Process* represents the interactions between the person and the environment, as well as influences those interactions have on the individual and the environment. *Context* comprises the immediate settings in which the individual develops, as well as the interactions between those settings, settings that do not contain the individual but that nevertheless exert developmental influence on her, and the larger sociohistorical environment. *Time* captures the timing of events in the life of the individual as well as the broader sweep of development. The PPCT framework is multidimensional, dynamic, context-bound, and person specific. In this section I will explore each element in detail and connect it to the study of college student development, particularly as applied to identity development.

PERSON

Including the person component in a developmental model would seem somehow redundant. How could we consider individual development without the individual? Indeed, the person is assumed to be at the center of most college student development theories, though rarely does he or she have an explicit place in them; the individual is the canvas on which development becomes evident, she is the vessel in which developmental change occurs, or he is a collection of demographic data that can be used to compare developmental and learning outcomes. On the other hand, some student development theories (e.g., Banning & Kaiser, 1974; Strange & Banning, 2001) emphasize the environment to the extent that individual characteristics, personal histories, and broader social contexts lose analytic meaning. Bronfenbrenner's explicit location of the person in the ecology model takes seriously the key elements of the developmental equation—person and environment—pointing not only to the occurrence of person-environment interactions but also to the nature of those interactions and the factors that lead to them.

It has been generations since the assumption could safely be made, if it ever really could, that students enter college having had substantially similar familial and educational experiences and resembling one another in terms of gender, race, class, religion, or ability. These differences are accounted for in a variety of theories (e.g., Cross, 1995; D'Augelli, 1994; Helms, 1995; Josselson, 1987; Tatum, 1995) and are used as variables to analyze a variety of postsecondary outcomes (e.g., Astin, 1998; Hu & St. John, 2001; McDonough, Antonio, & Trent, 1997; Pascarella & Terenzini, 1991; Terenzini, Cabrera, Colbeck, Bjorklund, & Parente, 2001). The person component in the ecology model includes a student's unique experiences and characteristics, including socially constructed identities (race, ethnicity, gender, sexual orientation, socioeconomic class, ability, etc.), prior academic performance and academic self-concept, political and social ideologies, and family background (Renn & Arnold, 2003). An appealing quality of Bronfenbrenner's model is that the meaning and influence of these nonenvironmental factors are assumed to shift across environmental and historical contexts (Arnold, 2000), a notion that, while it complicates research design, is compatible with the philosophy that identities are constructed and reconstructed in relationships across settings.

More important than these collections of experiences and characteristics, according to Bronfenbrenner, are an individual's ways of approaching interactions with others. Bronfenbrenner proposed that "the attributes of the person most likely to shape the course of development, for better or for worse, are those that induce or inhibit dynamic dispositions toward the immediate environment" (1993, p. 11). He called these attributes "developmentally instigative characteristics."

Bronfenbrenner (1993) posited four types of developmentally instigative characteristics. The first are those that act to invite or inhibit particular responses from the environment, such as a student's ability to pick up social cues in new settings. The second are those of "selective responsivity" or how individuals characteristically react to and explore their surroundings; the chosen environments of a student who consistently seeks the unfamiliar will be different from those of a student who seeks stability and familiarity. The third type are "structuring proclivities," which involve the processes by which individuals engage or persist in increasingly complex activities, including reconceptualizing and creating new features in the environment. In an unstructured curriculum with relatively few requirements, students will make different choices about the rigor and complexity of self-defined programs of study. Finally are the developmentally instigative characteristics related to "directive beliefs," referring to how individuals understand their agency in relation to their environments; a student who believes that she has the right and authority to name her own identity, no matter what those around her would call her, will react differently to her setting than one who is more inclined to accept an identity determined for her by others.

Differences in developmentally instigative characteristics account for some of the variability of college outcomes regardless of such nonenvironmental characteristics as race, ethnicity, gender, and age (Renn & Arnold, 2003), yet they are largely absent from some foundational student development theories (e.g., Chickering & Reisser, 1993; Perry, 1981). They would seem to account significantly for the *how* as well as the *what* of development and to explain why students who appear to be similar have such different learning and developmental outcomes and why students who appear to be very different may have very similar outcomes. Bronfenbrenner (1993) cautioned: "Developmentally instigative characteristics do not *determine* the course of development; rather, they may be thought of as 'putting a spin' on a body in motion. The effect of that spin depends on other forces, and resources, in the total ecological system" (p. 14). Thus nonenvironmental traits and developmentally instigative characteristics contribute to the shape of the developmental trajectory, bending it here and there according in part to what the individual brings to the encounter. We will later see how these differences affect the developmental trajectories of mixed race students.

An emphasis on interpersonal or person-environment interaction is certainly not unique to Bronfenbrenner's theory (see, for example, Banning & Kaiser, 1974; Holland, 1966; Moos, 1979; Tinto, 1993; Strange & Banning, 2001; Weidman, 1989), but the incorporation of an individual's developmentally instigative characteristics helps explain the process that occurs in these face-to-face interactions. In the next section, I explore the process more fully.

PROCESS

Critical to ecology theory, proximal processes are enduring forms of progressively more complex, reciprocal interactions between a developing person and the persons, objects and symbols in her or his environment (Bronfenbrenner, 1995, p. 620). This definition contains several key ideas: (a) processes are ongoing, enduring forms; (b) they are progressively more complex; (c) they are reciprocal; (d) they involve interactions between an evolving person and other people, or objects or symbols; (e) they occur in the setting containing the developing individual. These ideas are important by themselves but gain context when compared with college student development theories and research on college students. To fully describe the process components of the PPCT model, I will attend to them individually, illustrating how they connect to extant student development theories.

The idea that developmental *processes are ongoing, enduring forms* means that they comprise a dynamic, ever-changing system. The requirement that they be ongoing in nature evokes Alexander Astin's involvement theory (1984), which calls for sustained experience as a catalyst for development. Karen Arnold (2000) argued, for example, that "encounters with 'different' others will be ineffective developmental influences if contact is unsustained or superficial" (p. 9). She contrasted this experience with those to be had in "highly intellectual environments, such as those found at selective liberal arts colleges," where students are immersed in an intellectual faculty and peer culture.

Critical to the process component of development is the idea that individuals must encounter *increasingly complex environments* to which they must accommodate. Familiar to student development researchers and student affairs professionals in the form of Nevitt Sanford's theory of challenge and support (1960), Bronfenbrenner couches this concept as one of "forces" and "resources." In order to develop and change, an individual must encounter a variety of increasingly complex forces (challenges) and have the necessary resources (supports) to adapt to them. Too much force/challenge with inadequate resources/supports overwhelms the student, leading to paralysis; not enough challenge results in boredom or lack of stimulation. Of course, a student's personal background and developmentally instigative characteristics mediate this effect—to push two stereotypes, an adventure-seeking first-year student from an urban area may be more brave than a somewhat timid student from a rural community in tackling the campus bus system at a large institution in a busy city, just as that same adventure seeker might be frustrated by the lack of infrastructure at a small college in an isolated town, where her timid friend feels comfortably challenged negotiating the local Greyhound bus schedule for a weekend at home.

Reciprocity of the person-environment interaction is central to ecology theory because "the developing person is viewed not merely as a tabula rasa on which the environment makes its impact, but as a growing, dynamic entity that progressively moves into and restructures the milieu in which it resides," yet "the environment also exerts its influence, requiring a process of mutual accommodation" (Bronfenbrenner, 1979, pp. 21–22). This ongoing mutual accommodation manifests itself in changes in the individual and changes to the environment. It also involves an individual's developmentally instigative characteristics, such as tolerance for ambiguity and challenge seeking. According to ecology theory, "there is always an interplay between the psychological characteristics of the person and of a specific environment; the one cannot be defined without the other" (Bronfenbrenner, 1989, p. 225). For example, individual students in a seminar course will adapt to the expectations of the instructor and their peers, but they will also exert their own influence on the nature and direction of the course. The community of a residence hall floor will similarly influence individual behavior and development, just as it is influenced by the development and behavior of the residents.

Developmental interactions include *influential persons, objects, and symbols*. In his 1979 work, Bronfenbrenner proposed that these interactions occur "whenever one person in a setting pays attention to or participates in the activities of another" (p. 56). So the developmental process may be a result of indirect (paying attention to someone else's activities) or direct (participating in activities with someone else) interaction. Development may also occur in interactions with the physical or symbolic environment, such as when a student learns a new athletic skill, learns to connect her computer to the Ethernet in her new residence hall room, or is confronted with unfamiliar visual, textual, or cultural symbols (including those that abound in campus acronyms, abbreviations, and slang).

Critical to the process component of the ecology model is that *developmental interactions occur in settings that contain the individual*. On the surface, this element seems self-evident. Of course the person must be present in the setting where the interaction occurs if that interaction is to have an influence on her development; but as we will see in the next section in a discussion of the *exosystem,* one level of environmental context, some interactions that occur away from the individual may nevertheless exert an influence on development. The foci of the developmental process, however, are interactions that contain the individual—also called "proximal processes." Technology, of course, has deeply altered our ideas of what is meant by "containing" a person. We are "contained" by settings that are created online, on the phone, through our books, magazines, televisions, and other media that deliver the unceasing visual, textual, and auditory stimuli that have become what Kenneth Gergen has called the "multiphrenetic population of the self" (1991).

While these five elements—endurance, progressive complexity, reciprocity, interactivity, and proximity—frame the process component, the quality of various developmental processes may be further enhanced or inhibited by the nature of specific interactions and the ways in which those interactions fit into the larger context of developmental stimuli. In the next section, I will describe this larger context and then return to some of the ways in which the process is affected by the context.

Context

When considering something called an "ecology model," many people think first of the component Bronfenbrenner has labeled "context," for it is the environment surrounding an individual—her or his context—that comes first to mind when we think of ecology. Indeed, person-environment theories of development (Banning & Kaiser, 1974; Strange & Banning, 2001; Tinto, 1993; Weidman, 1989) draw attention to this element, sometimes to the exclusion of the person, process, and time elements also important to Bronfenbrenner. It is true that context plays a leading role in Bronfenbrenner's model, perhaps most strongly supported by process, then Person and Time. In this section, I describe four key elements of the context component and some of the ways in which contextual differences influence the developmental process.

According to Bronfenbrenner (1979), "The *ecological environment* is conceived typologically as a nested arrangement of concentric structures, each contained within the next. These structures are referred to as the *micro-, meso-, exo-,* and *macrosystems*" (p. 22, italics in original). Whether understood in relation to young children, as in Bronfenbrenner's work, or in relation to postsecondary students, the four levels of the ecological environment work independently and as a system to influence development through the processes described in the previous section.

Microsystems represent the most basic unit of the model and are the location of the proximal processes considered central to development. According to Bronfenbrenner (1993),

> A microsystem is a pattern of activities, roles, and interpersonal relations experienced by the developing person in a given setting with particular

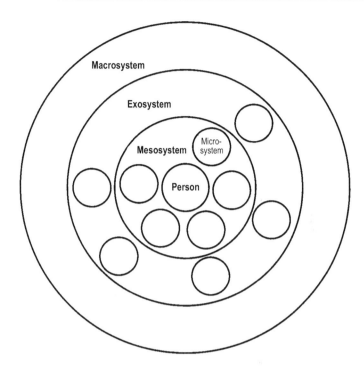

FIGURE 2.1
The Ecology of College Student Development

physical, social, and symbolic features that invite, permit, or inhibit engagement in sustained, progressively more complex interaction with, and activity in, the immediate environment. (p. 15)

In higher education, microsystems include academic settings (classes, labora-
tory and recitation sections, study and project groups), residential and/or family settings (residence halls, student apartments, family homes), formal cocurricular and/or community settings (student organizations, intercollegiate and
intramural athletic teams, performance groups, faith communities, community service sponsors), and informal social settings (friendship groups, dating
or partner/spousal relationships).

Microsystems are the settings where important relationships such as
those stressed by Astin's (1984) involvement theory, Vincent Tinto's theory
of student departure (1993), and John Weidman's (1989) undergraduate
socialization develop and are sustained. And whereas Astin, Tinto, and Weidman primarily addressed relationships in the lives of so-called traditional
students (i.e., first-time, full-time college students, attending college directly

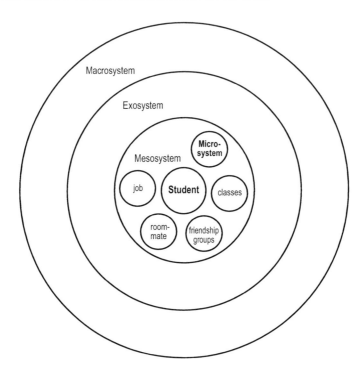

FIGURE 2.2
Typical Microsystems for a College Student

from high school and not supporting a household of their own), the ecology model is flexible enough to accommodate a broader array of students, including the working adult who is enrolled part-time—the so-called nontraditional student who now comprises over a third of the national undergraduate student body. For her, important microsystems might include workplace relationships, classes and study groups, partner and children, and community and civic organizations. Viewed as a problem, or at least a challenging anomaly, by Astin's involvement theory, this student would be viewed as no more or less challenging than other students for having microsystems not dominated by campus life.

Whether a student's microsystems exist primarily on campus or not, the microsystems are the setting of the proximal processes central to development. Participation in some microsystems will be entirely voluntary, the result of some developmentally instigative characteristic or personal preference (e.g., playing a club sport, writing for the student newspaper, living in a fraternity house). Participation in others may be more compulsory (e.g., tak-

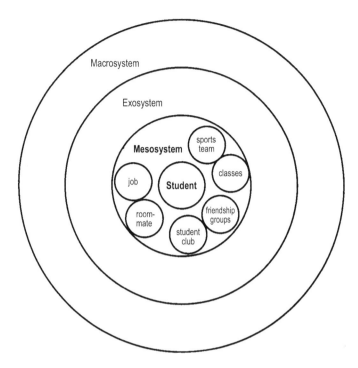

FIGURE 2.3
Typical Mesosystems for a College Student

ing a required course, participating in the basic training required of ROTC candidates), though the student ultimately has the option not to participate; of course, nonparticipation may lead to highly undesirable consequences, including not satisfying graduation requirements or losing a scholarship necessary for continued enrollment. A student's orientation to the microsystem may influence the degree to which that setting exerts developmental force, as may the experiences and predispositions the student brings to that setting.

Microsystems do not operate only as independent settings exerting forces on individuals; microsystems also operate with one another in *mesosystems,* creating an interactive developmental field in which an individual is embedded. The mesosystem is a web of involvements that "comprises linkages and processes taking place between two or more settings containing the developing person. Special attention is focused on the synergistic effects created by the interaction of developmentally instigative or inhibitory features and processes present in each setting" (Bronfenbrenner, 1993, p. 22). On campus, mesosystems might include the interactions between and among the various academic, social, co-curricular, and familial microsystems.

Karen Arnold and I have argued that such mesosystems are the mechanism by which campus peer cultures are created (Arnold, 2000; Renn, 2000, 2003; Renn & Arnold, 2003). This "mesosystem of peer culture," as we have called it, has been shown repeatedly to have a significant—perhaps the most significant—influence on student development and college outcomes (see, e.g., Astin, 1968, 1984, 1993a; Clark & Trow, 1966; Kuh, Hu, & Vesper, 2000; Newcomb, 1966; Pascarella & Terenzini, 1991; Tinto, 1993; Weidman, 1989). Peer culture sends powerful messages about the desirability and acceptability of certain identities, attitudes, and behaviors. As we will see in the coming chapters, the mesosystem of peer culture plays a crucial role in the identities of multiracial students, the approaches they take to identity, and the activities in which they engage to explore, claim, and signify their racial and ethnic identities.

While the power of peer culture in the development of student identity should not be underestimated, it is not the only operant mesosystem in this arena. Mesosystems formed by the interaction of on-campus and off-campus microsystems (e.g., friendship groups interacting with family or academic work with faith community) may also exert powerful influences on student development and identities. Messages received from friends may reinforce or call into question parental values, just as the curriculum might confirm or challenge the teachings of a religious tradition. The developmental challenge to the individual is to respond and adapt to these forces, as well as to exert his or her own force on these interacting environments.

Attending to the "synergistic effects created by the interaction of developmentally instigative or inhibitory features and processes present in each setting" (Bronfenbrenner, 1993, p. 22) gives power to the mesosystem as a developmental milieu. Forces and resources present in each microsystem interact in unique ways to create one-of-a-kind environments for each student. Indeed, even siblings attending the same institution, taking the same classes, and playing together on the same sports team would have different experiences based on their own developmentally instigative characteristics, preferences, and proclivities. Likewise, students from very different backgrounds, engaged in different activities, might have similar developmental outcomes depending on the combination and timing of various synergistic effects in the mesosystem.

A particular strength of the mesosystem is that it takes into account the unique—and unpredictable—nature of an individual's relationship with interacting microsystems. Whereas involvement theory (Astin, 1984) focuses on the microsystem as the level of analysis, comparing involvements in different arenas of campus life to see which have the greatest influence on student outcomes, the ecology model accounts for the effect of microsystem interactions in the mesosystem. This model is messier and more individualized, but in that sense it may be a more accurate depiction of the messy and

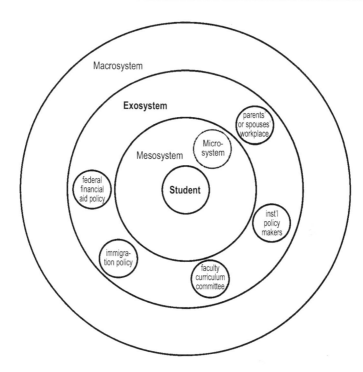

FIGURE 2.4
Typical Exosystems for College Students

individualized experiences of an increasingly diverse student population. I would not argue against the major tenets of involvement theory (such as the premise that the quality of the outcome depends in large part on the quality of the involvement), but I do argue that interactive effects are at least as important as the effects of individual microsystems. Amidst calls for the creation of "seamless learning environments" (Kuh, 1996), the mesosystem holds potential as a level of analysis that does not bifurcate student experience into academic and nonacademic, on campus and off campus, or faculty expectations and peer culture.

The *exosystem*, too, is important in examining student development and learning in a seamless fashion. Defined as "the linkages and processes taking place between two or more settings, at least one of which does not contain the developing person, but in which events occur that indirectly influence processes within the immediate setting in which the developing person lives" (Bronfenbrenner, 1993, p. 24). We are unaccustomed to considering environments that *do not contain* the individual in question. Why, we might ask, would they matter to development? What influence could they have if they do not contain the developing individual? In short, exosystems are important because they shape developmental possibilities and pose a variety of forces and resources to the individual.

More concretely, a residential student's exosystems might include a far-away family, parents' workplaces, and settings on and off campus, such as faculty committees and federal agencies, where policies are made that influence the individual. A marriage, separation, divorce, or sibling birth at home would affect most students. If a parent loses a job or gets a significant salary increase, the student might experience changes in financial forces and resources. Faculty decisions about graduation requirements or curricula would affect the student, as would changes in federal financial aid policy. An adult learner might be affected by changes in a partner or spouse's workplace, a child's day care setting or school, or decisions made at her own place of employment at levels to which she does not have access. Certainly Clinton-era changes in federal and state welfare policy have affected the lives of thousands of students, although they were not present when the changes were discussed or made. Through a direct domino effect (parent or partner/spouse loses job, student must seek employment) or through an indirect emotional effect (parent or partner/spouse loses job, student does not need to seek employment, but is prompted to worry about how she is meeting others' expectations), events in the exosystem exert developmental forces as well as present developmental resources.

Developmental forces and resources are also present in the *macrosystem*, defined by Bronfenbrenner (1993) as

> The overarching pattern of micro-, meso-, and exosystems characteristic of a given culture, subculture, or other extended social structure, with particular reference to the developmentally instigative belief systems, resources, hazards, lifestyles, opportunity structures, life course options and patterns of social interchange that are embedded in such overarching systems. (p. 25)

The macrosystem thus includes the sociocultural environment, made manifest in the proximal processes of student development. In the United States, macrosystem influences include patterns of social stratification and mobility, the economic system and capitalist ideology, a belief in the ideal of meritocracy and achievement of individual potential, as well as cultural understandings of gender, race, and ethnicity (Arnold, 2000; Renn, 2003; Renn & Arnold, 2003).

Theodore Wachs (1992) clarified the difference between macrosystems and cultures:

> While both macrosystems and cultures involve shared beliefs and values, macrosystems also can be defined based on shared resources, shared hazards,

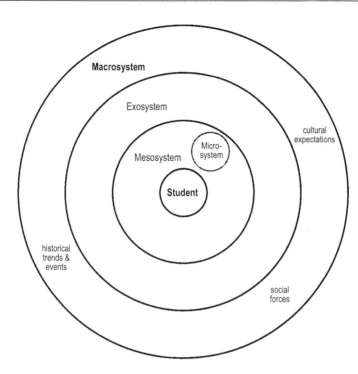

FIGURE 2.5
Macrosystem Effects on College Students

or shared historical events. Thus ethnic neighborhoods or eras (i.e. the "1960s"), while not fitting the definition of a culture, could fit the definition of a macrosystem. (p. 42)

Arguing that "macrosystem is not synonymous with culture," Karen Arnold (2000) explained:

> The macrosystem, therefore may be seen as heterogeneous, and student outcomes seen in terms of their "fit" with various macrosystems within and outside of higher education. For intance, a first generation college student might exhibit a poor fit with the cultural capital of the dominant elite as expressed in the proximal processes of interaction and rewards in peer groups and academic settings (Bourdieu, 1977). (Arnold, 2000, p. 29)

The distinction between macrosystem and culture or subculture is an important one in examining the college environment; "peer culture," as generally described and studied in higher education (e.g., Astin, 1993a; Clark & Trow, 1966; Feldman & Newcomb, 1969; Holland, 1966; Horowitz, 1987; Katchadourian & Boli,

1985; Kuh, Hu, & Vesper, 2000; Weidman, 1989) refers to the mesosystem level of Bronfenbrenner's ecology model. The macrosystem extends beyond and, indeed, encompasses wholesale the on and off campus cultures and environments influencing development.

Some examples of macrosystem influences may be useful here. Karen Arnold and I proposed that "who attends what college and on what terms might seem to be an individual or at least family-based decision, but the conditions that govern college-choice making are located in the macrosystem and only made manifest locally" (Renn & Arnold, 2003, p. 273). Fleshing out this proposition, we can easily conjure examples from the demography of postsecondary education today. Macrosystem influences maintained by educational traditions in geographic regions might propel high-achieving New England students to an elite private liberal arts college, while their equally talented and prepared peers in California or Michigan might elect an elite public research institution. Until 1996 only men could enroll in The Citadel and the Virginia Military Institute (both public institutions); until the "opportunity structures" located at these institutions—and the "life course options" supported by them—were made available to women, the potential for experiencing the developmentally enhancing influences of attending one of those institutions was limited to men. The macrosystem thus holds the developmental opportunities that will be made possible within the micro-, meso-, and exosystems, but it is not immune from influences arising from these systems; interactions between and among systems are a hallmark of the Bronfenbrenner ecology model.

Taken individually, the micro-, meso-, exo-, and macrosystems exert powerful influences on individual development; by taking into account the interactions between and among the systems, the entire context of the ecology model becomes not only more powerful, but also a dynamic, elastic environment that influences the individual and is influenced by her or him. While a number of person-environment theories go no further than the context—and, to be sure, there is plenty to explore in this component alone—Bronfenbrenner's ecology model holds the context as an important but not complete explanation for variations in individual development. Applying the context component as a whole to the higher education context (see figure 2.6), the multiple, interacting systems create a map onto which to plot developmental forces and resources. An appealing visual representation of the influences on an individual, it is nevertheless only one of the four components of the person-process-context-time framework. Just as the micro-, meso-, exo-, and macrosystems interact, so too do the person, process, context, and time components.

As I remarked at the end of the Process section, there are important ways in which aspects of the context (micro-, meso-, exo-, and macrosystems) might accentuate or diminish various developmental influences. Three

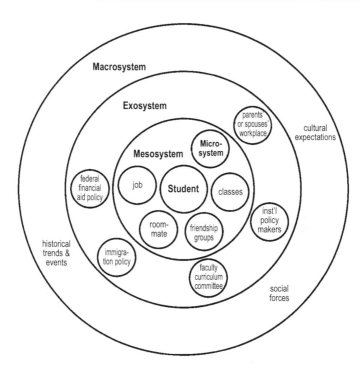

FIGURE 2.6
The Ecology of College Student Development

important ones involve the *degree to which settings are diverse*, the *degree to which settings are congruent*, and the *existence of ecological niches that favor different developmentally instigative characteristics*. I will describe each factor here and in more depth later when describing specific ecological effects on mixed race identity.

First, while the need for increasing complexity and a force-resource balance is critical for development, the *variety of settings containing an individual* can substantially enhance their influence. Bronfenbrenner (1979) hypothesized that "the positive developmental effects of participation in multiple settings are enhanced when the settings occur in cultural or subcultural contexts that are different from each other, in terms of ethnicity, social class, religion, age group, or other background factors" (p. 213). Thus, the development of an individual who participates in a culturally diverse array of micro- and mesosystems may be greater than that of an individual who participates in a homogeneous set of systems. Many college campuses, including the six involved in my study, offer a range of campus subcultures, even when the student body as a whole appears to be somewhat homogeneous. The benefits to a student attending an institution with a demographically diverse student body may be significant, as might the benefits of purposefully selecting activities and settings (such as cultural groups, study abroad programs, community service projects) that would bring a student into a range of settings.

Bronfenbrenner (1979) further hypothesized that "development is enhanced as a direct function of the number of structurally different settings in which the developing person participates in a variety of joint activities and primary dyads with others, *particularly when these others are more mature or experienced*" (p. 212, italics added). He specifically cited a higher education example:

> Based on this hypothesis, one could make the following prediction: holding age and socioeconomic factors constant, a young person entering college who has been closely associated with adults outside the family, has lived away from home, and held a number of jobs will be able to profit more from a college education than one whose experience has been more limited. (Bronfenbrenner, 1979, p. 212)

This structural and interactive variety is believed to require the student to adapt to a wider range of situations, leading to an increased scope and flexibility of cognitive and social competence. We sometimes see this phenomenon on campus among undergraduate adult learners or graduate students, who are better prepared to take advantage of the curriculum than their younger, often less experienced peers. Both kinds of heterogeneity of microsystem—among subcultures and with a wider range of ages within a microsystem—have the potential to enhance developmental processes.

A second contextual factor that might influence the process of development is the *degree of congruence or incongruence* between and among settings. By congruence I mean the extent to which the messages and developmental forces present in different settings are similar and convergent or contradictory and divergent. I do not propose this effect to be unidirectional, meaning that greater or lesser congruence results in greater or lesser development; rather, the degree of congruence has the potential either to enhance or to inhibit developmental processes. For example, on the one hand, a student whose family and school microsystems encourage traditional forms of academic achievement may, if he or she is inclined in that direction, benefit from the reinforcing mesosystem created by family and school; a student who is inclined toward musical performance or visual art, on the other hand, faced with the same congruent messages about traditional academic achievement might be paralyzed in the face of this family-school congruence. Moreover, the art-inclined student whose family supports traditional academic achievement but who ends up in the studio of a gifted artist and teacher who supports artistic accomplishment would experience incongruent messages from these microsystems (home and school). The incongruence might be perceived as more supportive than the congruent, but anti-art, message of the previous example; the incongruity might create more opportunities for individual development, as the aspiring artist sorted through the messages coming from family and school. Evoking John Holland's (1966) reliance on congruity and incongruity in an academic and vocational typology, I add the factor of interacting microsystems; whereas Holland focused on congruity between student and academic/vocational context, I focus in the ecology model on congruity between and among micro-, meso-, and exosystems as well as on congruity of messages with the receiver's inclinations and proclivities.

In describing the ecology of talent development in higher education settings, Karen Arnold (in Renn & Arnold, 2003) proposed that talent may be best enhanced in highly congruent environments. Drawing from her work with American Rhodes Scholars, she proposed that "congruence among individual characteristics, microsystems, and mesosystem could lead to the kinds of attitudes and behaviors that characterize Rhodes Scholars" (p. 279). She explained: "Rhodes Scholars might be expected to demonstrate a synergistic level of congruence between their immediate settings, in which family, peers, and faculty act as reinforcing sources of support for academic achievement and leadership" (p. 279). She cited the particular example of the U.S. Military Academy (West Point), whose "emphasis on character, scholarship, leadership, and athletics touches students through proximal processes in virtually all of the settings in which they are present" (pp. 279–80); according to Arnold, these norms, congruent and inescapable by West Point cadets, mirror the criteria for the selection of Rhodes Scholars. It is thus not surprising that West Point is the fourth-highest producer of Rhodes Scholars, joining Harvard, Princeton, and Yale in an elite cadre whose representation among Rhodes Scholars is deeply disproportionate to the number of students they graduate (Youn, Arnold, & Salkever, 1998). Congruity, in this case, breeds success.

Turning also to the potential benefits of incongruity, which feature strongly in the development of mixed race student identities, the key factor here would seem to be the potential for incongruity to pose cognitive, personal, and interpersonal challenges to the status quo. If, for example, you live in a family where parents and children are not of the same race but attend a school where teachers insist that there are "blacks" and "whites" and "asians" who can be grouped discretely, the messages about what it means to have (or be of) a race will be incongruent. Similarly, if you are the child of lesbian parents you may receive conflicting messages about "what makes a family" from home, school, and faith community. The child of an interracial or same-sex (or both) couple may receive incongruous messages, and these messages may prompt him or her to question the given-ness of categories seen by many as fixed and static. George Kich (1992, 1996) proposed that the questioning of these categories may itself prompt accelerated cognitive development and flexibility. It is therefore not necessarily the case that incongruity in context leads to inhibited developmental process, just as it is not the case that congruity leads unquestionably to enhanced development.

The third contextual quality that I will discuss in relationship to developmental process is the existence of *ecological niches*. Just as in biological ecosystems, some micro- and mesosystems represent "specified regions in the environment that are especially favorable or unfavorable to the development of individuals with particular personal characteristics" (Bronfenbrenner, 1993, p. 18). Institutions with special missions (military academies, single-sex colleges, historically black colleges and universities, tribal colleges, etc.) attract and support particular types of student bodies, acting as ecological niches that are especially favorable to students whose attitudes and characteristics are congruent with institutional philosophies and especially unfavorable to students whose characteristics are incongruent (Renn & Arnold, 2003). Ecological niches also exist within institutions, enhancing or inhibiting the development of students with different characteristics. The context of an ecological niche thus influences developmental processes in different ways, reinforcing certain development along certain lines and discouraging it along others.

These three factors—variety of systems, congruence or incongruence with systems, and ecological niches—illustrate the influence of context on process. Of course, they also illustrate the influence of person on context and process as well, drawing attention to the ways in which an individual's developmentally instigative characteristics draw her or him to explore a more or less limited range of environments, to interact with congruent or incongruent forces, and to experience supportive or unsupportive ecological niches in the environment. They call to mind Vincent Tinto's theory of student departure (1993), which posits that the extent to which students are integrated into academic and social settings in the collegiate environment influences the likelihood that they will persist. They also evoke the work of George Kuh, John Schuh, and Elizabeth Whitt (1991), who profiled "involving colleges" where students engaged in a range of related settings, received congruent messages about community and learning, and experienced supportive ecological niches.

Time

The final component of the PPCT model is time, represented in what Bronfenbrenner called the "chronosystem." Explicitly included in later iterations of the model, the chronosystem captures two perspectives of time: historical and personal.

> The individual's own developmental life course is seen as embedded in and powerfully shaped by conditions and events occurring during the historical

period through which the person lives. . . . A major factor influencing the course and outcome of human development is the timing of biological and social transitions as they relate to the culturally defined age, role expectations, and opportunities occurring throughout the life course. (Bronfenbrenner, 1995, p. 641)

The chronosystem thus operates at a sociohistorical level to make possible certain kinds of developmentally instigative opportunities (e.g., legal desegregation of public institutions or the admission of women to military academies), as well as at an individual level according to the timing of life events in the microsystems (e.g., a divorce, sibling birth, study abroad).

The chronosystem interacts closely with the macrosystem in conveying the element of time as manifest in changes in large cultural forces. The experiences of women students in the 1880s, for example, differed significantly from those of the 1920s, 1950s, or 1980s.[2] Attending college as a woman meant something different during these decades, as economic, educational, and cultural trends created time-bound cohort effects manifested in curricular choices, social life, and vocational decisions after graduation.

On an individual level, time can also be examined in relationship to the sequencing of events over the life course. A clear example involves the comparison of a student entering college full-time immediately after high school, who generally has different role and family expectations from the student who enters several years later, while working, partnering, and parenting. For these two students, the transition to college has a different meaning and consequences and will present different—though perhaps related—developmental forces and resources. The accumulation of experiences prior to and during college influences the person component of the PPCT model more than any other, and the chronosystem thus has individual as well as cohort influences.

Person-Process-Context-Time

The four components of the PPCT model interact to create a unique developmental environment for each individual. Although personal characteristics such as gender, race, and age can be separated out and "controlled for" in analyses of college student outcomes, the cumulative, dynamic interactions, influenced by developmentally instigative characteristics of people and environments, cannot be so easily parsed. The PPCT model proposes an explanation for the differential outcomes of students who appear to be similar; it also proposes an explanation for the similar outcome of students who appear to be very different from one another.

The fourfold approach of the PPCT model does not make for straightforward analyses of developmental outcomes in ways that can easily be generalized to large populations of college students. The model is not prescriptive or diagnostic. But because it accounts specifically for differing social, cultural, and historical contexts, it is especially useful in analyzing the development of students across institutional settings in light of dynamic, fluid notions of identity. In the remainder of this chapter, I discuss how the ecology model's flexibility and attention to context provide an alternative to the traditional, stage-based theories of identity development that predominate the college student development literature, focusing on the influence of the mesosystem of campus peer cultures on individual identity development.

ECOLOGY THEORY AS AN ALTERNATIVE TO STAGE-BASED THEORIES OF IDENTITY DEVELOPMENT

College student development theory derives significantly from the work of Erik Erikson (1968), who was a pioneer in extending Freudian constructs to explore development over the lifespan. Central to Erikson's work was the principle that development proceeds unidirectionally, through a series of invariant stages. Each stage is characterized by a *crisis* that must be resolved before further development can occur. Appealing in its treatment of the lifespan (versus Freud's emphasis on the first few years of life), Erikson's approach to development included a specific exploration of the identity crisis of adolescence, which became a starting point for subsequent researchers and theorists concerned with the experiences of college students.

Significant among these theorists was William Perry. In 1968 Perry published the results of several years of observation of and interviews with Harvard College men in *Forms of Intellectual and Ethical Development in the College Years: A Scheme*. The "Perry Scheme" followed a stage model and traced students' cognitive and moral development from the dualist, right-or-wrong orientation of younger, less experienced students to the relativist, differentiating orientation of their older, more experienced peers. Ideally, according to Perry, college men would arrive at a place where they could make commitments in relativism, recognizing the messiness of the world while also evaluating intellectual and ethical claims within a unified, mature worldview. Like Erikson, Perry posited a unidirectional model, where resolution of challenges at one level was necessary for movement to the next.

Also among the theorists following Erikson was Arthur Chickering, whose 1969 *Education and Identity*—revised with Linda Reisser and published in a second edition in 1993—introduced seven "vectors" related to the formation of identity, purpose, and commitments during the college years. Not a stage model, the vectors in their initial and revised form nevertheless implied an order to development that, while not subscribing strictly to Erikson's rigid stages, relied on accomplishment of some developmental tasks before others can fully proceed. In the vector model, identity development is understood generally to be achieving "that solid sense of self that assumes form as [other] developmental tasks . . . are undertaken with some success, and which . . . provides a framework for interpersonal relationships, purposes, and integrity" (Chickering & Reiser, 1993, p. 80). College students engage in a process of examining the systems of values and ethics taught to them by family and peers, creating new systems of beliefs and behaviors to match their self-definitions and lifestyles. They emerge from college with an identity forged in the academic and peer culture of the campus. This sense of self includes conceptions of body and appearance, as well as clarification of gender, sexual, and racial identity (Chickering & Reiser, 1993). An important addition to the student development literature, the seven vectors were the subject of substantial empirical investigation, a fair amount of which misinterpreted or overstated the sequential nature of the vectors, reinforcing the impression that the vectors were, in fact, intended as a stage model (for a discussion of this phenomenon, see Thomas & Chickering, 1984; Reisser, 1995).

Perry's scheme and Chickering's vectors form the foundation of what could be called a "canon" of college student development theory. They are taught in nearly all graduate programs that prepare college student affairs administrators, are frequently cited in research, and are part of the professional patois passed on to resident assistants, student leaders, and paraprofessionals through annual training and development programs on campus. Yet they also tacitly assert a linear, stage approach to understanding student development that often goes unquestioned in research and professional practice, laying the groundwork for unquestioned acceptance of other linear theories, such as those related to racial, ethnic, gender, and sexual orientation identities (e.g., Atkinson, Morten, & Sue, 1993; Cass, 1979; Cross, 1991, 1995; Gilligan, 1977, 1981; Helms, 1990).

Bronfenbrenner's ecology model, as described in this chapter, counters this tendency by calling attention to how individual differences and histories interact with dynamic environments to create unique patterns of developmental opportunities and outcomes. It provides for the possibility of ongoing identity construction and deconstruction in complex environments. It also provides for the possibility that individuals shape environments just as environments shape people, a concept not emphasized by Erikson, Perry, or Chickering and Reisser. While these foundational theories are important to understanding identity development, they treat identity as a fairly fixed notion that the student works to discover as he or she "finds" him- or herself in college.

In chapter 1, I discussed the influence of postmodernism on notions of identity and identity development. Faced with the prospect that college students will no longer be "finding themselves" but will instead be finding ways of constantly constructing and reconstructing identity in shifting contexts of face-to-face and cyber encounters with others (who are themselves constantly constructing their identities), postsecondary educators will find that the foundational student development theories will go only so far in guiding policy, programs, and practice. Rather than relying on models to help students achieve a singular sense of identity, they will need models that account for the increasing range of students' entering characteristics and identities, as well as the idiosyncratic ecologies of each student. If William Tierney (1993) is correct that identity depends on time and context, and individuals are "constantly redescribed by institutional and ideological mechanisms of power" (p. 63) such as those that might be encountered in micro- and mesosystems, developmental models that can account for fluidity, complexity, and context will become essential resources in the toolkits of higher education educators and policy makers.

Bronfenbrenner's ecology model contains the flexibility required to meet the postmodern call to understand identity as fluid, shifting, and contextual. Incorporating it into the body of college student development theory could provide a useful counterbalance to the dominant stage model approach to understanding student identities.

THE INFLUENCE OF COLLEGE PEER CULTURES ON INDIVIDUAL IDENTITY

A particularly useful application of ecology theory is in the study of college peer cultures and their influence on identity. As we will see in chapters 4 through 8, the mesosystem of peer culture was a key determinant in the racial identity choices of mixed race students. In this section, I will describe some of the developmental forces of the peer culture mesosystem especially relevant to individual identity development in college students.

The influence of peers on college students is well documented (e.g., Astin, 1968, 1984, 1993a, 1993b; Clark & Trow, 1966; Newcomb, 1966; Kuh, 1990; Kuh, Hu, & Vesper, 2000; Pascarella & Terenzini, 1991; Weidman, 1989). Alexander Astin asserted that peer groups are "the single most potent source of influence (1993b, p. 398). For the most part, though, the mechanisms through which peers influence student development and college outcomes have not been well described, a situation Kuh analyzed in his 1995 call to "cultivate 'high stakes' student culture research." If peer culture can be considered a mesosystem context, the person and process elements of the ecology model are very useful additions to studying its operation and transformative influence in students' lives. I offer an illustration from the area of racial identity development. Race is a socially constructed identity and as such is well suited to examination through a lens that filters development through a sociohistorical ecology framework.

RACIAL IDENTITY DEVELOPMENT AND PEER CONTEXTS

Whether one subscribes to a stage model orientation or to a more fluid model of racial identity development, the peer context is a critical feature.

The interactions between and among peer microsystems create a mesosystem of peer culture in which students, especially those who are full-time and residential, are immersed. Given differences in individual developmentally instigative characteristics, students will seek or avoid settings where members of various racial, ethnic, and cultural groups come together. These public and private settings, some formal and others informal, become places for students to "try on" different identities, to immerse themselves in groups of like others, and to experience belonging to race-based reference groups. Beverly Daniels Tatum describes such settings in her book "Why Are All the Black Kids Sitting Together in the Cafeteria?" and Other Conversations about Race (1995). Tatum and others (Cross, 1991, 1995; Helms, 1991, 1995; Phinney, 1990) described the ways that acceptance in or rejection from these groups may lead to adoption of an identity (identity achievement in James Marcia's terms), further exploration (moratorium), diffusion, or foreclosure. To best illustrate the influence of peer culture in the operation of stage models, I highlight three stages (or positions) common to stage models: encounter, immersion, integration.

As described in chapter 1, many stage models (e.g., Cross, 1995; Tatum, 1995) specify a stage of "encounter" in racial identity development. At this stage, the individual is becoming aware of his or her racial identity and how it operates in society. Campus peer culture may play a number of roles in this realization and exploration. For students who grew up in communities where theirs was the only family containing people of color, encountering an organized group of students of their race may be eye opening; likewise, students who grew up in communities where they were in the majority may encounter certain kinds of subtle and not-so-subtle racism for the first time on entering a predominantly white institution. Either of these experiences could be a developmental force as the student accommodates to a new understanding of race and racial identity. The same is true for white students, though they may be buffered by being part of the majority or by failing to notice discriminatory racial dynamics.

After the encounter experience, students of color are predicted to enter the immersion/emersion stage of development. On a campus where there is a critical mass of students of a certain race or ethnicity, opportunities for immersion in a racial identity are usually formed in and supported by peer culture. A student may belong to the Black Students Association, sing in a predominantly black gospel choir, take courses related to African American culture, join a black sorority, and live in a multicultural or African American focused living-learning community. She would have created for herself a fairly congruent, culturally focused mesosystem where she could explore her racial identity, quite possibly in the company of other black students much of the day. And, despite critics who would see her world as narrowly defined (though they would rarely offer similar criticism of a white woman who constructed her environment entirely in predominantly white settings), this immersion may be exactly what she needs to balance the experience of growing up in white American society and attending a predominantly white institution.

Another student, having experienced immersion, may emerge into a stage of integration, consciously seeking microsystems that emphasize a variety of identities. The student in the previous example might remain in the Black Students Association and sing in the choir but move into an apartment with a racially diverse group of women who met during a spring break service project in an urban women's shelter; she is then able to integrate her evolving sense of herself as an African American woman with her evolving concerns about women's issues and her sense of herself as a community activist. The messages about racial identity coming from each microsystem in this new configuration might not be as congruent as those experienced previously, but they might prompt development in different ways as the student manages challenges, supports, and ongoing questions about identity. As will become more clear in the following chapters, an ecological approach to studying racial identity works especially well in college environments, where peer culture may be magnified through residential students' total immersion in the setting.

SUMMARY OF THE ECOLOGY MODEL
AS APPLIED TO COLLEGE STUDENT DEVELOPMENT

Bronfenbrenner's PPCT model provides important advantages over developmental models that do not account simultaneously for person, process, context, time and the interactions among them. The model provides a heuristic for examining individual development, especially where interactions in the mesosystem affect the social construction of identity. In a world where "identity" has come to mean an ongoing dynamic process, rather than a static endpoint one reaches when one "discovers" oneself, the ecology model provides a lens through which to view the processes that happen when students encounter campus cultures created through the interactive web of academic, cocurricular, and social microsystems. The model also helps explain how the unique characteristics of each student shape development in ways that may not be predictable to educators attempting to influence development through environmental interventions and controls. It is useful not only for educational practice, however, as it can be used in research to examine the interactions of individuals and their environments. In the next section, I describe the research design I used to examine mixed race student identities through the lens of the ecology model.

USING THE ECOLOGY MODEL TO EXPLORE
MIXED RACE STUDENT IDENTITIES:
THE RESEARCH DESIGN

In order best to understand the context of the qualitative data I present in this book, it may be useful to understand how I collected and analyzed it. In short, I used ethnographic methods and grounded theory analysis to explore how college students with parents from more than one federally defined racial or ethnic background identified themselves and experienced the developmental influences of campus life. I conducted the study in four phases, on six campuses in three geographic regions, with a total of fifty-six undergraduate participants. In this section, I describe the campuses at which I conducted the study, the students who participated, the methods used to collect data, and the approaches used to analyze it. I also discuss some of the limitations imposed on the study by methodological decisions and circumstances. Readers more interested in the findings of the study than in the methods may want to go to chapters 3 to 9 and come back to this section later.

THE SIX CAMPUSES

In an effort to enrich the geographic reach of the literature on mixed race high school and college students, which has focused most often on the western United States (e.g., Field, 1996 in Colorado) and particularly on the West Coast (e.g., Cauce et al, 1992 in Seattle; Gibbs & Hines, 2001 and Wallace, 2001 in the San Francisco Bay area; Mass, 1992 and Williams, 1996 in southern California),[3] I selected three research sites in the Northeast (for phases I and II of data collection), two in the rural southern Midwest (Phase III), and one in the industrial northern Midwest (Phase IV). The six campuses represent a mix of public and private control; small (1,400 students), midsized (15,000–20,000 students) and very large (43,000 students) student bodies; most highly selective, selective, and nonselective admissions policies; and institutional type (community college, liberal arts college, comprehensive university, research university). One institution is Catholic, one is a former women's college, one is an elite private university, and one is in the Big Ten athletic conference. They are in state capitols, isolated farming communities, and leafy suburbs. Students are drawn to these institutions from local, regional, state, national, and international admissions pools. And while these six institutions certainly do not contain the universe of American higher education, I selected them because they provide important windows into disparate corners of that universe. In this section, I present a portrait of the six research sites, and in the next section I people them with the fifty-six mixed race students who participated in this study.

Northeast (Phases I and II)

Selected for their similarities (coeducational, private, primarily residential, focused on undergraduate education) and for their differences (size, selectivity, diversity of student bodies), the three institutions in the Northeast provided a solid base for understanding mixed race students' identity patterns and dynamics of peer culture.

Ivy University.[4] A private, coeducational, residential institution with an undergraduate student body of fifty-five hundred students, Ivy drew an international applicant pool and selected less than 20 percent of applicants for admission. Nearly one-third of the undergraduates were students of color from the United States and an additional 5 to 8 percent were international students. Students lived on campus from first through third year and then had the option of moving off campus, usually to apartments in privately owned houses in the neighborhood. Ivy University was the site of Phase I data collection (spring 1996) and one of three sites of Phase II (1997–1998). It is important to note that I was employed as a student affairs administrator at this institution during the first phase of data collection; my access to participants and information was therefore increased, though I was cautious about potential limitations placed on me by my dual role (administrator and researcher).

Catholic University. A coeducational, primarily residential university of approximately nine thousand undergraduates, Catholic University was located in the suburbs of a major metropolis in the Northeast. Students of color (known on campus as "AHANA" students, an acronym for Asian, Hispanic, African, and Native American) comprised 16 percent of the undergraduate population at the time of data collection; international students made up an additional 3 percent. Approximately 85 percent of the undergraduates identified as Catholic, though there was no requirement for participation in religious or faith-based activities on campus. Catholic University was considered highly selective, accepting about 40 percent of applicants for admission. About two-thirds of the student body lived on campus, which was preferred by many students, and the rest (usually sophomores and juniors, to whom campus housing was not guaranteed) lived nearby in apartments. Catholic University was a site of Phase II data collection (1997–1998).

Liberal Arts College. Founded as a women's college, Liberal Arts shifted its mission in the 1980s, admitting men, who at the time of the study comprised about 40 percent of the fourteen hundred students on campus. Twelve percent of the students were students of color, and 3 percent were international students. Liberal Arts admitted three-quarters of applicants, the majority of whom were from the Northeast. Liberal Arts was entirely residential; students were required to live in college-owned residence halls for four years.

Although Liberal Arts was located in a small town in a relatively undeveloped area, students had access by public transportation to two major urban areas in the region. Liberal Arts College participated in Phase II of the study (1997–1998).

Rural southern Midwest (Phase III)

Selected for their geographic proximity to one another and for the contrast they provided to one another and to the three institutions in Phases I and II, these institutions brought important regional racial dynamics—including communities descended from freed and escaped black slaves and the influence of migrant farm workers—to the study. Located in an area more stereotypically southern than midwestern in culture (think "grits and gravy" rather than "cheddar and brats"), these institutions were a two-hour drive to a major city. The collapse of the coalmining industry in the late twentieth century paralyzed the economic growth of the region, which was located in federal empowerment zone and rural health initiative territories. Both institutions in this region participated in Phase III of the study (2000–2001).

Rural University. Rural University was founded as a normal school and evolved into a public research institution with a strong focus on undergraduate education and a handful of graduate programs ranked among the top ten in the nation. Its eighteen thousand undergraduates came from around the world, though 80 percent were residents of the state. Nineteen percent of the undergraduates were students of color, and 4 percent were international students. Rural U was considered selective, accepting 69 percent of applicants for admission. Although located in a remote part of the state, Rural University attracted a large number of students from major urban areas, a circumstance that campus folklore attributed to the popular student claim that "Rural U was as far as I could get from home and still get in-state tuition." Rural U also attracted a significant percentage of students from small, homogeneous farming communities within one hundred miles of the campus. Several thousand students lived in campus housing, with the remainder renting in apartment buildings and trailers nearby.

Rural Community College. Ranked among the best community colleges in the nation, RCC had a very successful record of preparing students for transfer to four-year institutions, graduating students with associate's degrees, and providing workforce training in the region. Rural Community College enrolled about fifty-two hundred students in its transfer and career degree programs (another six thousand enroll in adult and continuing education courses). Nineteen percent of students at RCC were students of color, and a very small number were international students. Admission to RCC was open, and most students lived at home with parents, partners, or families.

Because of its proximity to Rural University, RCC was a feeder school to the four-year institution, and traditional-age undergraduates at RCC were frequent participants in activities and events at Rural University.

Industrial Northern Midwest (Phase IV)

Big Ten University. Big Ten enrolled over forty thousand students, thirty-five thousand of them undergraduates. A public land-grant university, Big Ten drew an international student body, with 3 percent international students. Admission to Big Ten was selective, with 65 percent of applicants being admitted. The university was located in a region that combined industry, government, and agriculture; because of its size, it contributed significantly to the local economy through employment, contracts, student expenditures, and the like. Eighteen percent of the undergraduates were students of color, and the international student and scholar population brought additional diversity to the predominantly white community in which Big Ten was located. Students from Big Ten participated in Phase IV of the study (2001–2002).

THE FIFTY-SIX PARTICIPANTS

Students who participated in this study met two basic criteria: they had parents from more than one federally designated racial or ethnic category, and they were in at least their second semester on campus. Currently, the U.S. government recognizes five racial categories (American Indian or Alaska Native, Asian, Black or African American, Native Hawai'in or Other Pacific Islander, White) and two ethnicities ("Hispanic or Latino" or "Not Hispanic or Latino") (OMB, 1997). Participants therefore were some combination of these categories (e.g., asian and latino; white and african american; black and hispanic).[5] In order to increase the likelihood that participants had been exposed to curricular and extracurricular opportunities on campus, the students were in at least their second semester on campus. Participants at the predominantly residential institutions (all except Rural Community College) were drawn from the population of students who had lived in college residence halls for the majority of their college years and who had lived away from home every semester while enrolled in college (i.e., in campus apartments, nearby student housing, or study abroad programs).

Students came to the study in a number of ways, which varied little from campus to campus. At all six campuses, I posted flyers advertising a study of "bi- and multiracial students" in high-traffic locations (such as student centers, the multicultural student programs offices, campus post offices, bulletin boards, laboratories, and locker rooms). I also utilized electronic bulletin boards, electronic mail lists of student organizations and institutional lists of self-identified students of color, personal contact in a few cases where I or a research associate knew of a student who was mixed race, and snowball sampling (Atkinson

TABLE 2.1
Institutional Summaries
(all data are from the year that research was conducted at the institution)

Research Phase	Institution	Number of Undergraduates	Students of color (U.S. citizens)	International students	Selectivity (Admissions rate)
I (1996–97) & II (1997–98)	Ivy University	5500	27%	6%	19%
II (1997–98)	Catholic University	9000	16%	3%	41%
II (1997–98)	Liberal Arts College	1400	12%	3%	75%
III (2000–01)	Rural University	18,000	19%	4%	69%
III (2000–01)	Rural Community College	5200*	19%	<1%	(open)
IV (2001–02)	Big Ten University	35,000	18%	3%	65%

* includes only transfer and career program students (six thousand additional students enrolled in adult and continuing education courses)

& Flint, 2001). Practicing maximum variation sampling (see Miles & Huberman, 1994), I selected students for participation based on gender identity, racial and ethnic heritage (including varying combinations of white parent with parent of color, and two parents of color), age, ability, sexual orientation, and class background. Appendix B contains an alphabetical list of all participants, their institution, class year, and heritages (table B.1), and a summary of participants by heritage groups (table B.2).

My criteria for sample size, both at individual institutions and for the total group, were *saturation* of information and *sufficiency* to allow others outside the sample to connect with the experience of those in it, as suggested by Seidman (1991). In Phase I (spring 1996), which was exploratory in nature, six students at Ivy University participated. Phase II (1997–1998) included eight students each from Ivy, Liberal Arts College, and Catholic University. Phase III (2000–2001) comprised six students from Rural Community College and eight students from Rural University, two of whom had also been community college students (one at Rural Community College, one elsewhere in the state). Twelve students from Big Ten University participated in Phase IV (2001–2002). While these fifty-six students cannot be considered representative of all mixed race students in the Northeast or the Midwest (to say nothing of the entire country), their experiences frame a window into the larger world of undergraduate experiences of students of color in general and mixed race students more specifically. Together with other recent studies that included multiracial college students (e.g. Kilson, 2001; Rockquemore, 2002; Rockquemore & Brunsma, 2002; Wallace, 2001), the participants in this study give voice to an important—and growing—population on campus.

DATA COLLECTION

There were four main components to data collection: individual interviews with the fifty-six participants, written responses by participants, a focus group of three or four students per campus (except at Big Ten University), and observations of and archival data about each campus vis-à-vis multiracial issues. I believed that students would express themselves differently through the different techniques; using a range of data collection strategies I hoped that all participants would find ways to express their understanding of themselves. Interviews provided an opportunity for individual students to respond in depth to questions about their college experiences and how they made sense of their multiraciality in the college setting. Written responses gave students a chance to reflect more deeply, in their own time and fashion, on how they made meaning of identity development. The focus groups accomplished several goals. They gave me an opportunity to watch how multiracial students interacted when asked to discuss their identity development; they provided students an opportunity to interact with their multiracial peers; they assisted in triangulating data; and they served as member checks. The archival research and observations provided background information about each campus milieu, particularly as it pertained to multiracial issues. In this section I will discuss each data collection method in detail.

Prior to the interview, all potential participants received an invitation letter from me about the study and signed an informed consent statement acknowledging potential personal risks and benefits of the study. Students also selected the pseudonyms by which they would be known during data analysis and reporting, including this book.

Individual Interviews

I conducted an individual interview with each participant; at Big Ten University, a research assistant and I conducted interviews together. Interviews ranged from forty-five minutes to two hours, and two-thirds of them were sixty to seventy-five minutes. Because of the more exploratory nature of Phase I, I conducted two interviews with each Phase I participant. I audio-taped all interviews for transcription and coding. Interviews followed the protocol included in appendix C, which provided open-ended questions for participant response. The interview questions for subsequent phases were derived from the results of Phase I (Renn, 1997) and reflected my interest in focusing on identity development in the college environment. Some of the questions came directly from Phase I, and some were developed to probe three major areas I identified as sites of identity development (peer culture, involvement in activities, and academic work). Each interview covered all of the questions on the protocol and also asked participants for more information on issues they raised that were not on the protocol. I ended interviews by inviting participants to add anything that they felt was important to the their understanding of their experience as multiracial college students or anything else that did not come up in the interview. Often this final question elicited important stories about a student's experience on campus.

Written Responses

At the end of the interviews, I gave participants a written prompt with instructions. I requested that they return their written response to me via mail or email within one week of the interview. The prompts were:

> Prompt A: First, describe something that happened to you in the past few days that related to your racial/ethnic identity. Then, tell me what that incident meant to you.

> Prompt B: Write about a time since you came to [school name] that you were aware of being multiracial. Again, please tell me what that situation meant to you.

While the majority of students required a reminder to return the written response, all but a few finally did. When the answers to these prompts are included as data in the book, they are presented exactly as written by the student (all punctuation, spelling, capitalization, etc.).

Campus Observations and Archival Research

I utilized campus publications, national publications that included information on each campus, Internet sites that referenced the institutions, and campus events to develop a profile of each campus vis-à-vis multiracial issues. When possible, I attended public events organized for or about multiracial students and made field notes to augment published and online sources. I was able to obtain poetry written by multiracial students about their experience as well as the script written by one participant for a performance art piece. Other participants gave me copies of papers or articles they had written about being multiracial.

Events included meetings and sponsored activities of monoracial campus groups (at all six sites) and organizations for mixed race students (at Ivy and Big Ten); panels on interracial dating (Ivy, Rural University, Big Ten); activities sponsored by historically black, latino, and "multicultural" sororities and fraternities (Ivy, Rural University, Big Ten); and two years of "Multiracial Heritage Week" activities at Ivy, each of which included a convocation with student speakers and a major lecture by an invited speaker. I attended both formally organized events (e.g., lectures, panel presentations, art displays, poetry slams, theater) and informal activities (e.g., open weekly meetings, socials). Through my professional work at Ivy prior to Phase I of this study I had previously observed and participated in numerous events for or about mixed race students. On the four campuses that at the time of data collection lacked a designated organization for mixed race students (Liberal Arts, Rural University, Rural Community College, and Catholic), I concentrated additional effort on organizations of monoracial students and on observations of student interactions in public social, recreational, and educational spaces (cafeterias, student unions, recreational complexes, libraries, academic lounges, and nearby off-campus establishments considered attractive "hang outs" for students of color).

With the help of bi- and multiracial students I had known before the study and those who participated in the study, I developed an archive of newspaper articles and publicity related to multiracial issues at Ivy from five years prior to the study. An organization of mixed race students was also quite helpful in collecting information about campus climate and multiracial students at Big Ten. At all institutions, I collected posters and flyers from events relating to issues of race, culture, or diversity sponsored by student groups and academic departments, and I monitored the daily or weekly student newspapers for any articles or letters related to race or race relations on campus. Archival materials augmented field notes from observations, facilitating the development of multitextured portraits of race, mixed race, and race relations at each campus.

Focus Groups

Focus groups served two important purposes: to bring together participants for discussion of mixed race issues on campus and to facilitate the research process through a member check. I conducted focus groups at the five campuses of Phases II and III, and the focus groups were comprised of volunteers from among the students interviewed at each campus. Focus group participants at Ivy had all encountered one another previously, in various activities on campus. At Catholic University, two of the four focus group participants knew one another through a friendship network that included a number of mixed race students. At Liberal Arts, Rural Community College, and Rural University, none of the participants had met prior to the focus group. I did not conduct a focus group at Big Ten because I had the opportunity to discuss emerging findings with a group of mixed race students, some of whom were interviewees and some of whom were not, and because scheduling an additional meeting of a subgroup of research participants proved infeasible.

Because I wanted to know if my developing analysis of data made sense to participants, I conducted member checks on each campus in Phases II and III by writing a summary of data collected in interviews, written responses, and field notes from that institution. I gave the summary to participants during the focus group sessions at these five institutions. The focus group protocol (included in appendix C) was designed to solicit feedback on how students perceived the accuracy of my summaries and the relevance of emerging codes and themes. For students not taking part in the focus group, I provided the same summaries and requested written feedback. Six participants chose to respond to the summaries. Information gathered during the member checks was incorporated into the study data.

DATA ANALYSIS

The data for this study thus consisted of audiotapes, transcripts, and field notes from the interviews and focus groups, the students' written responses, archival information and field notes from campus observations, and information gathered during member checks. In the first two phases, I framed my interpretation through grounded theory methodology (Glaser & Strauss, 1967) and developed the five-pattern schema of multiracial identity. In subsequent analyses, I compared data to the existing schema, refining and elaborating on the patterns when appropriate (for a discussion of using existing theories to guide qualitative data analysis, see Boyatzis, 1998; Coffey & Atkinson, 1996; Miles & Huberman, 1994; and Strauss & Corbin, 1994).

I began by hand coding transcripts of individual interviews. Based on the findings of Phase I and my decision to use the Bronfenbrenner (1979, 1993) ecology model as a conceptual framework, I anticipated the utility of codes relating to academic work, peer culture, involvement in activities, and identity development. In addition, I developed codes relating to family, international experience, race, culture, community, and personal development.

As I describe more fully in the limitations section below, I was concerned about how my identity as a monoracial white person and a college administrator might influence my data coding and analysis. To check my coding against that of a multiracial individual, I enlisted a biracial colleague familiar with qualitative research and identity development theory to code two Phase II transcripts and a written response. I also asked a multiracial Ivy University student who was not otherwise involved in the project to code two transcripts from interviews at the other campuses in Phase II. They independently agreed with my major codes, and each also made suggestions for modifying my subcodes slightly, which I did. I sought additional opportunities to present my data and emerging codes to colleagues from a variety of mono- and multiracial backgrounds and used their feedback to reshape my subcodes and focus my research questions. During Phase IV, I was assisted by a graduate student who identified as mixed race; her insights were invaluable additions to analysis of data from Phase IV and new interpretations of data from earlier analyses.

LIMITATIONS OF RESEARCH DESIGN AND METHODOLOGY

Like any example of research in higher education, my work with mixed race students is limited by a number of factors, some by design and others by default. I present them here so that my research can be interpreted in the context of these limitations. Key limitations include the nonlongitudinal nature of the research design, the nature of the sample, and my identity as a monoracial white woman.

First, although data collection spanned the years 1996 through 2002, the design was not a longitudinal study of the same fifty-six students over that time period. While the design illuminates individual identities at a given point in time, it does not capture the evolution of identities across time. Student accounts of their identity development play an important role in the telling of their stories, but the inability to follow up with students in the years following the interviews limits the findings in terms of identity *development;* the students still have plenty to say about mixed race *identities* on campus, but they simply cannot project their own future identities. In sacrificing a longitudinal design for geographic and institutional diversity, much is gained in terms of regional nuances and student experiences, but the outcome must be understood to be limited temporally.

The sample size and scope place additional limitations on the application of study findings. The experiences and identities of fifty-six students from six institutions form the basis for these findings. They cannot be considered to represent all mixed race college students in the United States any more than six institutions in three regions can be considered to represent the diversity of postsecondary education. Although I attempted to achieve a sample diversified along a number of characteristics (gender, age, year in school, racial/ethnic heritage, international experience, socioeconomic status, sexual orientation, physical and learning ability), the diversity of mixed race young people cannot be captured in any sample of fifty-six college students.

An important additional limitation of the sample, noted in chapter 3, relates to sample recruitment. Because students were recruited through flyers, email messages, and other communication to participate in a study of "biracial and multiracial students," it is not surprising that the majority of participants (fifty of fifty-six) identified in some way as mixed race, multiracial, biracial, or another similar term. While I attempted to counter this self-selection by contacting students whom I or others knew to be of multiple heritage, regardless of how they self-identified, the effect of the recruiting process on the apparent preponderance of participants who identify as multiracial cannot be underestimated. At the time of data collection, institutions were not required to collect data on individuals who identified in more than one racial category;[6] only Liberal Arts College was able to provide access to an institutional roster of students who identified in more than one category, to whom I sent a recruiting announcement. Maria Root described the challenges of conducting research on multiracial people (1992a, pp. 181–89), including past reliance on clinical samples and the difficulty of finding research participants who are not already self-identified as multiracial. Kendra Wallace (2001) was able to address some of these issues effectively in her study at one public high school and one private university by surveying 252 students about their racial heritage and selecting fifteen subjects from the sixty-three who indicated more than one racial heritage. While I avoided Root's concern about using clinical samples, my recruiting methods were not so broad as Wallace's and did result in a certain level of self-selection in the sample, a limitation that must be considered when interpreting the distribution of participants across the five patterns of multiracial identity.

The final limitation to which I would like to draw attention is the effect of my identity as a monoracial white woman. Not only am I white, but I am, as more than one of my research colleagues and participants has remarked, "really, really white," which I take to mean that my freckled pink skin, blue eyes, and red hair quite accurately give away my ancestry as descended from Swedes, Irish, Scots, Anglo-Saxons, Germans, and possibly other "really white" western and northern Europeans. In about a quarter of my interviews, a student would ask a question to the effect of, "You're white, right?" to which I often replied, "Yes. Hard to tell, huh?" But even when they did not ask, I was always aware of the potential influence on my research of my identity and of my privilege not only as a white person in the United States but also as a monoracial person in a nation that, for now, privileges monoraciality. A research assistant who conducted interviews with me at Big Ten University is also light-skinned, though she identifies as biracial. The influence of my and our racial identities—and physical appearances—on the outcome of data collection cannot be known but must be acknowledged.

Where I was able to take measures to balance my white, monoracial identity was in data analysis. As I described in the section on data analysis, I invited mixed race colleagues and students to code transcripts and to discuss their interpretations of the data. While my interpretations were often similar to theirs, they provided important insights into the mixed race experience on campus, as did my research assistants at Big Ten. The member checks were invaluable not only in bringing perspectives of mixed race individuals to the data analysis but also in bringing an undergraduate perspective; as a faculty member and former university administrator, my interpretation of student culture was from the perspective of an informed outsider, able to observe but not fully experience undergraduate peer culture. Thus the member checks and other conversations I had with multiracial undergraduates about my research provided essential lenses through which to view the data.

While these limitations are important to understanding my interpretations as presented in the text, they also provide opportunities for future research on the topic of mixed race students. Different procedures for sample recruitment and selection, a longitudinal design to follow one group of students, or different researcher identities would produce different data and, probably, different interpretations. Because the experience of multiracial college students is not well studied, additional data and analyses would be important additions to the literature on college students and peer culture. The contribution of this study, however, is in articulating patterns of racial identity experienced among a geographically diverse sample of college students from a range of institutional types and in applying an ecology model—with its flexibility and accommodation of fluid identities—to the study of college student identities.

In the next six chapters, I describe five patterns of mixed race identity in light of the ecology model, highlighting elements of each component—person, process, context, and time—that may have particular bearing on the patterns. Chapter 3 contains a description of the five patterns and information about the entire study sample and how they identified among the patterns. Chapters 4 through 8 focus individually on the patterns to create in-depth portraits of those identity patterns and mixed race students who choose to identify in those ways. Along the way, I refer to the elements of the Bron-fenbrenner model as developmental forces and resources, instigators, and inhibitors. There are other ways to examine the experiences of the fifty-six students featured in this book, but because the ecology model is such a pow-erful means to examine constructed identities in sociohistorical context, I use its concepts as a framework.

chapter three

Patterns of Multiracial Identity among College Students

> Sometimes I identify as biracial, sometimes I identify as hispanic, and sometimes I identify as half-hispanic, half-white. It depends.
>
> —Beth

MIXED RACE COLLEGE STUDENTS do not all identify in the same way. Some identify primarily with one of their heritages, some with two or more, and some as "multiracial," "biracial," "hapa," or some other term that indicates being mixed. Some students choose not to identify along U.S. racial categories by deconstructing race or by opting out of the categorization system. Many students fall into two or more of these groups by identifying situationally, according to social context. In fact, all but eight of the fifty-six students I interviewed identified in more than one way.

I call these five options "identity patterns" to indicate that they exist discretely, yet across the research group. The five patterns can be summarized briefly as:

1. the student holds a Monoracial Identity ("I'm black." "I'm asian.");
2. the student holds Multiple Monoracial Identities, shifting according to situation ("I'm half white and half Chinese." "I am Mexican and black.");
3. the student holds a Multiracial Identity ("I'm biracial." "I'm mixed.");
4. the student holds an Extraracial Identity, deconstructing race or opting out by refusing to identify according to U.S. racial categories ("I'm Jamaican." "I won't check any boxes." "I don't believe in having a race."); or

67

5. the student has a Situational Identity ("When I'm with my fraternity, I'm like them—white. When I'm with the Japan Club, I'm Japanese American. And when I'm home, I'm hapa.").

As will become clear later in this chapter and in the chapters that follow, these patterns are not exclusive, nor are they rigid or unchangeable. Students described periods in their lives when they were clearly in one pattern and other times when they were in a different pattern or patterns. Patterns are by their nature neither exclusive nor permanent.

It is important to understand that these patterns are not ordered developmentally; that is, one does not move from holding one monoracial identity to more than one, then to biracial, opting out of categories, and finally to situational identity. An individual may move from one to another depending on life circumstances, as will be illustrated later in the chapter, but it is not the case that he or she *must* proceed in a particular order or move from one pattern to another at all. As Maria Root (1996b) proposed and other researchers confirmed empirically (see Kilson, 2001; Renn, 1998, 2000; Wallace, 2001), it is possible that a multiracial person may have one or more of a number of racial and ethnic identifications over his or her lifetime and be considered psychologically healthy. Of course, it is not possible to hold only and always one monoracial identity and also identify situationally, but otherwise any pattern is compatible with any other pattern of the five.

While the patterns do not represent sequential development across the five, it is possible to detect some development within patterns.[1] For example, several students described growing up knowing that they were bi- or multiracial but not having a community of others with which to identify. When they got to college, they encountered informal and formal groups of mixed race students and began to publicly identify as biracial, multiracial, mixed, or hapa. Some students were deeply drawn to this new public identity and dropped their social connections with one or more of their heritage communities. This shift, from private to public multiracial identification and from public to private identification with monoracial groups, represents developmental change within the two patterns (multiracial identity and one or two monoracial identities), though it would be interpreted very differently by ecology theory (Bronfenbrenner, 1977, 1979, 1993) and by the linear models of identity development (e.g. Cross, 1991, 1995; Helms, 1990, 1995; Tatum, 1995). The factors involved in developmental change within patterns are the focus of much discussion in the next five chapters, each addressing one of the identity patterns.

THE FIVE PATTERNS

To set the stage for the chapters to come, I present here an introduction to the five patterns, describing them and creating a composite portrait of a student identifying in each. I also describe trends across the fifty-six student participants and discuss some of the general environmental factors that influenced student identities. In the chapters that follow, I draw in more detail on students' experiences to provide a richer description of each pattern and to illustrate the developmental diversity represented within patterns.

STUDENT HOLDS A MONORACIAL IDENTITY

Marta[2] has a mother who is white, of German and Scottish heritage, and a father who is second generation Mexican American. Marta herself has olive skin that gets quite dark in the summer sun, brown eyes, and straight, dark brown hair. Growing up in Texas, Marta participated in cultural activities of the Mexican American community, including dance classes, art exhibits, and festivals. She and her sisters spent a great deal of time with her father's parents and though they did not speak Spanish at home, they managed to converse with family and friends in a combination of Spanish and English.

Marta decided to go north for college, to attend an excellent preveterinary program to which she won a merit scholarship based on her high school grades and ACT score. Always strongly identified with her Mexican heritage, Marta arrived early at school for a special weeklong orientation for racial and ethnic minority students in the premedicine, preveterinary, and engineering programs. She enjoyed meeting the many other students of color who were strongly interested in sciences and engineering and was especially pleased to note the number of women among them. What surprised and disappointed her, however, was the relative scarcity of latina students, especially Chicanas. Expecting fewer latinas than she was used to in Texas, Marta still was not prepared to be one of just four latina/o students (and here they called them "Hispanic") of the one hundred new students gathered for the special orientation program. Nevertheless, Marta made friends and looked forward to moving into her residence hall, meeting her roommates, and beginning the school year in earnest.

On move-in day, Marta was overwhelmed by the number of new students and what seemed like the total absence of faces of color among them. Marta set up her side of the room, with pictures of her family and posters of some favorite Mexican art. She met her roommate, who was from a small, all-white community "up north" in the state, with whom she began a friendship based on mutual intellectual interests and similar habits of socializing and studying. The two struck out in their hall to meet other students, and Marta soon realized that she was the only woman of color on her floor other than her RA, another latina who was deeply involved in activities of the Organization for Hispanic Students (OHS). The RA invited Marta to an OHS social to welcome new students; Marta gratefully accepted and looked forward to the event.

At the social, Marta relaxed, realizing that although she was one of the few latinas in her residence hall, there was a sizable group on campus, made up of students from a variety of backgrounds—Mexican American, Puerto Rican, Cuban American, Latin American, and South American. Her RA introduced her to several returning students, and Marta met up with the three other premed, prevet, engineering students. Someone turned up the latin music, and Marta danced with her new friends, chatting back and forth in her comfortable Spanish/English mix. One of the returning students mentioned that they needed a first-year student on the social committee of OHS and suggested Marta volunteer for the position. For the first time since arriving for the pre-orientation Marta felt certain that she would find a place to fit in here.

When she returned to her residence hall, her roommate asked about the social. Marta filled her in, adding, "It's just so nice to find *my people* here." A bit perplexed, her roommate said, "Well, who are your people? I know from the picture that you're dad's Hispanic, but I thought your mom was white." "Oh," Marta replied, "she is. But 'my people'—'mi familia'—they're Mexican. I'm Mexican American. It's how I look, it's how I feel, it's what I am."

For Marta, how she *looks* and *feels* is what she *is*. Growing up with a strong Mexican American cultural background, she feels confident of her place in the latina/o community on campus. Although she finds common ground with her white roommate, she feels like she fits in with the Hispanic students, who welcome her into their student organization and community.

Many students of mixed heritage identify strongly with one of their monoracial or ethnic backgrounds. Of the fifty-six students I interviewed, twenty-seven (48 percent) did. For most students who have one white parent and one parent of color, this monoracial identification is with black, asian, latino, or native american heritage, though in a few cases students identified with the white culture and community and did not identify with their other heritage. Skin color, which I discuss in more detail later in the chapter, plays a role in students' ability to identify as white; students whose skin is noticeably dark are less able to choose a white identity without the interference of other students in that process.

A Monoracial Identity, whether of color or white, is one of the options for healthy resolution of mixed race identity. Students who have the cultural knowledge (language, history, literature, music, dance, food, humor, etc.) and physical characteristics (skin tone, hair texture, body type) to fit in with the monoracial group have an easier time than those who do not gain this knowledge before coming to college. On some campuses, however, where the communities of monoracial students of color are more open to diversity and less rigid about standards for membership, cultural knowledge and appearance are not barriers to mixed race students who want to identify with that monoracial group. It is not clear from the illustration, for example, if Marta would have been as quickly and warmly welcomed had her skin been lighter and her knowledge of the culture less rich. As we will see in chapter 4, a number of environmental factors play into students' desire—and ability—to identify with one monoracial category.

STUDENT HOLDS MULTIPLE MONORACIAL IDENTITIES, SHIFTING ACCORDING TO SITUATION

Kenji, who also goes by the nickname Ken, has a Japanese mother, who met and married a white American—Kenji's father—who was stationed with the military in Japan for several years. Born on the base in Japan, Kenji has been back to the island to visit his relatives and is close to his Japanese cousins. Ken's parents live in southern California, where they are active in the community of Japanese immigrants and Japanese-Anglo interracial families. They told Kenji and his brother that they were both Japanese *and* American, which the boys always took to mean "white American," and though they lived in a racially mixed neighborhood, the Catholic school they attended was predominantly white and latino.

Kenji is a junior at a midsized private university with a racially diverse student population. He has many good friends in the Japanese American student community, including officers of the Japan Club and the Asian Student Alliance (ASA), an umbrella group for the nine asian ethnic clubs on campus. He also has a number of friends who are Japanese and white, though he resists the "hapa" label that many of them use to describe their mixed heritage; Ken prefers to call himself "half-Japanese and half-white," a designation that he feels preserves the uniqueness of his family configuration. When pressed further, or around close friends, he is more descriptive, saying that he is "half-Japanese and half-Irish/German/Austrian/Swedish," calling on the nationalities of his father's parents and grandparents.

Kenji's cocurricular activities reflect his interest in identifying with his two monoracial heritages. As a sophomore Kenji lived in a residence hall as a specially trained Minority Peer Aide (MPA), providing residential counseling, support, and activities for and about issues for students of color. One of only twenty MPAs, Kenji was seen as a leader on campus and a spokesperson for asian concerns in his residence hall complex and in the MPA program. The university has a small but active residential fraternity system, and Ken pledged the historically white fraternity that his father joined in college. Ken now lives in the fraternity house where he is one of two men of color. Ken has been dating a white woman from his "sister sorority" since the middle of his sophomore year, a circumstance that, ironically, is viewed with less skepticism by his MPA friends now that he has left the program and moved into the fraternity house.

Although Kenji's friends in the politically and socially active community of students of color rarely attend fraternity events, and fraternity brothers rarely accompany him to cultural and social events with asian or other students of color, Kenji is comfortable with his "two worlds" and moves easily between them. He enjoys raising issues of diversity and tolerance within the predominantly white fraternity world, using the training he received as an MPA to give workshops and provide advice on making the recruiting and induction process more welcoming to students of color, though his efforts have met with little visible success. He also enjoys building bridges between the Asian Student Alliance and the interfraternity council; this year, the groups are cooperating in several community service and fundraising projects, including a mentoring program for asian immigrant youth, working on a Habitat for Humanity house with a Korean Presbyterian church, and cosponsoring a party to benefit the ASA's annual cultural show.

Ken takes a fair amount of good-natured joking from his MPA friends about being in a predominantly white fraternity, though he is sensitive to any intimation that he is any less asian for pledging. He knows that some "hard line" ASA leaders question his commitment to political solidarity and that a few have questioned his legitimacy as a leader in the asian community but believes that they felt that way before he joined the fraternity when they knew he was not "full Japanese." His response is to rely on his sense of identity, built on a lifetime of connection to both Japanese American and white communities, his friendships with students from different cultural communities on campus, and the knowledge that he is, in fact, "*both* Japanese *and* white, not *either* Japanese *or* white."

Relying on the principle of "both/and" has gotten Kenji far in his life on campus, participating fully in the community of students of color and a residential fraternity whose rituals and activities are rooted in a history of exclusively white membership and a tradition of heterosexualized and racialized matchmaking between members of affiliated fraternities and sororities. Accepted and valued in both communities, Kenji feels comfortable building bridges between them, using his insider status in each to make connections on campus.

Nearly half of the students I interviewed (twenty-seven, or 48 percent) identified in Multiple Monoracial Identities with two or more of their heritages. Most of these students (seventeen) had one white parent and one monoracial parent of color; the remainder had two monoracial parents of color (three), one parent of color and one mixed (three), one white and one mixed parent (two), or two mixed parents (two). Some described experiences similar to the composite sketch of Kenji, participating in microsystems distinctly connected to different parts of their heritage. Others experienced micro- and mesosystems that were themselves more mixed, sometimes connected to academic, athletic, or community service activities that attracted racially and ethnically diverse participants.

Students who identify with two or more of their heritages may do so because they come to college with cultural knowledge of both or because they seek out such knowledge (through classes, activities, and peer interaction) when they arrive in a supportive environment. Peer cultures play a key role in students' ability to identify with more than one heritage. Some microsystems are highly intolerant of students whom they see as disloyal or threatening; Kenji's decision to move into the predominantly white fraternity and date a white sorority woman could be viewed by some students as disloyal to the asian community, and conversely his decision to be active in the Japan Club and raise diversity issues in the fraternity could be seen as a threat to the traditional homogeneity of the residential fraternity system. Of course educators would like to see peer groups welcome such diversity and students like Kenji or those in my study who identified with more than one heritage, but the reality of campus life is that, depending on the dynamics of peer culture and the history of various key communities and organizations, students may encounter significant resistance to being "both/and." In chapter 5 I discuss these and other conditions influencing students' decision to identify with more than one racial group.

STUDENT HOLDS A MULTIRACIAL IDENTITY

Kim, the daughter of a light-skinned Cuban American mother and a mixed Cherokee and black father, always considered herself African American before going to college. She grew up in a predominantly white university town in the northern Midwest, where her parents settled after completing their medical residencies in the local hospital. While there were not many other black families, there was a small latino community and a growing asian immigrant community as friends and relatives of local families moved to the area to enjoy the social and economic mix of a university town that also supported light industry and a growing medical center. Kim was part of a culturally diverse circle of talented students taking advanced placement courses and participating in sports, arts, and student organizations at their well-regarded public high school. Kim decided to go to the state's flagship public university, located two hours away in a small city with a thriving multicultural community, enriched by a large international student and faculty population.

When she arrived at the university, Kim attended meetings and social activities of the Black Student Association (BSA). Though she was excited to be part of a sizable community of African American students, Kim was turned off by what she perceived as a separatist political agenda of the BSA leadership. She sometimes felt like an "imposter" in conversations about

black womanhood, because she could not trace her heritage through generations of black women ancestors, as was the custom among her female peers.
Over the course of her first year, she attended fewer and fewer BSA-spon-
sored events in favor of hanging out with a diverse group of students of color
who were less focused on campus politics.

At the start of her sophomore year, Kim got a job as a student assistant
at the Multicultural Student Center on campus. As the year progressed Kim's
supervisor, also a mixed race woman, asked Kim about her involvement in
campus activities and student organizations. Kim described how she dis-
tanced herself from the political activities of the BSA but wished for a way to
be more involved and to feel more genuine in claiming her black heritage.
The supervisor suggested that Kim try the Organization of Mixed Students
(OMS). Never having identified as mixed, and wondering how a group of
mixed students could help her relate more genuinely to just one of her heritages, Kim was skeptical but decided to attend an upcoming OMS meeting.

The meeting began with introductions by the dozen or so students present. Students gave their names and self-descriptions. "I'm Beth. I'm Hapa."
"I'm Keith—mixed black-French-German-Italian." "Robbie. Half-Japanese,
half-white, all American." "Cecilia. Biracial. Oh, Filipina and white."
"Margo. Usually I'd say 'mixed,' but today I'm feeling just Korean—I'll fill you
in later about what happened with my psych TA this morning." "Ouch. I'm
Peter. I'm mixed Jamaican Puerto Rican American." "Um, hi. I'm Kim. My,
um, mom is Cuban and my dad is black, and part Cherokee, too."

OMS president Robbie welcomed Kim and explained that the meeting
format consisted of announcements and organizational business followed by
group discussion of a topic. The topic for that meeting was "White Parents
and Their Kids of Color." The discussion ranged from very serious topics—
times when a student felt her white father had ignored racism directed at
her—to more lighthearted moments—sharing laughter about white mothers
who did not know what to do with their daughters' kinky hair. Kim listened
to the others, sharing their frustrations and humor. To her surprise and
delight, she felt like she belonged with this group. Her experiences were not
identical to Beth's or Keith's or Cecilia's, but she resonated with the experience of living with multiple cultures in her family while trying to fit into a
campus peer culture based on pride in monoracial group identities. Kim
became a regular participant in OMS activities and, as she told her supervisor, started seeing "mixed kids everywhere on campus—they're in the café,
the library, sitting on the quad—and I want to just go up and say, 'Hey, I'm
mixed too!'" Kim found, she said, a home on campus, a community of students who "got it" about being more than "both/and" in addition to being
more than "either/or."

Fifty of the fifty-six study participants (89 percent) identified in some
way as biracial, multiracial, mixed, or hapa, all terms indicating a category

unto itself, outside of the federal government's ostensibly monoracial categories or particular combinations of them.[3] Students identifying in this pattern were as likely to be men as women, to come from any of the campuses,
or to be of any given heritages. The terms they used to describe themselves
varied somewhat by campus, which could be attributable to regional factors,
peer culture, or the six-year spread in data collection. Earlier data collection
in the Northeast (at Ivy, Liberal Arts, and Catholic) yielded a number of students identifying as "multiracial" or "biracial," whereas later data collection
in the Midwest (Rural University, Big Ten, Rural Community College)
yielded more responses of "mixed" or "mixed race." The term *hapa* was used
across campuses and time frames, usually by students with some asian heritage
or exposure to hapa-identified communities on the West Coast.

A difference emerged within this identity pattern between students who
had the opportunity to claim some kind of public mixed race identity and
those whose mixed race identity was more privately held. For example, at Big
Ten and Ivy, multiracial students had established recognized student organizations that sponsored meetings and events and participated formally in student governance structures and alliances of organizations for students of
color. They thereby created formal public space for the deployment of mixed
race identity, an option not available on other campuses. An informal group
of multiracial students at Catholic University had coalesced and was moving
toward creating a formal student organization (which was recognized by the
university the year after data collection there). The informal group provided
a microsystem in which multiracial students connected with one another and
formed a community that supported claims to a bi- or multiracial identity
independent of monoracial categories or particular combinations of them.

At the other three campuses (Liberal Arts, Rural Community College,
Rural University) there was no formal or informal collective of multiracial
students. A few of the students indicated that they were aware of or knew
some other mixed race students on campus, but they did not seek each other
out or come together purposefully around their shared sense of nonmonora-
ciality. For these students, multiracial identity was privately constructed.
They did not have other mixed students with whom to discuss racial identities, to share stories of growing up multiracial, or to form a community on
campus. Lack of a critical mass was cited as a key factor at Liberal Arts College (where there were only 140 identified students of color on campus),
overall lack of student cohesion was most often cited at Rural Community
College, and a sense of apathy toward the issue emerged as a rationale at
Rural University. At all three campuses, though, a contributing factor may
have been the ease with which students felt they could move within the
mesosystem of peer culture. Comfortable moving between and among
microsystems, these students may not have felt a need to seek a group of like
others with whom to share their experience of being multiracial. Being mixed

was a private identity, shared with friends, but not a motivation to seek public deployment. In chapter 6 I discuss in depth this and other factors related to holding a bi- or multiracial identity.

STUDENT HOLDS AN EXTRARACIAL IDENTITY BY DECONSTRUCTING RACE OR OPTING OUT OF IDENTIFICATION BY U.S. RACIAL CATEGORIES

Jared describes his parents as "college-educated hippie wannabes" who met in the early 1970s and got married over the objections of their parents, who worried about discrimination the pair and any offspring would encounter living in their home state of Georgia. Jared's father, who is black, and mother, who is white, got married anyway, had two children, and stayed in the Atlanta area to remain close to both of their families. With the birth of Jared, the first child, the grandparents overcame their earlier objections and formed a strong support network that provided stability during Jared's parents' eventual divorce.[4] Jared's family was consistent in its message that he could decide for himself what he wanted to be called, and he identified as "half-black and half-white" for most of his childhood, preferring "biracial" as he grew older.

Jared is now a senior at a highly selective, predominantly white private liberal arts college with a substantial community of students of color (25 percent of the student body). In an interdisciplinary first-year seminar, he was introduced to the idea that race is socially rather than biologically constructed, an idea that resonated immediately with Jared. As a sophomore he did a class project on the history of racial categories on the United States census, arguing that the changes in the 2000 census were only the latest version of what he called "Official Racialization." Jared spent his junior year in South America as part of an interdisciplinary academic program that traveled to different regions to perform service, learn about local cultures, and document living conditions.

As a senior, he is writing a thesis that links industrialization with the disappearance of indigenous cultures and the rise of newly constructed regional cultures and identities; he compares ongoing industrialization with changes that occurred during European colonization of the Americas. He is well versed in the language and theory of postmodernism and uses it in his writing as well as in his way of understanding and explaining his place on campus, in the United States, and in the world. When asked, "What are you?" Jared responds with a brief analysis of racial construction, ending with an explanation that he does not subscribe to racial categories and therefore will not answer the question. On surveys and forms, he skips the question.

Jared is an outspoken critic of racial categorization. His childhood experience of being "half-and-half" laid the foundation for his skepticism; he understood from a young age that "race" is not something immutable whose so-called purity cannot—and should not—be sacrificed. Jared's faculty introduced him to cognitive tools and epistemological approaches for deconstructing the concept of race, and the curriculum provided ample opportunities to explore it in local, national, and international contexts.

From early childhood, Jared was immersed in microsystems that emphasized the individuality of racial identification. This immersion continued when he arrived on a campus where, at least in the curriculum, race was not taken as a given category. Jared repeatedly sought academic microsystems where he could explore the issue, and during his year in South America was transported into a different learning and developmental ecology. The interdisciplinary nature of Jared's first-year seminar, study abroad experience, and senior thesis represent an academic mesosystem made up of microsystems sending congruent messages about race and racial identity. It is not surprising that Jared applies these messages to himself and chooses to remove himself from the categorizations.

Like Jared, thirteen participants (23 percent) demonstrated a pattern I have called "Extraracial Identity." Four of the thirteen spent substantial amounts of time outside the United States while growing up, a factor that some attributed directly to claiming an identity not based on designated racial categories. Seven of the thirteen in this pattern (two of whom also had substantial international experience as children) attended the same institution—Ivy University—and were exposed to an intellectual and peer culture replete with references to postmodernism and deconstruction; I discuss this influence in detail in chapter 7, but the preponderance of students in this identity pattern from one institution (over half of all students in the pattern and also over half of the students from that institution who participated in the study) bears notice. Another trend among students in this pattern is toward juniors and seniors; only one first-year and two sophomores were among the thirteen in this pattern.

I classified students in the Extraracial Identity pattern who engaged four very different approaches to racial identity, but for whom the outcome was similar—an identity outside the designated categories. First, college students who were not marked (by physical appearance or name, for example) as having anything other than white heritage might choose not to adopt a cultural identity other than a homogenized youth culture in which whites have until recently been assumed not to have, or need, a racialized identity.[5] A second approach was that of resistance to outside definitions of identity categories; students engaging this approach refused to mark the boxes for race and ethnicity on official forms, for example, or to answer the "What are you?" questions posed by acquaintances and strangers. I recognized a third approach, which lay in the active intellectual engagement of the social construction race and purposeful deconstruction of its validity as a means of categorizing individuals. These students used the language of postmodernism and academic discourse to explain why and how they constructed identities for themselves outside the racial categories. The fourth approach was common among students with international experience or parents who were not born in the United States; recognizing the complicated sociocultural histories of their ancestors' homelands (including such factors as indigenous peoples, colonization, slave taking, and slave owning), these students simply did not recognize the categories designated by the United States government as having any meaning or relevance. "Race" was not a legitimate social category by which to sort people and group cultures.

The four approaches represent different degrees of personal and intellectual engagement of the notion of "race" as used in the United States, yet they might lead to similar answers to questions about identity. If asked, "Of what race do you consider yourself a member?" a student espousing any of the four approaches might answer, "None" or "The human race" and be consistent with her or his approach. Of course, their explanations would diverge, but the initial way in which they address questions of personal identity would be similar: "race" is not always meaningful personal identifier.

Where this identity pattern, taken from any of the four approaches, runs into trouble is in its seeming naiveté. It is all well and good to deconstruct racial categories as Jared did, but is he not still going to be seen as a man of color and suffer discrimination? How can we build antiracist alliances if we refuse to acknowledge the legitimacy of racial categories? Does not such a stance play into the strategies of those who seek an end to affirmative action and other identity-based programs?[26] One of my interview participants recalled a quote from a lecture she attended given by philosopher Naomi Zack: "Race isn't real, but racism is." Making sense of this paradox is no small matter, and I discuss the cognitive challenges and possibilities of such a stance when I describe this identity pattern in chapter 7.

It is worth noting that no students I interviewed engaged exclusively in this pattern; that is, all thirteen identified in one or more other patterns in addition to sometimes taking the deconstructionist/opting out stance. In fact, none took the hard line stand that the fictional Jared did in always declining to identify racially in some way. In part this finding is an artifact of my recruiting strategy (I sought "bi- and multiracial students," an invitation not likely to attract individuals who claimed no racialized identity), but it may also indicate that holding such an approach to racial identity is a difficult stance to maintain in the face of powerful forces on campuses that are organized in part around racial identities. In chapter 7 I discuss the complexities of the Extraracial identity pattern as well as some of the ecological factors that contributed to students' ability to consider and decision to adopt this against-the-racialized-mainstream pattern.

STUDENT HOLDS A SITUATIONAL IDENTITY,
IDENTIFYING DIFFERENTLY IN DIFFERENT CONTEXTS

Lena, whose father is African American and whose mother is Filipina, was born in the Philippines and moved to the United States two years later at the end of her father's military assignment. Like many families with a career military member, they moved several times while Lena and her sisters were growing up, and they were stationed overseas as well as around the United States. As a child, Lena identified as biracial and had opportunities to learn about her Filipina as well as her African American heritage. Unsure what she wanted to do but aware that she enjoyed working with children, Lena decided after high school to get a job as an aide at a daycare center near her home. Two years later she began to take classes part time at the local community college to become certified as a teacher's aide, which would allow her to take on more professional responsibility.

Now working thirty-five hours a week at the daycare center and in her fourth semester as a part-time student, Lena is also involved in the student government at the community college. She represents the Black Student Caucus and chairs a task force charged with helping the predominantly white student government recruit more students of color for leadership positions. Because of this leadership role, other students, faculty, and administrators see Lena as a spokesperson for students of color, a responsibility she accepts gracefully though warily. Often, she is asked to speak about "What's the black point of view" about a hot topic on campus, to which she responds that there are as many different points of view as there are black students and her point of view is X or Y.

Lena participates in Filipino Alliance social activities, through which she met her boyfriend, whom she calls "whole Filipino," and a number of other students who share her mixed Filipino heritage. To save money, Lena lives at her parents' home, and she has remained close to her extended family in the United States and the Phillipines. She is an active member of a predominantly Filipino Catholic parish, leading activities for preschool children while their parents are at Mass. She teaches them simple phrases in Tagalog, as well as Filipino songs and stories. In this setting, Lena feels "very Filipina," aware of her mixed heritage only on those occasions when a child points out that her skin or hair look different from theirs; then she explains, "Filipinos come in lots of colors. You're lighter and I'm darker, and we're both Filipinos."

Lena is comfortable with different aspects of her identity in different situations. At home, she describes herself as biracial, aware of the cultural influences of her parents and grandparents. At school, she is publicly identified as black, mainly because she has taken on a leadership role in that student community. But she also participates with the campus Filipino Alliance and dates a Filipino student. Lena identifies through her church as Filipina, aware of her biraciality when the issue of race is raised by others. Lena experiences her identity as biracial, black, or Filipina, depending on the setting.

Ultimately, thirty-four (61 percent) of the fifty-six participants in my study held Situational Identities, depending on their experience of different microsystems. Common combinations were students with Monoracial Identity who also identified sometimes as Multiracial (seven) and students who combined Multiple Monoracial and Multiracial identities (twelve). Twelve students combined Multiple Monoracial Identities with Multiracial *and* the Extraracial Identity pattern. As I noted in the previous section, all thirteen students who identified in the Extraracial Identity pattern also identified Situationally.

For some students, the shift between identity patterns was smooth and comfortable, while for others the transitions were more abrupt and fraught. Negotiating the boundaries of peer microsystems was especially challenging on campuses where the boundaries of identity-based groups (e.g., organizations of ostensibly monoracial students of color, such as a Black Student Alliance or a Japan Club) were carefully policed by members who, often tacitly but sometimes openly, assessed the authenticity and legitimacy of claims to group membership. On campuses where group membership was more fluid, students described easy transitions among groups and untroubled foregrounding of different racial identifications in different circumstances. This particular factor of individual microsystems—the ease of entry into different groups—created a powerful ethos in the mesosystem as students came to understand explicit and implicit identity politics on campus, sometimes by violating the tacit rules constructed through peer culture.

Identifying differently in different situations was once seen as a weakness in identity development; according to many stage models, the goal of developing racial identity is to have a unitary identity that is integrated into the personality and is carried across contexts, perhaps more salient in some than others, but constant nevertheless. James Marcia's designation of "identity achieved," with its implication of finality, has been used by identity theorists (e.g., Josselson, 1987; Phinney, 1990) to indicate this "successful" attainment of healthy racial identity. In such a viewpoint, deploying different identities in different settings may indicate less maturity in racial identification.

I argue the opposite, that the ability to read contexts and construct one's identity in relation to specific contexts is a highly evolved skill requiring emotional maturity and cognitive complexity. George Kitahara Kich (1996), in fact, argued that the process of asserting a marginalized, nondichotomized gender, sexual, racial, or ethnic identity enhances an individual's ability to handle the ambiguity inherent in such social constructions.

> A person's degree of emotional/cognitive/social flexibility (the ability to tolerate and to manage increased levels of complexity and differentiation) may be understood as a developmental consequence of a healthy adaptation to life. . . . People learn and develop competencies as they journey over the difficult terrains of their racial and sexual lives. Flexibility of constructs, relational competence, and adaptability are potentially the skills of living with difference and in the margins. (Kich, 1996, p. 275)

And, in keeping with Maria Root's proposition that there is more than one possible healthy outcome of biracial identity development—more than one appropriate approach to "border crossing"—the idea that identity could be deployed situationally by well-adjusted, intellectually and emotionally mature individuals forms the core of this identity pattern. It is this pattern, and the implication that fluidity could mark advanced development rather than indecision or immaturity, that most directly challenges the applicability of stage-based (mono)racial identity development models to the experiences of mixed race college students.

TRENDS ACROSS THE FIVE PATTERNS

With a nonrandom sample of fifty-six, it is important to interpret data trends with caution. It is also, however, interesting to note some trends that cut across the five patterns. Examining data by gender, heritage (one or two parents of color, race/ethnicity of parents, etc.), and institution reveals differences in identity choices that bear additional investigation with larger samples or by grouping criteria. I will discuss trends within patterns in the next five chapters, but an overview may be of interest at this point.

Gender

Identity patterns differed by gender, both in the number of identity categories students occupied and in the identities they chose. Across the sample, students identified in an average of 2.70 patterns, but the men averaged 2.10, and the women averaged 3.03. In other words, women more often fell into a greater number of identity patterns than did men. Whereas the majority of the participants (forty-eight of fifty-six) identified in more than one pattern, all eight students who occupied only one identity pattern were men. The five students who identified only as Monoracial were all men (Bob, Fred, John, Mark, and Sapo), as were the three who identified only as Multiracial (David, Dwayne, Steve).

In addition to influencing the total number of identity patterns students occupied, gender may also have been a factor in students' choices of identity patterns. Gender differences, sometimes sharp, appear in each category. Women were more likely than men to choose Multiple Monoracial Categories, Multiracial, and Extraracial. Men were more likely women to choose one Monoracial Identity.

Scholars of the mixed race experience have proposed explanations of gender effects in the identities of multiracial people (see Allman, 1996; Streeter, 1996; Twine, 1996), though the gendered construction of racialized identities—and the racialized construction of gendered identities—remain empirically underexplored (three exceptions are Herschel, 1997; Rockquemore,

TABLE 3.1
Number of Identity Patterns by Gender

	One pattern (e.g., just Monoracial Identity or just Multiracial Identity)	Two patterns (e.g., Multiple Monoracial Identities and Situational Identity)	Three patterns (e.g., Monoracial Identity, Multiracial, and Situational)	Four patterns (e.g., Multiple Monoracial Identities, Multiracial, Extra-Racial, and Situational)	Average number of identity patterns per participant
Men	8	2	8	2	2.10
Women	0	9	18	9	3.03
Total	8	11	26	11	2.70

TABLE 3.2
Distribution of Participants across Identity Patterns by Gender

	Monoracial Identity	Multiple Monoracial Identities	Multiracial Identity	Extraracial Identity	Situational Identity
Men (20)	12 (60%)	5 (25%)	15 (75%)	2 (10%)	8 (40%)
Women (36)	15 (42%)	22 (61%)	35 (97%)	11 (31%)	26 (72%)
Total (56)	27 (48%)	27 (48%)	50 (89%)	13 (23%)	34 (61%)

2002; and Root, 1997). Sociologist Kerry Ann Rockquemore (2002) argued for a gendered analysis of identity construction among biracial black/white individuals, concluding,

> Because of the scarcity of marriageable Black men and the high probability that educated and affluent Black men will marry white women, the interpersonal tension between Black and biracial women currently runs high. That tension, at a time when multiracial people have identity options, has created a push factor for many biracial women, effectively driving them away from a Black identity and toward an exclusively biracial identity. (p. 498)

While the data from my study do not support the assertion that biracial women are selecting an *exclusively* biracial identity, they do lend support to the assertion that women are less likely than men to choose a monoracial identity pattern and more likely to choose a bi- or multiracial pattern. Students themselves offered explanations for gender differences in identity choices of mixed race men and women, which I discuss in the context of specific identity patterns in the following chapters.

Heritage

I am often asked if mixed race students identify differently depending on their ethnic and racial heritage. In my study, some trends appeared that bear further investigation with a larger sample. Students with two parents of color (as opposed to one parent of color and one white parent) were less likely than other students to be in the Monoracial Identity pattern (33 percent), more likely to be in the Multiple Monoracial Identities (75 percent), and much more likely than others to experience a Situational Identity pattern. Conversely, students with

TABLE 3.3
Distribution of Participants across Identity Patterns by Heritage

	Monoracial Identity	Multiple Monoracial Identity	Multiracial Identity	Extraracial Identity	Situational Identity	Average number of identity patterns per person
Two Parents of Color (12)	4 (33%)	8 (75%)	10 (83%)	5 (42%)	11 (92%)	3.17
One Asian & One White Parent (16)	8 (50%)	8 (50%)	15 (94%)	2 (13%)	9 (56%)	2.63
One Black & One White Parent (13)	6 (46%)	5 (38%)	13 (100%)	1 (8%)	7 (54%)	2.46
One Latino/a & One White Parent (5)	5 (100%)	0	2 (40%)	1 (20%)	0	1.60
One Pacific Islander & One White Parent (7)	3 (43%)	4 (57%)	7 (100%)	3 (43%)	5 (71%)	3.14
One Mixed & One White Parent (3)	1 (33%)	2 (67%)	3 (100%)	1 (33%)	2 (67%)	3.00
Total (56)	27 (48%)	27 (48%)	50 (89%)	13 (23%)	34 (61%)	2.70

one latina/o or hispanic parent and one white parent were most likely to hold Monoracial Identity (100 percent) and least likely to hold Multiple Monoracial Identities (0 percent) or Situational Identity (0 percent). Students with two parents of color averaged 3.17 patterns, whereas the five students with one latina/o or hispanic parent and one white parent averaged 1.60.

Another notable trend appeared among students with one black and one white parent; these students were least likely to be in Extraracial Identity pattern. Only one of the thirteen black/white mixed students (Amy) engaged in this pattern. A significant literature (see Davis, 1991; Rockquemore, 2002; Rockquemore & Brunsma, 2002; Spickard, 1989; Williamson, 1995) supports the notion that race relations in the United States are most often conceptualized with blacks and whites on opposite ends of a spectrum, and the literature on college student cultures depicts a dichotomous view of campus race relations (see Tatum, 1995). Given this societal and campus milieu, it is not surprising that most students with black and white heritages identified as one, both, mixed, or situationally. Students with black heritage may not have felt as able to engage an Extraracial Identity, because peer cultures exerted a press toward racial identification.

Institution

While the sample size at each institution is too small to generalize to entire institutional cultures, there were some trends by institution that merit notice. Looking across the identity categories, students varied by institution in the number of identity categories they occupied. Ivy University averaged the highest (3.07), with Liberal Arts averaging the lowest (2.25). Correspondingly, when examining institutional differences within identity categories, Ivy students were the most likely to practice Situational Identity (86 percent), and Liberal Arts students were least likely to practice this pattern (25 percent).

At Ivy University students were also much more likely to be in the Extraracial Identity pattern. Half of the Ivy students (seven of fourteen) indicated this pattern, whereas only one student per sample at Catholic, Rural Community College, Rural University, and Big Ten did so; two students at Liberal Arts College were in this pattern. In the Situational Identity pattern, Ivy and Liberal Arts stood out. What conditions might have contributed to these differences across campuses? The answer appears to lie in institutional culture as promulgated by peers and by faculty.

The curriculum and campus peer culture at Ivy strongly supported postmodern discourse and challenges to the construction of social categories. Students were exposed to postmodern theory in courses, campus lectures, and even the student newspaper. In some student circles, discussion of deconstructing race was commonplace, and students had developed their own

TABLE 3.4
Distribution of Identity Patterns across Institutions

	Monoracial Identity	Multiple Monoracial Identity	Multiracial Identity	Extraracial Identity	Situational Identity	Average number of identity patterns per participant
Big Ten University (12)	6 (50%)	8 (75%)	10 (83%)	1 (8%)	6 (50%)	2.58
Catholic University (8)	4 (50%)	4 (50%)	7 (88%)	1 (13%)	5 (63%)	2.63
Ivy University (14)	5 (36%)	6 (43%)	13 (93%)	7 (50%)	12 (86%)	3.07
Liberal Arts College (8)	6 (75%)	2 (25%)	6 (75%)	2 (25%)	2 (25%)	2.25
Rural Community College (6)	3 (50%)	3 (50%)	6 (100%)	1 (17%)	4 (67%)	2.83
Rural University (8)	3 (38%)	4 (50%)	8 (100%)	1 (13%)	5 (63%)	2.63
Total (56)	27 (48%)	27 (48%)	50 (89%)	13 (23%)	34 (61%)	2.70

shorthand for it. One Ivy participant (Luz) said, "You know, I can deconstruct this and reify that, and blah, blah, blah." In contrast, students at the other institutions had not been exposed as broadly to constructionist ideas and language; campus programs designed to enhance diversity and community tended to focus on differences and commonalities among groups rather than examining the social construction of those groups. There was not substantial peer support for theoretical exploration of racial identity, and students were less likely to engage in the Extraracial Identity pattern.

Differences in the Situational Identity patterns can also be associated with campus peer culture. The two extremes—Ivy and Liberal Arts—had very different campus peer cultures. At Ivy, peer groups drew very clear boundaries around identity-based groups, relying on shared knowledge, experiences, and physical appearances to mark insiders and outsiders (Renn, 2000). Mixed race students could participate in various student communities but felt compelled to identify strongly with whichever community they were in. So at the Black Student Alliance meeting, Eleanor summoned her knowledge of the black experience in America; at the meeting of the mixed race student group ("Spectrum," a pseudonym), she relaxed into a biracial identity where it mattered less that her mother was white and her father was black.

At Liberal Arts College students described the ease with which they moved from social group to social group. At Liberal Arts, boundaries between peer groups were less rigidly policed than they were at Ivy; students could move easily among them, carrying more or less the same identity to each. Students considered having a Situational Identity less important, because there was less need to shift between and among racial identities when moving from one group to another. The importance of peer groups and group boundaries will be clear in the chapters related to each of the identity patterns.

RELATIONSHIP OF THESE PATTERNS TO OTHER RESEARCH ON MULTIRACIAL IDENTITY IN COLLEGE STUDENTS

Other researchers have found that mixed race people identify in ways similar to the five patterns I drew from my study data, though not all use the same categories or have found five. A comparison of the findings of Kendra Wallace (2001), Marion Kilson (2001), and Kerry Ann Rockquemore and David L. Brunsma (2002) provides a larger scholarly context for understanding the findings presented in this book.

Although the four studies drew from samples limited in their generalizability by size, selection, and geographic reach, it is interesting to compare the identity choices and patterns across the total group of three hundred. A comparison of these data must be interpreted with much caution, given the aforementioned limitations imposed by sampling, the differences in research

TABLE 3.5
Distribution of Participants across Identity Patterns (Renn), Visuals (Wallace), Choices (Kilson), and Categories (Rockquemore & Brunsma)

• Monoracial Identity (Renn)	• Multiple Monoracial Identities (Renn)	• Multiracial Identity (Renn)	• Extraracial Identity (Renn)	• Situational Identity (Renn)
• Home Base/ Visitor's Base (Wallace)	• Both Feet in Both Groups (Wallace)	• Sits on the Border (Wallace)	• Raceless Identity (Kilson)	• Shifting Gears (Wallace)
• Monoracial Identity of Color (Kilson)		• Biracial or Multiracial Identity (Kilson)	• Transcendent Identity (Rockquemore & Brunsma)	• Multiple Descriptors (Kilson)
• Singular Identity (Rockquemore & Brunsma)		• Border Identity (Rockquemore & Brunsma)		• Protean Identity (Rockquemore & Brunsma)

(continued on next page)

TABLE 3.5 (continued)

Renn (56)**	27 (48%)	27 (48%)	50 (89%)	13 (23%)	34 (61%)
Wallace (15)**	11 (73%)	5 (33%)	6 (40%)	N/A	11 (73%)
Kilson (52)**	34 (65%)	N/A	17 (33%)	10 (19%)	10* (19%)
Rockquemore & Brunsma (177)***	29 (17%)	N/A	103 (58%)	23 (13%)	8 (5%)
TOTAL (300)	72 (24%)	32 (11%)	73 (24%)	23 (8%)	45 (15%)

*This is the number who responded to "multiple descriptors"; it does not include other individuals who may also have identified situationally. These ten individuals were also added to appropriate categories (monoracial of color, biracial/multiracial, raceless).
**Totals across rows do not equal number of participants in each study, and percentages do not add to 100 because the majority of participants indicated more than one category.
***Total across row does not equal 100 percent because some data were considered missing.

methods, the generational spread of participants (born in the early 1960s to early 1980s), and the time periods of the data collection (Kilson: 1993–1994; Wallace: 1996; Rockquemore & Brunsma: 1997–2001; Renn: 1996–2002). Even with these caveats, it is interesting to note the variety of ways in which mixed race students and other young adults across the United States identified themselves.

Kendra Wallace (2001) created four visual prompts from the strategies Maria Root (1996) proposed for resolving biracial identity: (a) *Home Base/Visitor's Base*, representing "the mixed heritage person mostly in one community of heritage, while interactions with the other community occur through occasional visits to this other 'base'" (Wallace, p. 121); (b) *Both Feet in Both Worlds*, for a person "not split between two worlds, but firmly grounded in both worlds at the same time" (Wallace, p. 125); (c) *Life on the Border*, for "someone who views their own identity essentially mixed or multifaceted" (Wallace, p. 124); and (d) *Shifting Identity Gears*, portraying "parts of an individual's identity shifting into the foreground, while other parts shift into the background as the person moves across social contexts" (p. 127). Wallace used the visuals to prompt discussion in interviews with fifteen high school and university students and found that "all the subjects identified with at least one visual, and fourteen out of fifteen identified with at least two" (p. 121). Although she did not indicate the identity patterns of each student, she indicated that eleven (73 percent) identified with the Home Base/Visitor's Base visual, five (33 percent) with the Both Feet in Both Worlds, six (40 percent) with Life on the Border, and nine (60 percent) with Shifting Identity Gears.

Wallace's visuals and the identities they represent correspond to four of the five patterns in my data. Home Base corresponds to the Monoracial Identity pattern, Both Feet in Both Worlds to Multiple Monoracial Identities, Life on the Border to holding Multiracial Identity, and Shifting Identity Gears to Situational Identity. Wallace did not include a separate pattern for Extraracial Identity, perhaps because Root did not present this option as an independent strategy. Wallace did, though, describe the ways in which students resisted racialization, such as when she summarized students' discussion of "being both/and" (pp. 147–52). Furthermore, it can be argued that in a society premised on an assumption of monoraciality, anyone who resists a monoracial construct (as represented by any of Wallace's four visuals) is opting out of racial categorization.

Marion Kilson, who in 1993 and 1994 interviewed "young adult Biracial Americans" born in the 1960s, used a different system to indicate how her participants self-identified, including an option to indicate a "raceless identity" similar to the Extraracial Identity pattern I use. She divided her fifty-two respondents into two groups, those who used "single descriptors" and those who used "multiple descriptors" (Kilson, 2001, p. 42). Forty two, or 81 percent of the total group chose single descriptors, the majority of whom (twenty-five, or 48 percent of total) chose a "monoracial identity of color such as 'African American' or 'Black'" (p. 42). Eleven (22%) used "a biracial or multiracial identity such as 'Black-and-Korean' or 'African American-and-Syrian'" (p. 42). Six (12 percent) chose what Kilson called a "raceless identity such as 'Other' or 'Human'" (p. 42). The remaining ten respondents used multiple descriptors. Six (12 percent) used "multiple self-descriptors for their racial identity," including "those claiming both an identity of color and a Biracial identity such as 'African American or African American-and-Irish' or 'Black or Biracial'" (p. 42). Three (5 percent) were among "those asserting both an identity of color and an ambiguous or raceless identity such as 'Mixed or Other' or 'Black-and-Korean or Other'" (p. 42). And one person (2 percent) indicated "raceless self-decriptors like 'Other and Unknown'" (p. 42).

The five patterns I use relate to Kilson's self-descriptors as follows: of the single descriptors, her Monoracial Identity of Color is a more specific description of my Monoracial Identity pattern; Biracial or Multiracial Identity is the same as Multiracial Identity pattern; and Raceless Identity is very similar to my Extraracial Identity pattern. Kilson's multiple descriptors are most like my Situational Identity pattern. Although it at first appears that none of the respondents identified with Multiple Monoracial heritages, as in Wallace's Both Feet in Both Worlds visual, Kilson discussed the situational nature of biracial identity by noting that "in addition to such primary public self-identification, Biracial Americans acknowledge that they may change their racial self-descriptors in different social contexts" (p. 42). Examples given include a man of "European American/African American-Native American parentage"[7] who identified situationally with his Native American heritage in relation to his work, which he said has "a lot to do with nature and the environment and that [heritage] is a really good tie-in" (Kilson, 2001, p. 42, brackets in original).

Sociologists Kerry Ann Rockquemore and David Brunsma (2002) studied college students with one black and one white parent, whom they labeled "biracial." In the survey portion of their mixed-methods study, Rockquemore and Brunsma examined the identities of 177 college students from a community college and a private university in Detroit. Twenty-five of the survey respondents also participated in in-depth interviews. All data were collected between 1997 and 2001. Rockquemore and Brunsma created "tentative descriptive categories for the ways that black/white multiracial people understand their biracialism: (a) a border identity, (b) a singular identity, (c) a protean identity, and/or (d) a transcendent identity" (p. 41). They viewed the categories as "ideal types" that were "not necessarily mutually exclusive" (p. 41).

Rockquemore and Brunsma's Border Identity resembles my Multiracial Identity pattern, including students whose identity "highlights an individual's existence between two socially distinct races" (Rockquemore & Brunsma,

2002, p. 42). Rockquemore and Brunsma further divided this category into those whose Border Identity is validated and those whose Border Identity is unvalidated. A total of 58 percent of their respondents fell into one of these groups of Border Identity. Rockquemore and Brunsma's Singular Identity category corresponds to Monoracial Identity, and they classified 17 percent of their respondents in this category (14 percent identifying as "exclusively black (or African American)," and almost 4 percent as "exclusively white (not black or biracial)" (p. 47). The Protean Identity category represents "biracial identity as [the] protean ability to move among cultural contexts" (Rockquemore & Brunsma, p. 48), be they white, black, or biracial. Like my Situational Identity pattern, this category included those students who consider identity to be fluid and shifting according to context. Four percent of Rockquemore and Brunsma's participants fit in this category. Finally, the Transcendent Identity category corresponds to my Extraracial Identity pattern. Thirteen percent of the sample was in the Transcendent Identity category.[8]

Although the labels used for identity categories differ across the four studies, it is clear that these five patterns of identity hold for college students in a variety of settings across nearly a decade of research. And while research methods were not consistent across the studies, the similarity among findings is interesting and points to directions for future research with mixed race college students. Of particular interest to college educators and administrators may be the specific factors of postsecondary institutions that lead to these five identity patterns. I turn now to one of these factors, the role of campus peer culture, which is a major feature of the five chapters that follow and address each of the identity patterns.

ROLE OF PEER CULTURE IN FORGING PATTERNS OF IDENTITY

A constructionist perspective on racial identity formation (e.g., Cerulo, 1997; Cornel & Hartmann, 1998; Rockquemore, 2002; Rockquemore & Brunsma, 2002) holds that "racial identities are considered to have emerged from the tension between the definition of self assigned to an individual by out-group members and the definition of self constructed by that individual" (Rockquemore, 2002, p. 487). A symbolic interactionist perspective posits "identity as a reflexive process, influenced by both external constraints and individual agency" (Rockquemore, 2002, p. 487) and a "negotiated process by which individuals understand themselves and others and evaluate their selves in relation to others" (Rockquemore, 2002, p. 488). In either case, the role of individuals in the immediate environments—the microsystems and mesosystems in ecological systems theory—is considered critical to identity formation. They are either the "out-group members" against whose definitions an individual reacts or the "others" with whom one negotiates identity through coded, symbolic interactions. Peer culture, according to constructionist and symbolic interactionist theories, is an important locus of identity construction and maintenance. This importance extends well beyond the theoretical into the everyday lives of mixed race college students.

Like the real students from whose experiences they were composed, Marta, Kenji, Kim, Jared, and Lena spend most of their waking hours immersed in peer culture, and it is within this environment that identities are formed and negotiated. The openness of microsystems to individuals of different identities creates an ecological press on identity and identification. Kenji's membership in a white fraternity was seen as disloyal to the asian community, but Lena's participation in the Filipino community was supported by friends and family. Identity-based microsystems are bounded by spoken and unspoken rules about who can enter, when, and under what conditions. Cultural knowledge, humor, behavior, and physical appearance constitute common rule categories that cut across campuses (see Renn, 2000; Rockquemore, 2002).

Peer culture is formed by the interactions between and among various campus microsystems, and the ways that tacit and explicit group membership criteria reinforce or contradict one another become part of the larger culture. Though Kenji's fraternity brothers rarely ventured cross-culturally in their extracurricular lives, neither did his friends from the Asian Student Alliance; peer culture supported separate spheres of student involvement. From the two microsystems, Kenji got the same message: Stick with your own people. The challenge for Kenji, of course, is that his "own people" were in both spheres. On some campuses, like Lena's, the mesosystem of peer culture supports more fluid identification, allowing students more easily to identify differently in different situations.

The messages Kenji and Lena received from their peers required different responses and decisions about identity. In part these responses are guided by developmentally instigative characteristics. The drive to find a place on campus to "fit in"—as Marta did at the social for latino students and Kim did at the meeting of mixed students—is an important characteristic influencing identity and identification. The strength of the desire to self-label—exemplified most keenly by Jared's response to "What are you?" questions—represents another developmentally instigative characteristic that influences individual responses to the mesosystem of peer culture. In the chapters that follow, the importance of the role of peer culture and interactions between individuals and their environments will become clear in the context of the five patterns of identity.

chapter four

I'm Black—Monoracial Identity

Really I just think of myself as Chicano. I grew up with the language, the food, the culture. I look Mexican, I don't look white. So people just assume I am, and that's how it is.

—Juan

LIKE THE COMPOSITE Marta introduced in chapter 3 and study participant Juan, nearly half (twenty-seven), of the mixed race students I interviewed identified exclusively or sometimes in the Monoracial Identity pattern. They called themselves by many terms—"biracial, mixed, black," "Chicano or mixed," "biracial Chinese American," "half American, half Japanese," "Mexican American," "biracial or black," "half Filipino," "Jamaican, multiracial, or black," and "black"—but they shared the experience of identifying with just one of their monoracial heritage groups.

In this chapter on the Monoracial Identity pattern, I describe trends among the twenty-seven students in this pattern, characteristics and experiences they shared, and influences of the peer culture mesosystem leading to identification in this pattern. Portraits of four students who identify primarily as monoracial illustrate characteristics, experiences, and peer influences on the group.

CHARACTERISTICS OF THIS PATTERN

Students who identified in the Monoracial Identity category were those students who some or all of the time identified with just one of their monoracial heritage groups. They stood in contrast to those students who some or all of the time identified with two or more heritage groups (in the Multiple Monoracial Identities pattern). For example, a Monoracial Identity student with one asian and one white parent might identify exclusively as asian, or she might identify sometimes as asian and sometimes as mixed. Another asian-white mixed student who identified sometimes as asian, sometimes as white, and sometimes as mixed would have been in the Multiple Monoracial Identities pattern, as were those students who identified as "half-X and half-Y." Most often, students identified with the heritage of a parent of color rather than a white parent, though two students (Mark and Fred), both light-skinned men, identified strongly as white at the time of their interviews.

TRENDS WITHIN THE PATTERN

While nearly half of the participants (48%) identified sometimes or always with only one of their monoracial heritages, the 27 students in this pattern were not evenly distributed across the sample. Men were more likely to identify this way (60%) than were women (42%). Students with two parents of color or one mixed parent and one white parent were less likely (33%) than students with one parent of color and one white parent (54%). All five students with one latino/a and one white parent identified in this pattern; four identified with their latin heritage, one with his white heritage. Students with Monoracial Identity were more likely to be in their first two years of college (18, or 67%) than in their last two (9, or 33%). And they were found more often at Liberal Arts College (6, or 75% of LAC participants) and less often at Ivy (5, or 36%) or Rural Comprehensive University (3, or 38%). These trends thread throughout the chapter, in participants' voices and experiences, to create a broad portrait of mixed race college students who identify with one of their monoracial heritage groups.

PORTRAITS OF STUDENTS WHO CHOSE THIS PATTERN

MARK

> I identify more with my mother's side. She's white. My father is Mexican. Growing up I lived with her, and he wasn't there after maybe two or three years. So the most experience I've had with his side of the family, like his brothers and sisters and my grandparents, there are a lot of them that lived in [nearby state], but not too many, so I mostly grew up with my mom's side of the family. So it seems like I've always identified more with her side than with the others just because that's what I've experienced most.

Mark was a light-skinned, blue-eyed man at the end of his sophomore year at Big Ten University when we met for an interview. He came from a small town "up north," where the lack of diversity in his public high school was "boring" because "everyone was the same"—meaning white and mid-

TABLE 4.1
Distribution of Students in the Monoracial Identity Pattern
by Gender, Heritage, Class Year, and Institution

		Total in sample	Identifying in this pattern
Gender	Men	20	12 (60%)
	Women	36	15 (42%)
Heritage	Two Parents of Color	12	4 (33%)
	One Asian & One White Parent	16	8 (50%)
	One Black & One White Parent	13	6 (46%)
	One Latino/a & One White Parent	5	5 (100%)
	One Pacific Islander & One White Parent	7	3 (43%)
	One Mixed & One White Parent	3	1 (33%)
Class Year	First Year	14	6 (43%)
	Sophomore*	17	12 (71%)
	Junior	11	3 (27%)
	Senior	14	6 (43%)
Institution	Big Ten University	12	6 (50%)
	Catholic University	8	4 (50%)
	Ivy University	14	5 (36%)
	Liberal Arts College	8	6 (75%)
	Rural Community College	6	3 (50%)
	Rural University	8	3 (38%)
	TOTAL	56	27 (48%)

*Throughout the text, *sophomore* refers to a second-year student at any institution, including the community college, although this term is not universally used in two-year colleges.

dle class. His precollege micro- and mesosystems of family, school, and community formed a predominantly white milieu in which he developed an essentially monoracial white identity. Mark transitioned into the larger and more diverse environment of Big Ten by being "a lot more outgoing than in high school. I've had to be more forward and outgoing. And that's a good thing."

At the time of the interview, Mark was preparing for another transition, from two years in the residence halls with friends to the off-campus house of the predominantly white fraternity he had joined earlier in the year. It was clear that the fraternity comprised a peer mesosystem that would become the context of a number of Marks' microsystems, because as he said, "I spent a lot of time this year with that, because it takes up a lot. Having all kinds of things to do. . . . I wasn't set on joining a fraternity, but I got there and it was really cool. All of the guys were just regular people and so I loved it." Involved in the fraternity and other college activities, Mark was not drawn to participate in activities of the hispanic/latino student organizations. "It just didn't interest me. If something else came along from [those groups], I certainly wouldn't just turn it down."

Racial identity "has never been a big deal" to Mark. Asked about his comfort discussing his mixed Mexican and white heritage, he said, "It hasn't ever really bothered me to talk about it, but I don't wind up talking about it too much just because most people don't ask. Unless they see my [Mexican] last name, most people can't tell there's anything like that." Mark was aware that his physical appearance did not mark him as other than white and that his unmarked appearance provided a measure of privacy in regard to others' speculation about his ethnicity; this privacy was rare among other study participants, whose "racially ambiguous" appearances invited questions and comments that sometimes prompted identity shifts and redefinitions. For Mark, though, the transition to Big Ten was more about adjusting to the size and diversity of the student body than about personal explorations of racial identity.

There were, however, elements of the ecological system at Big Ten that set Mark thinking about racial and ethnic identity. Asked if he would use a specific term to describe his identity, he replied, "*Mexican American,* but I hardly ever use that, because how often do people ask that? And it's only in those situations like, 'Which box do I check?' Yeah. Exactly. That's pretty much the only time that I use it." On institutional forms, Mark checks the "hispanic/latino" box, though he said,

> It's frustrating sometimes. Because I'm always confused. I always debate for that one second on which I should check. I think in high school I started wondering which one I should really check. . . . It was never really too big a deal. I was just always unsure. Cause was it the one that *I* identified with most? Or was it what I was? And obviously, it's what I was, so it wasn't ever really too big a debate.

As a result of checking the "hispanic/latino" box on his college application, Mark was automatically placed on mailing lists of various campus organizations, offices, and programs serving students of color. For the most part, these groups operated in Mark's exosystem; he was not directly involved with them, yet they influenced features of his immediate environment, not least of which were their frequent communication efforts. These communications had a direct influence on Mark's identification process:

> I get all the emails and messages from the minority aides, and all the groups like that, which sort of keeps reminding me that I do have that other section of my personality or whatever you want to call it. So yeah, I think it's made me more aware, plus having other students like that around also helps.
>
> I'd say Big Ten is more comfortable. It wasn't *uncomfortable* in high school, but it's nice to know that there are other people like me around, which is kind of nice, but it hasn't really affected me too much as far as a big change in how I think about things. But it's just kind of nice to have there. To know.

So while identifying personally with his white heritage, Mark did not deny his Mexican heritage. The micro- and mesosystems of his environment before college supported his identification with his mother's white family and the homogeneous community in which he lived; at college, Mark was glad to know that there were other students like him with "hispanic origin," but he did not identify with the latino community, seek courses with content related to his Mexican heritage, or explore his racial identity beyond the periodic completion of institutional forms. The only participant to identify primarily as monoracial and white, Mark was comfortable treating his mixed heritage as a matter of fact rather than a matter of identity.

DEE DEE

> It's something that now I struggle with, how some multiracial people, who look just like me, but they don't say they're black. Some would say they're black, but some wouldn't, and I'm just like, "What do you mean? What's wrong with being black?" (laugh) . . . Of course being black in America is based on different cultures and traditions. It's a way of thinking about how you define yourself, and if you don't have the same definition as me, of course you're going to have some difference in how you think about yourself.

Dee Dee described her heritage as "African American and South Asian." She identified primarily as black, though according to the situation might also deconstruct racial categories or opt out of self-definition, characteristics of the Extraracial Identity pattern. Dee Dee was a senior at Ivy University, having spent her junior year in Spain and Egypt on study abroad programs. Her early childhood was spent in a racially and ethnically diverse neighborhood in New York City, playing with the black, asian, latino, and white children whose parents worked on the nearby military base. A move to a predominantly white area in the Midwest was "startling" to eight-year-old Dee Dee, prompting her to be more aware of her dark brown skin and thick black hair. In response to the move from diverse to more homogeneous micro- and mesosystems, Dee Dee became "deeply rooted in my culture." She remembered her teenage self: "I knew what it was about and that I was *fierce* and that I was so *down*, and just all this crazy stuff." Asked why she chose Ivy, Dee Dee responded

> I was working on this project writing about colleges and researching them, and I went into the [guidance counselor's office] and picked up the book, and thought, "Oh, interesting, I think I'll apply." But I didn't think I'd get in or anything. . . . And my friend Amelia, she went to [another elite college]. We were the only two people out of our class who went to Ivy League schools. The others went mostly in state. I always liked the idea of these two black girls going off to the East and everyone just being like, "Wow." (laugh)

Four years after her decision to go "off to the East" Dee Dee was no longer the same "black girl" from Saint Louis. Immersed in a peer culture at Ivy that required evidence of racial and ethnic "authenticity" for entrance to the politically active Third World student community,[1] Dee Dee found her voice as a black woman in multiple contexts: leadership in her residence hall, becoming a women's peer counselor, and the classroom. Though not in a formal leadership role in the Third World community, Dee Dee felt like an insider in the African American student peer mesosystem:

> There's like the black vernacular and how we use it, and how people revert to that in situations when it's not even necessary. You know, just to talk, we just do that amongst ourselves. You just automatically do it for some reason. But you can't assume that someone at [Ivy] is going to speak it. But with people that you know, you do.

Dee Dee described the most significant influence on her identity as her two semesters abroad. Her experiences in and out of the classroom in Spain and Egypt deeply influenced her thinking about race, culture, and identity.

> Until I went abroad, I automatically assumed that the experience was the same for black students from Africa, or the U.S., or the Caribbean, and now I really see the difference. And there's black latinos, too. . . . Now that I've gone away, especially since going to two different countries, I came back with a much greater sense of culture. And not just necessarily race, and that's a big thing, but what culture means to race and how it defines race.
>
> Before I went, there was white, black, and asian. And I didn't realize how a person from Southeast Asia could be just as dark as I am, but their language, their customs, their traditions are totally different and totally shape their experience, and especially here in America, where there's so many— what is there, like 260 million people?—of all different races, of all different cultures, and each one of those factors in. So my racial experience counts just

as much as my cultural experience in defining who I am and how I live. Race is a very hard thing to define. Culture is a little bit easier to define by traditions, customs, ceremonies. It's not based on physical characteristics.

Definitely, going abroad was one of the most important experiences of my life. Now, it's easy for me to just say, "Take me as for what you see me." Whatever you're comfortable with. If you're comfortable defining me as black, that's fine. But then also in saying "I'm black" limits what blackness is and how it transcends cultures.

I've learned so much in the past year about culture. And what it means to be a person and how my culture, especially going to Egypt, how in some ways it's just me and how my experiences in the first part of my life, being pretty much impoverished, and how that's affected my experience. How that's affected my black experience, and how it's affected my experience here at Ivy, like how I feel about what's mine and what's not mine. Being black was all I had, but now that I've been away I know there's just something very different about being black and being a woman and being not rich, but not destitute, about being acceptable to do things that upper-class people do. All those things, under the heading of race, on top of being—feeling—stronger at times.

It's just much more complicated now, race and culture, it's more complicated now. It's not like I can just give one definition of "This is being black" because I'm black. Now, I ask, "what does it mean to be black?" What does blackness mean in America? In Africa? In Europe? And in all these other places how does my skin tone affect me and how I'm seen?

Dee Dee complicated the idea of race by placing it in an international context, where it became clear to her that culture, not so-called race, is what differentiates groups of people. So her self-definition as black took on cultural nuances that situated her as specifically *African American*, within particular social and cultural contexts in the United States.

Pressed to define further what that black identity meant to her as someone with African American and South Asian heritage, Dee Dee elaborated:

Sometimes people infuriate, well, really bother me, when they use "multiracial" or "biracial." I think that by and large to say that, especially if they're of African American heritage, which is a combination of native american and black anyway, it's already in there. And if they're of African and European heritage, regardless of whether they look like me in our skin tones, certain features definitely look different from native Africans or native West Africans, and to say "biracial" is just to say "Oh, I'm just, whatever." There are just very big differences in who we are, and to negate that, regardless of whether it's a good thing or a bad thing, is to negate the cultures native americans have had, and the role Europeans have had, in our heritage. Saying "multiracial" creates an artificial separation.

My mother being South Asian is not something that's common. So sometimes I'll just say, "I'm black. My mom is South Asian." But to say "biracial" or "multiracial" erases all that.

Here Dee Dee balances internal and external definitions of "black." To her, being black in America already meant being of mixed heritage; Dee Dee's black identity encompassed her fully, and to say "biracial" was to create an unnecessary category. But Dee Dee was aware that she operated in a society that did not share her understanding of black-as-mixed heritage: "I think in places where there's so much mixing, take a place like Brazil or Puerto Rico, I'd be like, 'Oh, I'm multiracial,' you know?" So she settled for exerting her personal definition—"I'm black"—within the monoracial context of campus and U. S. cultures, knowing that when she wanted to be fully descriptive of her heritage in ways that others could understand, she must add "My mom is South Asian." Dee Dee's way of making meaning of U.S. racial categories rendered this private-public distinction neutral; she felt no apparent disjuncture in presenting her self-definition to a world that she knew did not fully understand its meaning.

RENEE

My mom always told me that it didn't matter what I called myself. I'd always be "that black girl" from [town]. And I think she was mostly right, at least about what the white girls thought. But the other black girls, they weren't always so sure, you know? But I had my best friend, Dawn, and she was all black and she didn't take crap from anyone and she and I did everything together in high school. And she made sure the other kids knew that I was "down" with the community. So that made it easier to hang with the black kids, too, so pretty much everyone decided it was okay for me to be black, if that's what I wanted to be. And it was.

In her second year at Rural Community College, Renee was planning to complete her general education requirements and transfer to Rural University. She lived at home with her African American mother and two younger brothers. Their father, who was white, lived a two-hour drive away in the nearest city, and Renee saw him "on holidays, usually on breaks, and stuff like that." Renee's mother had moved home with the three children, to the rural community in which she grew up, when she and Renee's father divorced six years prior to the interview. Renee described the transition from a predominantly white suburb to a racially diverse, but highly segregated, small town as

hellish, just awful, I hated it down here. I missed my dad and my friends. I didn't talk to *anybody* for the longest time—they all thought I was this really snotty girl from the city who thought she was better than the rednecks and "niggahs" down here. And they were right. I *did* think that at first. Okay, for a long while I thought that.

After what Renee described as "several knock-down, drag-out fights" with her mother and threats to move back to the city with her father, Renee settled somewhat unhappily into school, vowing "not to make friends with these girls, ever." The school was technically integrated, with black, white, and a few Mexican American students sharing academic and athletic microsystems but sharply segregated in social microsystems. Interracial dating "didn't happen—no way!" and Renee struggled to fit in with either the white or black girls. The ice melted with her friend Dawn when they worked together on a social studies project about the history of the region: "And when I told her about my family and how my great-great-great-or something-grandparents had been slaves, she said, 'Geez, girl! You really are a sister!' And we've been friends ever since." Following that breakthrough, Renee made her way with Dawn's assistance into the black peer culture in her high school.

Renee's ACT scores and high school grade point average were not high enough for her to be admitted to the regional university many of her friends—including Dawn—would attend, so she took a teacher's advice and enrolled in the college transfer program at Rural Community College. Renee found the classes "okay, nothing too challenging," and became involved in the Black Student Organization (BSO). In this new environment, old tensions arose with some of the other women in the group:

> One day [my first year] I walked into the [BSO] lounge and one of these girls—she's really pretty and she *pretends* to like you, but she really doesn't—she sees me and she stops talking all of a sudden—like that!—and she and the other girls look at me like, "Would you get her? Sister thinks she's all that 'cause she's 'high yelluh,' but she *ain't* all that at all." And I just walked over to get my books that I left there before class and I pretended I didn't notice, but you couldn't *not* notice. It was that cold, you know? Like ice in there. So I left. Fast.
>
> But some of them were nicer, mostly the lighter girls. Not as light as me, sometimes, but lighter than that ones that gave me The Look. And now I know enough girls—light and darker ones, too—and they know me and who I am and we don't have to play that game anymore of who's got better hair and who's too dark and who's too light. We do stuff together for BSO, and that's where I've been able to show them what I'm really about, like planning stuff for [new student orientation day] and making sure the new black kids know we're here for them. So doing that has made them see that I'm there to put in the time and all like that. I guess they think I'm black enough to poster campus! (laugh)

In the black student peer mesosystem, Renee has encountered similar developmental prompts as those she encountered in her rural high school. Not readily accepted by all of the other african american women, she had to reassert her black identity through participation in a legitimizing activity, involvement with the BSO. Eventually she found black women who accepted her fully as part of the community, leaving aside the tacit competition for male attention that is implied in the comparison of skin tone and hair texture in many black women's communities.[2]

The discovery of and immersion in microsystems that supported Renee's black identity formed a foundation for her involvement in campus activities, an important element in college student development (Astin, 1984). Renee was nominated by her peers and selected by a committee of students, faculty, and administrators to participate in the college's annual Martin Luther King, Jr. Day program. The event reinforced Renee's black identity and had a lasting impact on her.

> The best was when I introduced the Dr. Martin Luther King Day speaker this year. That's when I really, really felt like I wasn't looked at like "Renee that 'high yelluh' girl" but as "Renee, African American." Cause everyone saw me and knew I was there because I'm black. And my mom came and my brothers did, too. And for [my brothers] I think it was important to see me as black and to know that they can be strong, proud black men if they want to. That's what I want them to know. That they can be as black as they want to be. That was the best.

This recognition of her contribution to the college community, and the black community in particular, prompted Renee to reflect on her experience of Rural Community College:

> I didn't expect it to be much of anything. I just thought I'd take classes and finish and go up to [Rural U]. That's all I figured on. But it's been so good to have a *place* here. And I think I'll miss it next year. Yeah, I will. I really will.

Involvement in the black student mesosystem created an unexpected link to the community college for Renee. It challenged the black identity she had struggled to establish in high school, then reinforced it when she persisted in her involvement with BSO. Renee's developmentally instigative characteristics—those that led her to become involved and to persist in the face of negative responses—prompted her to claim and reclaim a "strong, proud, black" identity.

SAPO

> "What are you and where are you from?" Yeah, definitely people ask that, especially when you get to college and everyone's asking, "Where do you come from?" In class, we were talking about the different questions of "Where are you from?" "What country do your ancestors come from, where were you born, where are you coming from high school?" So people come to

you and ask you that. I say I'm from Boston, but I'm originally from California. If they ask me what ethnicity I am or what my name is, I'll say Mexican American.

Sapo's Mexican father and Irish mother worked with the United Farm Workers of America and spoke Spanish at home in a Boston suburb. Sapo played basketball on his public high school's team and was recruited by a number of Division III colleges because of his athletic and academic talent. He chose Liberal Arts College (LAC) because "it's a good place to study, it'll challenge you academically." Having lived in a number of ethnically diverse communities growing up, Sapo found LAC's student body fairly homogeneous. He noted that there were some tensions between the college and the "white, working class town" in which it was located, attributing these to students' unwillingness to look outside their immediate environs.

Sapo described the peer culture at LAC as one in which students could move easily from one group to another, a contrast to his high school, where

> I hung out with mostly minorities because I would play basketball. The other four guys of the starting five players were black, and I grew up with them since I was little, since I first got there [at age nine]. So when I came here it was very different. When I first got here, it was pretty much just hanging out with the basketball team, because when you get here you just want to stick around the same people. But then you kind of branch off. Everyone's together at first, and then people just branch off their different ways. It's a really friendly atmosphere.

And in this "really friendly atmosphere" Sapo sought out friends across a range of groups, from athletes to "people who are really into their books" to "alternative kids" and groups of students of color.

> I meet people in class, in dorms, obviously because that's where you live and spend a majority of your time. And I've never really clicked to one friend or friends. I just kind of like to roam, freelance. I like to meet a lot of different people. I think it's selfish if you just stay in one group of friends, even though that's fine, if you feel comfortable. But the way I see it is there's so many different people, I might as well get acquainted with all of them I can.

Sapo moved with ease among these groups, "roaming" as he called it, without a sense of pressure to conform to a particular racial or ethnic identity.

Although he moved among groups, Sapo identified strongly with his Mexican heritage and participated in activities of the Latino Students Association (LSA), attending social and educational programs on campus and in nearby cities. Sapo had also chosen a Latino studies major:

> I guess you could say from the influence of my parents. Spanish is spoken at home. Just from growing up, it influenced me to want to learn more about

> Latin America. I've taken some good classes in Hispanic Studies. Like now
> I'm taking a class about Latin America, and it's in Spanish. I like that class
> a lot, because that's one of my main interests, Latin America.

Electing to participate in academic microsystems that supported his Mexican American identity provided important opportunities for Sapo to expand his cultural knowledge and to consider if he wanted to make a career in an area related to his cultural, political, and economic interests in Latin America.

Sapo acknowledged his biracial heritage, but also acknowledged the difficulty of creating a separate "biracial" identity group on campus:

> Biraciality is kind of a complex subject. Like if you have a group of biracial
> students, they're not all the same biraciality, they're all different ethnicities.
> So there's not an event where you can say, "This is for biracial students,"
> because only a few people would go. So it would be hard to have events
> specifically for those couple of people. Like I said, I think biracial students
> have already gone off with their own [monoracial] groups and defined what
> they are by hanging out, or they've gotten in touch with one of their sides.

It is important to note here that Sapo was one of only 150 students of color on a campus of 1,400 enrollment. The issue here was one of critical mass; there was not a critical mass of students identifying as biracial to create a separate reference group, as existed formally or informally at other campuses in the study (see Renn, 2000, for a discussion of critical mass and its role in the creation of mixed race space). But given Sapo's observation that biracial students are "all different ethnicities," he might not see a need for a biracial collective on any campus. In his worldview, students have "already gone off with their own groups," as he had with Latino students.

Moreover, Sapo postulated that "a lot of biracial students are pretty open-minded because they're more than one ethnicity, so they have to look at both of them." Echoing the "advantaged" approach to the study of mixed race taken by Weisman (1996) and Kich (1996), Sapo presents mixed heritage as a privileged vantage point from which to observe racial, ethnic, and cultural issues on campus and in the broader society. He said

> I think it's sometimes hard to be biracial because you're not classified as one
> thing. You're bi, you're different things. But I think it definitely outweighs
> all the negative aspects. There's a lot more benefits, because you're part of
> different cultures. I think it just opens up your mind if you're brought up in
> a biracial household with different cultures kind of intertwined with your
> upbringing. But I think it goes both ways. It's emotionally draining and
> there are lots of benefits to it, too.

This mixed review captures the complexity of Sapo's experience. At the point of the interview, he identified as Mexican American, enjoying activities of the Latino Students Association and choosing a Latino studies major. Influenced by his parents' professional and political activism on behalf of a largely immigrant labor force, Sapo was using the resources of Liberal Arts College to learn more about his background through an academic, cultural, and social lens.

THE ECOLOGY OF MONORACIAL IDENTITY

How do students such as Mark, Dee Dee, Renee, and Sapo come to identify more strongly with one monoracial heritage than with one or more others in their background? Like these four, most of the twenty-seven students in this identity pattern also engaged in other identity patterns, commonly the Multiracial Identity pattern. When they identified with a specific racial or ethnic group, however, they chose just one. What features of campus life influence these identity choices? The ecology model and the key themes of space and peer culture are useful for examining the ways in which interactions between and among personal characteristics, microsystems, and mesosystems create developmental presses that led students to choose this identity pattern at the time of the study.

Personal Characteristics

Students who chose Monoracial Identity described family structures and perceptions (their own and others) of their level of cultural knowledge as important factors in identity. They also described behaviors and attitudes depicting a variety of developmentally instigative characteristics, such as a propensity to persist in uncomfortable situations, to probe and explore identity, and to resist external categorization, that would contribute to identity formation. Physical appearance also played a role in choosing Monoracial Identity. These elements combined uniquely in each participant, as they do in every student who comes to higher education, yet there are commonalities among the group that bear discussion.

Cultural Knowledge

Having—or lacking—*cultural knowledge* was a major factor in students' choice of the Monoracial Identity pattern. Some students believed that they lacked cultural knowledge of one or more of their heritages, and they therefore stayed away from groups whom they perceived, correctly or incorrectly, to require this cultural knowledge of group members; conversely, some students came to college lacking cultural knowledge and used the rich curricular and co-curricular opportunities available to them to gain knowledge about their heritage. A student might choose to identify in the Monoracial Identity pattern in either case, though for very different reasons.

Family was a key element in forming students' sense of themselves as culturally knowledgeable and in the personal characteristics they brought to college with them. Study participants came from a variety of family constellations. The presence or absence of family members from different heritage groups played a significant role in cultural acquisition if not in actual identity. For example, on the one hand, Dan grew up on the East Coast with his white father, stepmother, and half-brother, though he had a strong sense of himself as Chinese.

> My childhood was really monocultural. My mother was Chinese and my dad is white, Italian, and my mother died when I was two and a half, so from that, I never had a direct Chinese influence in my growing up. So that just kind of made it falling into, especially in my town, the mainstream white culture. I never had Chinese culture, which to me is different from not having a Chinese identity, because I've always known I was Chinese and I've always said I was Chinese and Italian. I would never switch it, I would never start out with Italian. I would always put Chinese first, because from when I was little, I knew I was different and I actually think I really enjoyed being different, along with its hardships, but I was proud of it.

On the other hand, Jennifer grew up in the Midwest surrounded by Filipinos:

> Both my parents are involved with a community of Filipinos that I basically call my aunts and uncles. We're really close to them. The person who recommended I come to Catholic U was from part of that group of friends. I spend Christmas with them, I spend Thanksgiving with them, I see them when I go home, I'm good friends with all the kids. And I think that has brought the Filipino culture a little closer to myself. Just because it's more different than what everyone else does, it stands out more to me.

Tim's latina mother included extended families from both sides in holiday celebrations, though he believed that, "my [white] grandparents really just don't get why the music can't just be country-western and the food can't just be hamburgers. They think that in America everything should be *American*, which means *white* to them, I guess." Dan, Jennifer, and Tim had very different experiences of family and culture, gaining varying degrees of cultural knowledge along the way; yet they all came to college with strong monoracial identities, which they enriched through academic and cocurricular activities related to those cultural groups.

A perceived lack of cultural knowledge prompted some students to choose academic microsystems that focused on the acquisition of cultural knowledge. Juan focused on the economics of Latin America, Renee took courses on African American literature and history, and Sapo chose Latino studies: "I guess you could say from the influence of my parents. Spanish is spoken at home. Just from growing up. It influenced me to want to learn more about it, which is why I chose the major." Jennifer took a course on Filipino Americans and learned that she had more cultural knowledge than she had thought.

> I'm actually taking a class on perspectives on Filipino Americans right now. So that has been really an eye opener for me—learning more about my father's culture and its progression in the United States. It's not something you run across everyday, so I told my Dad about it and he was like, "Oh, you should take it," and so I did. I'm taking it as an elective. I guess I just wanted to know more about it, although by taking the class, I realize that I know more than I thought I did.

Within courses, several students elected to do projects relating to a single monoracial identity. Mike wrote articles on local black politics for a journalism course, Tim used his family's Mexican heritage as the focus of a writing assignment, and Vincent used the occasion of a course assignment to talk to his mother about his Chinese heritage. Academic choices sometimes immersed students in microsystems related to their identities and sometimes caused students to raise questions and issues about their heritage in family microsystems. In either case, these microsystem interactions created opportunities for students to subscribe more strongly to Monoracial Identity.

Students often felt that other microsystems, such as monoracial peer groups on campus, required a certain level of cultural knowledge for membership. Lack of language skill was often cited as a reason for feeling excluded from these groups, as Clarice indicated.

> Sometimes I feel the differences just because I never learned Hindi or Marathi or anything or my dad's language. I never learned any of that because my parents didn't want to push one culture or the other onto me. They just let me develop my own and I never had a desire to do it.

Even Dan, who strongly identified as Chinese, described his sense of not having enough cultural knowledge and his perceptions of how cultural knowledge affected how welcome students were in the monoracial groups at Ivy University:

> And I still don't know anything about Chinese culture, besides my grandmother talking a little about it. And I didn't feel like I could fit in completely, because there are a lot of asian americans that kind of like lost their culture and they kind of feel like they can't become involved and they can't be a part of the scene, because culture's such a big part. And obviously it depends, but it's just hard to feel that you should be part or be involved without it. And you feel like they treat you with this little bit of contempt for you because you don't know.
>
> The asian americans who are "down" with it are involved, heavily. Like they're the heads of [Asian Student Alliance] and [Minority Peer Aides] and

stuff like that. But then there are a lot of asian americans who aren't much involved. Stereotypically, they're like pre-med, and they're not necessarily viewed as part of the "Third World" title by other asian american students.

Though this effect was particularly strongly felt at Ivy, it permeated the other five campuses as well, calling into question students' claims to legitimacy and authenticity in monoracial groups of students of color. Cultural knowledge as a personal characteristic was a factor in students' ability to identify publicly as monoracial, though students did not include cultural knowledge as a criterion for their personal definitions of identity.

Physical Appearance

Outward appearance—skin tone, hair color and texture, eye color—shaped the identity choices of many students who identified as monoracial. For better or for worse, the power of skin tone, facial features, hair color and texture, and body shape to influence racial identity remains extremely strong. Root (1997) and Rockquemore (2002) argued that this is a particularly gendered phenomenon, with women more subject to scrutiny based on physical appearance. I concur with their analyses, given the propensity of women in my study to discuss the role of their physical appearance in identity and the relative lack of importance of appearance to men's identity choices.

For some students, physical appearance was congruent with a monoracial identity. Fred identified primarily as white and said,

> For me, I think it's a little different because some people don't even realize that I'm half-Japanese. Actually, one of my good friends for a year or two just found out last semester. He was talking to my friend and they were talking about it, and they actually made a bet about me. He didn't believe it, he was talking to my roommate, and he was surprised.

Other students held monoracial identities but in appearance did not conform to expected campus norms. Eleanor described the influence of her "black body" on her identity as a black woman:

> When people talk about identity and beauty and exoticism and hair, you know, well, I like my hair short, I don't have this exotic look that some biracial or multiracial women fit the image of. So identifying as a multiracial woman hasn't really been part of my growing up process. Or like with body image issues. People say I have the "black body" or something. So I haven't had to deal with a lot of the images that multiracial women generally deal with.
>
> But I could never choose to be white, you know, I never *would* choose to be white and I *could* never choose to be white, so I think that some choices aren't available based on the way that you look. So it has something to do with how you look that you have certain choices.

In Eleanor's case, identity options were limited by physical appearance, based on how others perceive the multiracial individual.

Princess, too, identified as black in part based on her appearance. As a child she was subject to race-related teasing because her white mother did not know how to help her style her tightly curled black hair:

> We lived in the south, so I mean, I get dark in the summer, and I had an afro until I was 12 years old because my mom didn't know about relaxers and that whole deal, and I was always made fun of, you know? They called me this and that, and I didn't know why—I just thought I had curly hair or whatever. And at parent-teacher conferences, my mom was like, "Hi, I'm Princess' mom," and she has platinum blonde hair, really blue eyes, really fair skin, and there she is with her little black child. So that was always interesting. I'd ask her, "Why am I . . . ?" And she would say, "Well, honey, it's because you are black."

The sharp difference between Princess' and her mother's appearances brought Princess' black heritage to the forefront and contributed to her strong sense of black identity. Princess perceived that based on her appearance, others on campus identified her first as black, then possibly as latina or mixed, any of which were fine with her, "so long as when they get to know me they know I'm black." For Eleanor and Princess, then, physical appearance confirmed personal identity, a congruence that supported their monoracial senses of self.

For other students, however, a "racially ambiguous" physical appearance was not congruent with their monoracial identities and contributed to some stress in regard to being accepted as members of those monoracial communities. Students described times when they felt their physical appearances influenced others' first impressions:

> You're always scared that people aren't entirely accepting of you, like especially when you walk through the door and people look at you like, "Hey, you're not Chinese." . . . My sister really identifies with the white side, and we've had some conversations about that. She doesn't make an issue of it, and outwardly she's fine with that. But she also looks pretty white, so it's easier. (Phil)

> At Catholic U I've never felt comfortable in joining any of the AHANA[3] Asian clubs, though they send me things all the time. I remember I went to a meeting once when I was a freshman. And I walked in, and I felt really uncomfortable, like people were looking at me like, "Are you *sure* you should be here?" (Jennifer)

The similarity in these examples—walking into a monoracial student group—is striking and speaks to the power of physical appearance in peers' perceptions of mixed race students' authenticity and qualification for group membership. Most often, these peer judgments are tacit, though occasionally they are articulated publicly. Marisa, who identified (among other labels) as black, was at a meeting of the Black Student Association (BSA) at Liberal Arts College when physical appearance was explicitly raised as a matter of group membership:

> I remember attending meetings of BSA and it was kind of like deciding, I think it was this year, deciding who should be accepted into the BSA, like your origins and if you're African American, something like that.
>
> I remember a student looking around and he says, "I don't mind if she and if that one stays." I just said, "What do you think I am?" It was kind of separating. People who just look at me, they figure I'm hispanic or some other category.

Phil identified as Chinese, Jennifer as Filipino, and Marisa as black, but their appearances did not clearly mark them as insiders in these groups. Unlike Eleanor and Princess, they did not perceive an easy, nonverbal connection to other students who identified as they did. This incongruence between physical appearance and identity—an incongruence that is not limited to mixed race individuals but extends also to anyone who does not easily fall within expected norms for physical expression of gender, race, class, ability, or sexuality, among others—created developmentally instigative or inhibitory moments as students managed the impact of repeated, daily interactions where they had to decide how to respond to nonverbal and verbal "What are you?" questions and challenges.

Developmentally Instigative Characteristics

In addition to cultural knowledge and physical appearance, students had a number of personal characteristics related to propensity to probe and explore the concepts of race and racial identity, to resist or adopt external categorization, to persist in identifying privately and publicly in a variety of ways. Although Bronfenbrenner did not deal specifically with the development of racial identity, these propensities fall under the rubric of the *developmentally instigative characteristics* he assigned to individuals. As an example, Dan, who identified primarily as Chinese, wrote about an his response to an exercise he led during new student orientation:

> We did an exercise dealing with race relations and it was the first time a lot of people had gone through something like that so it was a very uncomfortable experience for a lot of people, but it definitely helped me formulate, like I actually went back to my room and wrote this thing, I don't really know what it was, I just started thinking and wrote a couple pages about just, issues of race and institutionalized racism and so I just kind of went on this tirade for like an hour or two, I wrote some things, this vision of me writing this question on "Dan's Thoughts on Race."

And I guess a lot has just been thinking on my part, outside of any type of meeting or anything, like a class. It's just been independent—influenced by classes and stuff—but independent. Like last year I thought a lot more about identity issues, and this year I'm thinking a lot more about what to do. Just taking it outside of a personal realm, like a lot of issues as far as community and action and questions and stuff like that, where last year it was more personal. I think that everything I do influences that. I guess there's just seeing stuff and talking with people that makes me think and gets me thinking, and then I get frustrated and want to do something about it.

Dan's reflection on the exercise did not confirm or challenge his own racial identity, yet it provided an opportunity to place his racialized experience in a broader context of community and activism. This private exploration of the ideas of race and racism led, in Dan's case, to more extensive involvement with the community of students of color at Ivy; these involvements in turn provided new microsystems for identity exploration. So Dan's developmentally instigative traits—his intellectual interests in exploring concepts related to race, identity, and community—led him to further involvement around these issues and additional micro- and mesosystem interactions related to his own identity.

Personal traits of some students led them to academic courses, student organizations, friendship groups, off-campus programs (community service, study abroad, etc.) where they, too, engaged ideas about race, culture, and identity. On the other end of the spectrum, some students were inclined to limit their exposure to multiple new environments, but for each student, a unique combination of factors led to a unique developmental environment, even within a single institution. I turn now from the personal characteristics of cultural knowledge, appearance, and developmentally instigative characteristics to the environmental systems in which students developed and deployed their identities, beginning with microsystems and continuing with mesosystem influences on students' monoracial identities.

MICROSYSTEMS

Dee Dee, Renee, Mark, and Sapo described a number of college microsystems that influenced their identities. Dee Dee's study abroad experiences in Spain, where she was expected to represent Americans generally and American blacks specifically, and then in Egypt, where she deepened her knowledge of African cultures and history, reinforced her sense of herself as black while also broadening her understanding of that identifying term. Renee encountered both challenges to her authenticity as a black woman (from the women in the BSO lounge, for example) and powerful affirmations of her black identity (in her role in the Martin Luther King Day program). Sapo selected a major that created a number of course-related microsystems that supported his Mexican American identity. In each case, students put themselves in microsystems that influenced—either by congruent reinforcement or incongruent challenges to identity and ideas about race—their monoracial identities. For other students, too, academic, organizational, and social microsystems formed important venues for developing and expressing a monoracial identity.

Academic Microsystems

Academic microsystems could be places that supported monoracial identity, as Sapo experienced in his Latin American studies major, or they could be settings where racial identity was challenged or received unwanted attention. Eleanor's Introductory Spanish professor required students to make family scrapbooks as a way to practice using Spanish terms.

> The family album was lying open on my desk and my Spanish professor (of Haitian descent) picked it up. He was shocked! The first 10 or so pages are black-and-white pictures of my Scottish-Irish-Canadian great-grandparents, grandparents, mother, and aunt. He thought that my family album did not belong to me. He was extremely surprised to find out that these people were my relatives. As I recall, he said, "I would have expected this from others in the class, but not you . . . I thought you were Black." I responded with "I am Black!!!"
>
> Anyway, the class was very amused with my presentation about my "colorful" family and very ignorant about the laws prohibiting interracial marriages. My professor was stunned to realize that my state of Virginia was the last state to legalize interracial marriages in the late 1960s. Needless to say, it had been common knowledge to me for a while. My professor also asked me if I ever felt caught between two worlds (i.e., tragic mulatto) or if I had problems identifying with black or white people. Furthermore, he asked me if I considered myself to be black or white. Being that he didn't give me the option of both, I said that I considered myself to be black, which I do in most cases.

As described in the previous section, Jennifer took a course on Filipino Americans, and other students used academic assignments to explore their heritage. In these ways, students publicly or privately asserted their place in monoracial groups.

Social and Recreational Microsytems

Social and recreational microsystems also formed environments that supported monoracial identity or exploration of a racial heritage. In student organizations, campus programs, and living groups, participants encountered prompts to the formation of monoracial identity. At Rural Community College (RCC), for example, Jack was asked to lead the Black Students Association "even though they knew I wasn't fully african american, but because I knew the ropes, I could run the group." In Jack's case, organizing skills trumped racial identity in a formal microsystem in need of leadership. He embraced his black identity, and because of his leadership role in BSA was accepted as a black man at RCC.

Eleanor was a member of a black women's group at Ivy and described the ways in which involvement in this group influenced her self-identification:

> I was elected to be chair of the black women's group my sophomore year, and I was like, "Wow!" and I knew I was very good at organizing and I knew all the resources, but I was like, "Me? Head of black women?" . . . I knew, going to a women's high school my identity of "woman," you know, was very much set. And my identity as "biracial" or "black" was set. And putting the two together and identifying as a black woman hadn't really been set. But I was bringing a different experience to the black women's community. That I was still a black woman and if I felt like I could handle the responsibility then they wanted me to take it on. And then there's also this thing of being known as the closeted biracial person the last couple years, cause I took on a lot of black student positions.

While chairing the black women's group supported the monoracial (black) identity Eleanor held and chose to express most often, the leadership position also called into question her membership in the community of biracial students on campus. She was "closeted," a position not well respected on her campus.

Marisa, whose appearance did not immediately mark her as "black enough" to belong to the Black Students Association at Liberal Arts, nevertheless identified as black. At a preorientation for new students of color, she gravitated toward other black students though, as she wrote, she did not "completely fit in."

> I remember connecting with the black students and the Spanish students, and that was really good. So I connected with these students and we said, "We're going to stick by each other, help each other through this." We talk about missing our families, and so through time we connected. I became part of the Black Students Association on campus and also started networking with other groups, like the asian group and the hispanic group, because at the same time although I identified with the black students, I really didn't feel I completely fit in.

The microsystem formed in the Black Students Association supported Marisa's identification, at the same time drawing attention to the fact that she was not exactly matched to the existing categories. This incongruity led her to become involved in other race-specific groups. By the time she was interviewed, she was the chairperson of an alliance of organizations of students of color where, ironically, she had to resist gentle pressure from the BSA to allow them favored status on various campus committees. It was not unusual for students who claimed Monoracial Identity to experience a sense of not completely fitting in, though many students persisted in their identity choices, finding microsystems where they were supported as being mixed race *and* claiming one primary identity.

Unlike Eleanor and Marisa, who were deeply involved in public campus roles related to identity and therefore exposed to broader judgment about their identity choices, Bob was prompted more privately to explore his racial identity by an interaction with his residence hall roommates. One of his roommates was taking a course related to race and ethnicity, which led to conversations in the room about the derivation of racial categories in the United States. The conversations were the catalyst for Bob to learn more about his heritage.

> I say I'm hispanic, I guess. Mexican American descent. Actually it was brought up in my room. One of my roommates who's in that [American Thought and Language] class, Race and Ethnicity in Today's Society, he had been talking about it, and basically, you're classified as hispanic, but you could be Spanish and caucasian or you could be Mexican American and caucasian. So actually now, when someone asks me what I am, I say hispanic from Mexican descent. So that way they know, and not just hispanic, cause I could be anything. Cause usually in high school, it was just hispanic, cause I didn't really learn much about it until this year when I talked to my grandma about it.
>
> [KR: What prompted you to talk to your grandma about it?]
>
> Cause we had that conversation, so I was curious, so I called her. And we were talking about it as a room, with my roommates, and then she cleared it up for us.

The microsystem of Bob's living quarters provided a direct developmental prompt, which was derived from the exosystem influence of the roommate's class. Bob was not in the class, but its curriculum affected him indirectly through his interactions with the roommate who was in the class. This example of interacting systems illustrates the complex environmental web that is central to Bronfenbrenner's ecological systems theory; development can be instigated by factors not immediately present to the individual. In fact, it is difficult to discuss the influence of single microsystems without escalating to the next level of interaction, the mesosystem, where multiple microsystems interact to create a developmental milieu rich with congruent and incongruent messages about race, identity, family, and community.

MESOSYSTEMS

. Mesosystems are created when more than one microsystem interacts. For participants, these were created through the interaction of microsystems comprised of family and peers, academic and student organization settings, or multiple campus microsystems (e.g., an athletic team, a performing group, friendship circles, roommates, etc.). Students who identified strongly with Monoracial Identity sometimes found mesosystems that supported their chosen identities, but they just as often found mesosystems that contained both support and challenge. Negotiating the incongruent messages often provided developmentally charged moments, where the decision to claim a Monoracial Identity was either strengthened or called into question. Mesosystems were the location where these congruent and incongruent messages met; in this section I describe a number of mesosystem interactions related to the development and assertion of a monoracial identity.

Seeking to deepen her connection to her Filipino heritage, Kira joined a Group Independent Study Project (GISP) to learn Tagalog. She learned that language had the power to make her feel included in the Filipino community, but at the same time it could put her in the position of excluding cultural others.

> And I took the GISP this year because I've always wanted to learn Tagalog, because I feel that I should, that it's part of my heritage. And I hadn't been taught it when I was younger because my dad didn't want my mom to teach me it. So I felt pretty upset about that, the fact that in some ways I could understand why my dad didn't want my mom to teach me it, because then he wouldn't understand it. . . . So I felt bad towards my father, there was a little anger, even though I understood the reason.
>
> And so I took the GISP. And in the beginning I was scared to tell him about it. We had to plan the class last year, and all through that I didn't tell him. I was very vague when I would tell him about what courses I was taking, like "Oh, I'm going to take these three classes and I don't know what my fourth class will be." And basically when it came time to decide, I was talking to my mom and I told her. And later my dad called and left me a message on my machine saying, "Well, I don't know how wise of you it is to take this course. You don't know what your concentration is yet." And yeah, that's a legitimate reason. I don't know what my concentration is yet and maybe I should be exploring other things. But in other ways, this GISP doesn't come around every year and I wasn't sure if I'd have another chance before I graduate. And it was really important to me, and so finally I was able to talk to him about it.
>
> And so even now when I go home, I just try not to emphasize the fact that I'm taking the GISP. I'm also studying Spanish this year, so sometimes when I'm at home I practice speaking Spanish with my sister and my mom,

but I try to avoid practicing my Tagalog when he's around, because I feel bad that he's being left out. And he wouldn't have been able to learn it because he doesn't pick up a language very quickly. And over Thanksgiving it was really weird because a lot of my mom's relatives come over and so I wanted to practice speaking some Tagalog and I told them I was taking it. And they were like, "Oh, she's learning Tagalog finally." And all my relatives were really excited. And I remember that my mom and my dad and my grandmother were in the kitchen getting food ready and everyone else was looking at my books and quizzing me, and I felt really bad because at that time it was only my dad and my sister in the house who didn't understand at all what they were saying. And at that point I was like, "Oh, God. Why did I do this? Why did I take this?" Because I don't want to be shutting him out. And I don't want it to be used against him. Sometimes I really want to explore my Filipino side for myself, by I don't want to hurt my father with it. (Kira)

For Kira, the acquisition of language related to her Filipino heritage involved risking the security of her relationship with her white father. In one microsystem—the Tagalog GISP—she was gaining important cultural knowledge, which had ripple effects in two other important microsystems, her immediate and extended families. The mesosystem created by the joining of immediate and extended families at Thanksgiving dinner demonstrates an incongruous system of beliefs and values, causing Kira to question, "Why did I do this?" Kira answers her own question ("Sometimes I really want to explore my Filipino side for myself" and "I've always wanted to learn Tagalog, because I feel that I should, that it's part of my heritage"), revealing developmentally instigative characteristics that lead her to risk conflict in important relationships for the sake of claiming her Filipina identity. The mesosystem created by the interactions of family and academic microsystems was the environment in which these characteristics operated to influence Kira's identity.

Kira also encountered the forces of a different mesosystem, the mesosystem of peer culture. After a challenging first year of trying to figure out where she fit in on campus, she had decided to take the independent study course in Tagalog as a sophomore. She also decided to go to Filipino Alliance (FA) meetings, in spite of plans not to participate in that group or the campus group for mixed race students (Spectrum). She talked about the difficulty of being a biracial first-year student and her sense of inauthenticity in a peer culture that strongly supported monoracial students of color.

I think the whole summer [after my first year] I went home and it seemed that every part of me became legitimate again, and I thought everything was set. I always viewed myself as having a Filipino side and a white side, neither of which is really defined, and neither of which is really valid, because there's nothing that is, I guess, essentially Filipino or white (laugh) about being some of each. But I felt I had that balance and I felt comfortable with myself and I came back this year, and partly because I didn't have time, I was planning not to go to Spectrum meetings or Filipino Alliance meetings. But then it just happened that some friends are doing a GISP on Tagalog this year, and I *did* go to the FA meeting, and somehow I feel like within myself I'm trying to legitimize myself as a Filipina, valid, without seeing myself so much as being biracial.

The Tagalog GISP and the Filipino Alliance microsystems work together as a mesosystem of peer culture to support Kira's sense of herself as a "valid" Filipina. Indeed, she is aware that she is influenced by peer culture not to behave in ways that will be seen as white or as not "Filipina enough."

And now I've found out that sometimes I suppress my white side or whatever that I randomly characterize as being white. And sometimes I feel off-balance because I'm not allowing myself to enjoy or spend time with what I really enjoy. Partly because I feel that if I do that then maybe I wouldn't legitimately be Filipina or part Filipina. Which is really weird to think, even if that's not what makes someone Filipina, but I guess in terms of other people's acceptance of me I feel that.

Because of the strong monoracial peer culture at Ivy, Kira's monoracial Filipina identity comes at the expense of some activities that she might "really enjoy."

Although Kira described some peer pressure about the definition of being "legitimately Filipina," her decision to identify monoracially seemed like it was an independent choice on her part. Other students at Ivy described campus peer climates that discouraged multiracial identities and favored monoracial categorization. Kayla attended a student-sponsored panel about interracial dating and described her experience:

There was a lot of antagonism there. People were accusing other people of trying to quote "escape their blackness" by identifying as biracial. . . . And it makes me wonder if I'm ever going to be able to get married. Because everyone there seemed to really want to preserve their culture. And they felt like an intermarriage would be totally going against that. You know, someone was saying that being a Hindu Indian is so much of part of who they were they couldn't even imagine being with someone who wasn't.

The construction of a peer culture mesosystem that privileged monoracial over multiracial identity contributed to some students' sense of acceptable public identities. The unique developmentally instigative traits of each individual (e.g., propensity to resist external pressure to identify in one way or another or ability to maintain private identification while deploying a different public identity) determined how his or her interactions with the environment would influence racial identity. There were, however, other factors in the mesosystem that exerted influences on the selection of Monoracial Identity and continued to influence identity while students exerted their monoracial selves.

Significant among these factors was the extent to which students could move easily among campus subcultures while maintaining Monoracial Identity. At four institutions (Big Ten, Rural University, Liberal Arts College, Rural Community College) students described fairly fluid environments where movement among groups was easy and unremarkable. At two institutions (Ivy University, Catholic University), students described very rigid boundaries between peer groups, with implications of group membership reaching beyond personal identity into broader experiences of peer culture. The ability to maintain Monoracial Identity while moving among and between campus peer groups was affected as the rigidity of group boundaries interacted with individual characteristics.

Sapo maintained his Mexican American identity across the fluid boundaries at Liberal Arts College, where Audrey also exerted her black identity in multiple settings.

> [KR to Sapo: Do you feel like as a biracial student you have a place at LAC, that you fit in somehow?]

> Sure. I feel like if you want to hang out with a certain group, then you can. There's no barriers to anything. If I want to go to a [Latino Association] meeting, and then I'll go to a different group meeting. There's definitely stuff for me to do, both cultural and noncultural. . . . And when you meet different people, they affect you in different ways and you see stuff that you hadn't previously, which causes you to think differently and do different stuff than you did before. (Sapo)

> I find that the sports teams are very together and they're very supportive of each other, where it's the same thing with the a capella [singing] groups and the different groups on campus. I see more of a socializing between groups. . . . I've met people through [my singing group] and through the theater department, definitely through Christian Fellowship and the track team. And they do different things, like the theater department people will go to improv shows, and the Fellowship people will go to Christian concerts. So I have many different friends who may not be interested in the same thing, but all the things they're interested in are all the things I'm interested in! (Audrey)

Sapo and Audrey experienced peer culture at Liberal Arts as an environment of multiple groups of students in which meeting "different people" who "may not be interested in the same thing" was comfortable, in part because there was the freedom to "hang out" with a variety of groups. The peer culture mesosystem featured a fluidity of group membership that allowed Sapo to go from the latino student organization to other groups with "no barriers to anything." Later in her interview, Audrey said, "It's just too small a place to go changing how I feel about myself every time I move around campus. We all end up in the commons [dining hall] together anyway!" The fluidity among groups and the small campus size supported those students who chose to maintain a fairly consistent and public monoracial identity.

A large campus, too, can provide an environment that is fluid and supports mixed race students' choice to identify monoracially. At Big Ten University, a campus roughly thirty times larger than Liberal Arts College, Bob experienced an openness to moving among groups similar to the one described by Sapo and Audrey.

> I think there's a lot less racial tension here than it would be in other situations where the majority of students were white. More people come out about what they are, like being gay or talking more about their race and being more comfortable with their ethnic background. And people seem more open here than they do back home. So I can go to football games, participate in [residence hall] government, study, go to the rec center and play basketball or tennis. . . . It seems like there's not a lot of racial tension here, so it's comfortable, no matter what you are. You see everybody and no one picks on you cause you're black or cause you're Mexican or cause you're white. It's just relaxed and comfortable.

In this "relaxed and comfortable" environment Bob was prompted by conversations with his roommates to explore his Mexican American heritage. Whether or not Bob continued to develop his Mexican American identity after his participation in the study is not known, and his perception that the campus was relatively free of racial tension could have changed if he became more closely aligned with other students of color. But at the time, Bob's sense of the peer culture supported his claim to a monoracial Mexican American identity, regardless of how much knowledge he had about his heritage.

At Catholic University, however, students described a campus dominated by a "white, jock-y" culture. Many students of color participated in the mainstream campus culture, but there was a parallel culture of AHANA students, the students of color who identified strongly with their cultures and were socially and politically active on campus in student organizations based on monoracial groupings (e.g., Black Students Alliance, Asian Students Alliance, etc.), similar to the self-labeled Third World community at Ivy. In addition to creating some pressure to conform to "legitimate" or "authentic" displays of monoracial identity, participation in the AHANA student culture required adherence to rigid boundaries between the mainstream ("white, jock-y") culture and the AHANA groups. This rigidity led some students to claim a private monoracial identity but avoid public identification with monoracial groups. Jennifer, for example, identified as Chinese but did not participate in the Chinese student organization or asian student clubs:

I definitely see that people stick to their groups at this school. It's very cliquey. That is another reason why I have chosen never to join those groups, because I never wanted to be part of those cliques. I wanted to make my friends on account of who they were, not what they were. If you go to the Commons, that dining hall, you just see groups over here, groups over there, and I just don't know. I find that amazing. I never quite have understood that.

The message she received from these groups was "not an appealing one," and Jennifer preferred to identify as Chinese and as biracial to a network of friends who were for the most part outside the AHANA student culture.

Finally, although peer culture might determine public claims to monoracial identity, students sometimes resisted these messages and created their own ways to own an asian, black, or latino identity. They used the public spaces of friendship groups and student organizations, as well as the private spaces of intellectual activity and personal reflection to assert monoracial identities and locate nonjudgmental support for them. Some found it in family, though others used campus resources to build a foundation of cultural knowledge that families had not or could not provide. Guided by their developmentally instigative characteristics and personal histories, they built monoracial identities that were resilient to the forces of peer culture that might offer resistance.

SUMMARY

Students' experience and reading of campus peer cultures influenced which identities were available for them to claim publicly and, as important, which were desirable to claim in a particular campus context. The students highlighted in this chapter—Sapo, Renee, Dee Dee, and Mark—and others whose experiences illustrated environmental influences on identity fit, at least some of the time, in the pattern of Monoracial Identity. Many of the same micro- and mesosystem influences, however, led other students to other identity patterns. In the next chapter, I will describe students who fit the Multiple Monoracial Identities pattern and how their experiences of the campus environment supported those identity choices.

chapter five

I'm Asian and Latina—
Multiple Monoracial Identities

I just say, "I'm Vietnamese American," and that to me means I'm
Vietnamese and I'm white. That's how I identify it as. And then
they usually say, "Well, are you mixed?" And I say, "Yeah, I'm
mixed with French and Vietnamese." And they're like, "Oh,
okay." I think they get the Vietnamese and French rather than the
Vietnamese American when I say that.

—Kimlien

TWENTY-SEVEN STUDENTS I interviewed held Multiple Monoracial Identities, like Kimlien and like Kenji, the composite portrait presented in chapter 3. The majority of participants in the study described two parental heritages (e.g., one asian and one white parent; one black and one latino parent,
etc.), thus when they were in this identity pattern they held two monoracial
identities; a few students had three or more heritages, and they might identify simultaneously with each. Students in this pattern described themselves
in many ways, including, "black and Italian," "half-hispanic and the other
half is a mixture of a lot of things," "half-Japanese," "half white, half Filipino," and "multicultural—I'm American Indian-white-black and white-
black-American Indian again."

   In this chapter I describe students who identified in the Multiple Monoracial Identities pattern, some common characteristics and experiences these
students shared, and the influence of developmental environments on racial
identity. I feature three students who identify with more than one racial
group to illustrate the characteristics, experiences, and peer influences on students in this pattern.

CHARACTERISTICS OF THIS PATTERN

Students who classified in the pattern of Multiple Monoracial Identities were those who identified as "both x and y" or, for some, "half x and half y." Most also identified at times as Multiracial, some were in the Extraracial Identity pattern, and many identified Situationally according to interactions in the immediate environment. Students in the Multiple Monoracial Identities pattern were those with "both feet in both worlds" (Root, 1996b; Wallace, 2001), who engaged both (or all) of their heritages on a regular basis. Like Kimlien, quoted above, these students identify with more than one heritage, and when one of those heritages is white, they often identify with a specific national, cultural, or ethnic group rather than simply as white.

TRENDS WITHIN THE PATTERN

Among students identifying in the Multiple Monoracial Identities pattern, differences emerged along the lines of gender, specific heritage combinations, class year, and institution. Because of the way I defined identity patterns, very few students (two) were in both the Monoracial Identity pattern and the Multiple pattern; thus, many of the trends within the Multiple pattern are the inverse of those seen in the previous chapter in the Monoracial Identity pattern. For example, whereas men were more likely than women to identify in Monoracial Identity (60 percent and 42 percent, respectively), men were less likely than women to identify in the Multiple Monoracial Identities pattern (25 percent and 61 percent).

In terms of racial heritage, students with two parents of color or one white parent and one mixed parent were more likely (75 percent and 67 percent) than students with one white parent and one parent of color (41 percent) to identify in this pattern. No students with one latino/a parent and one parent of color identified in this pattern; all five identified in the Monoracial Identity pattern. I attribute the differences in identity patterns among students with different racial heritages, and specifically among the number of different heritages for each participant, to the salience of racial and ethnic groups of color in the United States and the relative lack of awareness of white culture. A student with two parents of color is more likely to be aware of those cultures than a student with one white parent and one parent of color. Indeed, many of the students with white heritage experienced that identity specifically through an ethnic or religious group (Italian, Irish, Hungarian Jewish, etc.).

Students in the Multiple Monoracial Identities pattern fell across all class years and institutions, with no especially remarkable trends. Sopho-

TABLE 5.1
Distribution of Students in the Multiple Monoracial Identities Pattern
by Gender, Heritage, Class Year, and Institution

		Total in sample	Identifying in this pattern
Gender	Men	20	5 (25%)
	Women	36	22 (61%)
Heritage	Two Parents of Color	12	8 (75%)
	One Asian & One White Parent	16	8 (50%)
	One Black & One White Parent	13	5 (38%)
	One Latino/a & One White Parent	5	0
	One Pacific Islander & One White Parent	7	4 (57%)
	One Mixed & One White Parent	3	2 (67%)
Class Year	First Year	14	9 (64%)
	Sophomore	17	4 (24%)
	Junior	11	6 (55%)
	Senior	14	8 (57%)
Institution	Big Ten University	12	8 (75%)
	Catholic University	8	4 (50%)
	Ivy University	14	6 (43%)
	Liberal Arts College	8	2 (25%)
	Rural Community College	6	3 (50%)
	Rural University	8	4 (50%)
	TOTAL	56	27 (48%)

mores were least likely (24 percent) to be in this pattern, while first years, juniors, and seniors were more likely than would be expected (64 percent, 55 percent, 57 percent). Again, the sophomore trend is the inverse of the trend toward Monoracial Identity among students in this year. Similarly, trends across institutions were roughly inverse, with Liberal Arts College having the lowest percentage (25 percent) among the institutions and Big Ten having the highest (75 percent). At Catholic, Rural Community College, and Rural University, exactly half of the participants fit this pattern.

PORTRAITS OF STUDENTS WHO CHOSE THIS PATTERN

SUMMER

> I grew up in L.A., and my mother's Korean, and my dad is half—well, his
> mom is Scotch-Irish, and his dad is Latvian Jewish, that's where the "Gold-
> man" [last name] comes from. . . . I feel like I'm equally Korean as I am Irish,
> or have this Jewish heritage.

Summer grew up in a multicultural household, where her mother made
meals that drew from American and Korean tastes ("The food that we ate,
it was always Korean rice and then steak, or kimchi, Korean food, and then
green beans."), décor was international ("We'd have Korean rugs, but then
an American stereo system and books."), and traditions were honored from
Korean, Jewish, Buddhist, and Christian culture ("Like Korean Children's
Day where you give kids money in red envelopes, and then there was this
Buddhist thing where cats were bad, so we weren't allowed to have any cats,
but if there was ever a spider in the house it meant good luck. You can't
touch the spider, you have to leave it alone."). Summer internalized what
she characterized as "Korean values" related to education, hard work, and
achievement, and also enjoyed "white American" activities like "hanging
out after school with people." Summer enjoyed her culturally diverse public
school through sixth grade and then attended an "all-girls, private, very traditional upscale private school," where the student body was predominantly
white. She chose Catholic University because she wanted to be in a city on
the East Coast, although at the time we met in her senior year, she said she
wished she had gone to Berkeley, which would have been more "diverse and
culturally interesting."

The transition from Los Angeles to a comparatively homogeneous white,
Catholic institution provided a substantial jolt to Summer's developmental
ecology and prompted her to consider her racial identity and her environment in new ways.

> I think a lot of it was being taken out of that environment where I had the
> luxury of being around people who were very educated about others. I felt
> like coming here I had to do so much soul-searching almost, because it was
> so frustrating to come here. People would say the most stupid things, like I
> was walking down the stairs and one girl said, "She's in my country and she
> should speak my language," and she was going off on this. I just felt like I've
> heard that so much, not just with ethnicities, not with just cultural igno-
> rance, but people will say, "fag" or stuff, and I just wasn't used to that, and
> it really bothered me.
>
> And I didn't have a single Asian friend freshman year or sophomore
> year, so it was really hard for me. I would go to a party and I'd look all around
> and be like the only non-completely white person here, and then I would

realize, once I mentioned it to my roommates and they were so oblivious, which I don't blame them, but they all come from small towns and just knew of one asian person. And they would say, "Wow, do you really notice that? Do you really think about it?" My answer was, "I don't think about it that much, but being here now I do notice it." I have started to think about it and so I really had to kind of think about how important it was to me. I realized how important diversity was to me, definitely.

For her first two years at Catholic, Summer surrounded herself with an "L.A. crew" of white women who met early in their first weeks on campus and formed a bond based on the common experience of being three thousand miles from home.

Summer described the climate at Catholic University as one with a mainstream, predominantly white culture and a parallel culture of AHANA students who were politically and socially active in a more or less separate sphere, a description that matched my campus observations. Although Summer herself held a strong Korean identity, she experienced the Korean student culture as especially cliquish even within the AHANA community. About the climate for students of color at Catholic she said

> I think it really depends on how you look at it. I think a lot of them are really happy with just being together. I know Koreans are just by nature like that, and you can see that in Koreatown, in L.A. They really like being together and they stick together really closely and they totally enjoy that. I've had a lot of Korean kids in my Japanese classes and they really, well, I don't think that they really have a problem with [the climate] because they are totally satisfied with just having their Korean friends.
>
> Then I think there are people who are minorities that really want the integrated kind of atmosphere, and I'm one of those people. I was so used to having all different kinds of people, even outside of school. I mean, I had friends who were like ex-Crips and stuff, I had all these different kinds of friends and I loved it, and I thought it was the most enriching thing, and here [at Catholic] I thought that all the Koreans are the same, and that was really boring to me. So I think it really just depends, and some people are totally happy with the segregation. It's definitely segregated, very, very segregated, and some people like it and some people don't. I guess it just depends on what kind of person you are.

As a result of her disinterest in joining this separate—and, to her, separatist—peer culture, Summer formed friendships with a variety of students, mostly white, who participated in the dominant campus culture.

> Before [going to study abroad junior year], most of my friends were white, and I just never thought about it that much. It was either I joined the AHANA groups and had all asian friends or I hung out with everyone else.

So it was like two really separate paths I could have taken, and very rarely can you do both here. Even the Korean kids in my Japanese class, they'd be like, "You're Korean? You don't act like it, you don't look like it." They were like, "Well, you must not be because you don't hang out with us. You can't be Korean." It's just kind of weird.

Although Summer eschewed the social and political asian student culture on campus, she engaged directly with her asian heritage by enrolling in Asian studies courses. When she learned that Korean language classes were not available to students not majoring in Korean studies, she decided to learn Japanese and to study abroad in Japan her junior year. Summer recognized the irony of being of white and Korean heritage and going to study in Japan, noting in her program, "a lot of half-Japanese people were getting a feel for their roots." Summer took the opportunity to go home for a weekend with a Korean friend from the Japanese university, an experience that had a profound influence on her sense of identity.

I'd never been to Korea before so that was really amazing to me. We did some sightseeing, and went to this Korean Heritage Museum. So I did the whole thing, and it helped me understand my mom so much better and where she came from. And I watched these cultural dances, and things my mom had dragged me to when I was younger, that I hated, that I thought were so boring, that I thought were so cool now.

Like Dee Dee, whom I highlighted in the previous chapter, Summer found study abroad to be not only a rich academic and cultural immersion experience, but also a chance to reconsider her ideas about race, culture, identity, and community. It was also a chance to get away from the United States and to reflect on her first two years at Catholic.

So a lot of it was maturing and realizing more about myself, and finally getting to be in Asia and stuff like that. I think that's what really changed me, having the two contrasts—being here for two years and not having any Asian friends to being there where I had Korean friends and half-Korean friends, and half-Japanese friends, half-Chinese, Russian-Chinese, Mexican-Korean, the craziest mixes. And it was awesome and I loved it.

Shortly before Summer left for Japan, she met a small group of other mixed race students at Catholic. As she planned her return from the study abroad year, she faced a difficult decision about housing selection for her senior year. Although she had remained with the white women of the L.A. crew for two years, she had grown tired of the "big, white, jock-y guys" they hung around with. She took a risk and committed to a housing group with the new friends, and although she missed the familiarity of being with her group of white friends, she was enjoying the "more liberal vibe" of the new group. She said, "I'm so thankful for this group of friends because they're more laid back and they're just more interesting. And we have our little half-asian jokes. It's cool for me, so I'm grateful for that."

Summer found a way to stay connected to her group of white friends who were in the more dominant campus culture, but she also found ways to express her asian identity. She had grown decreasingly comfortable in the majority milieu, but she retained a strong sense of her white—and particularly her Jewish—heritage, remarking that it was especially interesting to have a distinctly Jewish name at a Catholic university. She firmly embraced her "half-Korean, half-white" identity and found a group of other "half-asian" students to share it with.

BETH

> It seems like most people who are biracial pick a side, and I have chosen not to do that because I am both. Actually I am more than both, but I am a lot of things on my mom's side and a lot of things on my dad's side. It just so happens that my [paternal] grandma was born in Mexico and my grandparents on my mom's side were born here. So I don't really pick a side. But sometimes people, when they hear my name, want to know why I'm not dark. Why I have blond hair. Why I am articulate and don't have an accent. Then I explain that I am Mexican *and* anglo *and* more than that, too.

Beth grew up in a small industrial city in the Midwest, where she lived with her second-generation Mexican American father and her mother, "a mixture of a lot of things," including Austrian Jew and anglo American. After graduating from a large public high school Beth attended an area junior college full time for a year before she started to work full time, which she did for eight years before returning to the junior college to complete her associate's degree. The year prior to the interview, she transferred to Rural University because she was interested in biology, and friends told her that Rural U was the best in-state school for doing research in the natural sciences. Beth was preparing to take the LSAT in order to apply to law school to pursue a career in environmental protection law.

Beth drew on her experience at the junior college when deciding how to become involved in activities at Rural U. She had joined the hispanic student organization at the junior college to expand her social and support network, a strategy that was successful. She used the same strategy to get involved at Rural U:

> So being involved in the organization in my junior college kind of set me up for wanting to be involved in the Hispanic Student Council (HSC) here and kind of made that transition. It was a good organization to belong to,

because right away I had people show me around and I felt more at home because there was a common interest there. The cultural aspect was something that helped me to adjust.

Given the opportunity to represent HSC to Rural U's undergraduate student government, Beth declined, having decided to limit her involvement to internal organizational matters so that she would have time to focus on her academics and her student worker position in the financial aid office. It was a difficult decision, but she felt it was "the right choice because I need this experience to get out in the work field, and once I have a job I will be able to give back to my community." Her community, Beth explained, was "minorities and hispanics, but also first-generation students who are white or poor or both."

Beth's biracial heritage and her simultaneous identification with different aspects of it came through strongly in her discussion of religion, family, and community. Although her father's Mexican family was strongly Catholic, Beth's mother's family included Austrian Jews, Lutherans, and other Christians. Beth felt that to her Mexican relatives, "If you are not Catholic then you are considered different or even weird in some cases, so it's complicated." In spite of strong cultural and ritual Catholicism in her family, Beth and her siblings had all left the church for other faith traditions, a move seen in the family as a rejection of Mexican culture and an embrace of the non-Mexican heritage that the siblings shared with their mother. Indeed her own parents' marriage was considered controversial not necessarily because of her mother's race but because "religion is a very important part of Mexican culture, and in some ways it can be hindering because they don't want you to marry outside of the Catholic church." More than just "hindering,"

> There was actually a split in our family as far as relations go because my grandma wanted, well she was raised Catholic, and then there was another part of my family someone married into, someone who was Lutheran. It made a split in our family and our family is not as close because of that. It took many years to find that out, but that is what it boiled down to.

In spite of her father's strong desire that she remain in the Catholic church, Beth joined an interdenominational, international, Christian church in Rural U's small town. She experienced membership in this church as "not so much rejecting my Mexican side, but holding onto that while also being more on my mom's side." She said, "My father has accepted it only because he doesn't have a choice." In addition to discussing implications for identity of her decision, Beth in part attributed her openness to racial, ethnic, and cultural diversity to the international church.

Beth cited two other factors in her openness to diversity: her nontraditional student status and her mixed heritage. The life and work experience

Beth brought to Rural U allowed her to "see some things I might otherwise miss, you know, in the getting used to college and trying to figure things out." Beth also noticed demographic differences between the junior college and Rural U, and she particularly noticed a greater diversity within the hispanic student community at Rural U, where "you have Puerto Ricans, you have Mexicans, you have Guatemalans. You name it." Beth felt that she was in a better position than traditional age students to appreciate the diversity, because she had already "seen a college without so much of it."

It was her biracial Hispanic and white identity, however, that Beth cited as the most important factor in her appreciation of domestic and international diversity.

> I honestly don't know what has opened my eyes to different races other than maybe being biracial. That is the only thing that I can attribute it to. My father is Mexican, but he was schooled very untraditionally. He didn't have a formal education so a lot of his philosophy and thinking has rubbed off on me. He knows so much about history and about language and how they evolved, and I have gotten some of that from him. So I am not afraid to go up to somebody and say, "Where are you from?" or "Your accent is so beautiful, what language do you speak?" or "Where is that at?"

In addition, Beth felt personally affected by racism directed at others because, "There are things like that that do affect me because like I said, I am all of these things. I am not just white. I am not just Mexican. . . . So it is important to me and it is a personal issue with me when I see them being discriminated against."

While her Mexican heritage helped Beth connect with issues for people of color, her white heritage helped her feel connected with students in the white majority at Rural U. She found some students of color at Rural U closed off to interactions and cultural sharing with white students.

> When I first came here I had the attitude that anglo people, or non-hispanic, non-black people just don't want to be exposed to the cultures, but what I found is that it goes both ways. There are minorities, whether it be african americans or hispanics or whatever, they are kind of afraid to share their culture. And me being biracial I am not afraid at all, because I know both sides of it. And I know people. I have a lot of friends who are white, and a lot of friends who are hispanic and a lot of friends who are african american, so I see all sides of the picture, and I want to learn as much about other people's cultures as I want them to learn about mine.
>
> I have more in common with non-Mexicans because they are willing to share whatever it is that they are proud of versus Mexicans, who want to keep kind of to themselves. I don't know why that is. Maybe there is the tension again of me being biracial, but I haven't figured that out yet.

Beth's bicultural background facilitated her connection with both whites and hispanics yet made her somewhat different from both groups. Being "not just white . . . not just Mexican" was a challenging but ultimately more comfortable position for Beth than choosing to identify with just one heritage.

KIMLIEN

> My asian friends came over and they're like, "Well, what are you doing? Are you going to the New Year's party?" It's for our New Year—for our Chinese and Vietnamese New Year. And I'm like, "Yeah, I'm gonna go." And they said, "What are you going to wear?" And I was thinking, "Well, that's a good question. Should I wear my aó dai, which is traditional Vietnamese dress? Should I just wear dress clothes, like a sweater and some slacks or a regular dress?" And I think that was kind of hard for me. I'm thinking, "What should I wear?" Cause I didn't really feel like I had the right to wear my aó dai, because I'm not full, but then I felt it would be bad for me to show up in regular dress clothes. I actually did end up wearing regular dress clothes to the party.
>
> And some were wearing aó's, some were wearing regular dresses, so I didn't feel that bad. I was like, "Yay, I fit in! And I don't feel so bad," which is really good, that people can integrate like that. But I did feel kind of out of place, like I should have worn my traditional dress rather than plain clothes.

The dilemma of what to wear to a New Year's party is not an unusual one for a college student, but Kimlien's dilemma was about more than matching her shoes to her dress; in her case it was a matter of representing the Vietnamese part of her heritage with her aó dai or wearing the "regular dress clothes" that signify white American culture. Kimlien's father is French American and her mother is a Vietnamese-Chinese American who immigrated to the United States with her mother during the Vietnam War. Kimlien's mother was sixteen years old when Kimlien was born, and Kimlien takes great pride and inspiration from her mother's ability to finish high school and college while raising two young children.

Indeed, it was her mother who decided Kimlien and her sisters should have names that reflected their mixed race heritage.

> I was very proud of my mom, because she gave me not only an American name but a Vietnamese name so I don't forget where I'm coming from. I thought that was very important, to not let a kid forget where they're coming from. Not only are they *this*, but they're also *that*.

Kimlien's childhood involved cultural elements of both "this" and "that," as she grew up in an urban area and then moved to a small town, where she was "the only asian, mixed or otherwise" in school. Of the experience she said, "It was really hard to fit in or identify with anyone, because I wasn't really white but I wasn't really asian. I was just kind of there."

Kimlien chose Big Ten University because an uncle, also Vietnamese and white, and his black girlfriend had gone there. At a precollege summer program Kimlien learned that a handful of Big Ten students were attempting to form a mixed race student organization. After she arrived for the regular academic year, she was contacted by one of the student organizers and "that's just how [the group, Hapa] evolved. It became something more than just an idea. It became an actual group." Hapa was open in theory to any student on campus but limited in practice to students with asian heritage; Kimlien explained, "We're trying to keep the Hapa group right now to hapas, and because it's really hard to find other people specific you want to identify with." Through Hapa, but also in other venues on campus, Kimlien encountered mixed students, a source of solidarity, and common understanding.

> I get really excited when I find other people that are mixed, and I'm like, "Oh my god, I'm mixed too!" Especially, it's so exciting to find someone that is like you, 'cause they know the issues that you've been through. It's a lot of fun. I like it.

The connection with other mixed Vietnamese and white students, in particular, provided Kimlien with a sense of belonging, accentuated through her experience in the student group Hapa.

Interviewed in the spring of her first year, Kimlien had taken a leadership role in Hapa, maintaining the group's web page and being elected to represent the organization on the executive board of the Asian Student Alliance (ASA), an umbrella group comprised of Asian and Pacific Island ethnic and national organizations (e.g., Japan Club, Korean Student Alliance, Hawai'i Club, etc.). As an official representative to ASA, Kimlien found that she was "finally accepted into the asian community as one of them." In this microsystem, she could merge her asian identity with her mixed identity to create a sense of authenticity and legitimacy in the eyes of her peers.

Like other participants in the study, Kimlien's claim to her heritage had been challenged by other students. On one occasion, Kimlien was called a "banana," a term used to insult someone deemed "yellow on the outside, white on the inside." She said, "I met this one Vietnamese guy, and he called me that because I was mixed and he felt that I had no right to be calling myself asian because I was mixed." Kimlien recalled this incident as one of the occasions when she felt forced to choose and defend a single identity, in this case asian: "I guess, that's the time when I really defended my asian-ness. And I was like, 'Listen here: I'm just as much asian as you are.'" Indeed, Kimlien's participation in Hapa at Big Ten had sharpened her awareness of her asian identity.

> Most of the time, people will put you where they want to put you, whether
> you're white or asian. But there are times when I'm like, "Excuse me, you
> know, I am asian too" you know. And other times I'm like, "Oh, whatever,"
> like I really don't care. I'm not going to make a big fuss out of it. I guess since
> I joined the Hapa group I do make more of a fuss of it now than I used to.
> Like with the terms *oriental* and *asian*, cause calling a person oriental is sort
> of like calling an african american person—it's a very put down term. And
> I now get really offended by that. "No, I'm not oriental, I'm asian." I think
> now that I'm here, I get more offended than when I was back at home.

The network of mixed asian students at Hapa provided Kimlien with support for her mixed identity while also bolstering her exploration of her asian heritage.

While exploring her asian roots and mixed heritage, Kimlien maintained a strongly bicultural identity. Growing up she had experienced the very separate spheres of her mother's, father's, and grandmother's households, the first two of which were culturally white, while the third was Vietnamese; in college she selected elements of many cultures to create physical, social, and psychological environments in which she was comfortable.

> In my room, in my dorm room, I get to decide what I want up, which I really
> like. But when I go home, my mom is now remarried to my stepdad, who is
> also white, and so at that house there's no asian influences at all and at my
> dad's house, not any more. So the only time I get the asian influence is when
> I go to my grandma's, so it's still like that now. Home is just this and this,
> and grandma's house is asian. But I like it up here, cause I get to decide what
> I want.
>
> In my room I have a Chinese lantern with my name written on it in
> Japanese. Cause I'm taking a language class right now—Japanese. I want to
> learn about East Asian culture since I didn't get much of it growing up. And
> I have my red envelopes up and I have sayings on the wall written in Viet-
> namese, like "I love you"—I have my little good luck cat from Japan and
> stuff, so there are little asian influences that remind me, "You're not just
> what people think you are—you're something more than that." Little
> reminders. I have a little jade pendant that is very popular in Vietnamese
> culture, so I always wear that, cause my grandma always has a jade pendant.
> So now I'm just like grandma. (laugh) I really love it.

The idea that she is "more than" what people think she is sustained Kimlien, even as she explored a variety of asian ethnicities and an emerging public hapa identity. Cultural symbols served as "little reminders" that she has a legitimate claim to her heritage.

At the same time, as someone whose "skin tone is a very olive color" Kimlien "could pass for Italian," a situation that often led to "What are you?"

inquiries, to which she invariably replied, "Well, I'm mixed Vietnamese and French." She experienced these questions as attempts to make her choose between her "asian-ness" and her "whiteness," a choice she would not make except when she felt forced to defend her asian heritage, as she did when called "a banana."

At the time of her interview, Kimlien was operating comfortably in mainstream white culture and increasingly comfortably among her asian peers. She had found a space in Hapa where she was welcomed and supported, and she was creating other spaces on campus, including in her residence hall room, in which to express various facets of her identity. Occasionally faced with a need to chose between her identities—when confronted by a peer or when deciding between outfits for a cultural event—Kimlien resisted monoracial categorization in favor of bringing her whole self, her bicultural and mixed race self, to the table.

THE ECOLOGY OF MULTIPLE MONORACIAL IDENTITIES

Summer, Beth, and Kimlien identified in the Multiple Monoracial Identities pattern. At times they identified more strongly with one heritage than others, at times they identified as multiracial, and overall they could be said to exhibit the Situational Identity pattern. But the fact that when they identified by heritage it was with more than one also placed them in the Multiple Monoracial Identities pattern. Like half of the study participants, they chose to explore and claim multiple heritages. The ecology model provides a useful framework for understanding how these students negotiated identity-based spaces and peer culture on campus. The model also provides a framework for understanding how students' individual characteristics contributed to their identity choices as they moved among microsystems and mesosystems.

Personal Characteristics

Like their peers who chose Monoracial Identity, students who chose Multiple Monoracial Identities came to college with unique sets of family experiences, physical appearances, and developmentally instigative characteristics. Students in this pattern described times when they felt like they possessed or lacked cultural knowledge, met or did not meet peers' judgment of racial "legitimacy," and experienced support or challenge to their chosen identity pattern. Although they were resisting the cultural norm of claiming a single monoracial identity, they seemed to move more easily among campus groups than the students described in the previous chapter who chose Monoracial Identity. Like those other students, however, students claiming Multiple Monoracial Identities were subject to the developmental presses of peer culture and exerted their own influence back on the environment.

Cultural Knowledge

Cultural knowledge factored into students' decisions to identify in the Multiple Monoracial Identities category. Family constituted the primary precollege microsystem for the acquisition of cultural knowledge. In many cases, growing up with parents from different backgrounds created a rich environment in which mixed race students could learn about both (or all) of their heritages. Cultural knowledge provided relatively easy entrée into monoracial peer groups on campus, where, as noted in the previous chapter, boundaries were often drawn between cultural insiders and outsiders. Summer came from a household that was bicultural, "in every sense that there could be, . . . the food that we ate, . . . the way the house was decorated," religion, and school and extracurricular activities. The experience of having her mother bring Korean dumplings and Korean sushi as refreshments for Summer's gymnastics team exasperated Summer—"I'd be like, 'Mom, don't bring that. Be like the other moms. Why can't you bring *normal* food?'"—but also prepared her to joke and laugh with other Catholic University students about the experience of being the child of a Korean immigrant.

Several study participants in the Multiple Monoracial Identities pattern were the children of immigrant parents or had substantial international experience prior to coming to college. Often, they equated "American" and "white" and rarely articulated the conflation. But in their homes, American *did* mean white, at least until they realized that Americans are categorized in a number of racial groups. Some of these students were aware of being bicultural, but also of their parents' attempts to assimilate into mainstream, white American culture. Their acquisition of both cultures facilitated their identity with more than one heritage. Dave, the son of a white American mother and Iranian[1] father, said,

> Growing up was very balanced. My parents tried to give me an American influence and an Iranian influence. There was actually more American in my house than there was Iranian. But definitely they tried to give me a strong Iranian background, too. Growing up was mixed culturally. I definitely got doses of both.

Dave felt comfortable identifying with his white heritage *and* with his Iranian heritage and enjoyed the flexibility his bicultural identity provided: "If I get into an argument with my father, I'll joke around, 'You're Iranian, you won't understand.' And if I'm arguing with my mother, I'll joke, 'You're American, you don't understand.'"

Erika spent her first twelve years in Japan with a Japanese father and a white American mother who had lost her ability to speak following a stroke; Erika was sent to boarding school in the United States to learn the English her mother could not teach her and to "know more about my American side, my American-ness." In another asian-and-white family, Elektra attributed her mother's reluctance to teach her Chinese to her mother's desire for Elektra to be "more American, more white," even though she taught Elektra to cook Chinese dishes and to celebrate Chinese holidays. For Dave, Erika, and Elektra, home was a place where two cultures coexisted and where they were encouraged to explore both to varying extents.

Students whose parents were not immigrants also had opportunities to explore cultural knowledge in ways that facilitated their decision to identify with Multiple Monoracial Identities, though some encountered obstacles. Jeff's second generation Japanese American grandparents were interned during World War II and had not taught Jeff's father much about Japanese culture. "So in terms of my Japanese side, we'd always have a big New Year's dinner, but other than that it wasn't too much emphasized," in contrast to, "On my mom's side, for culture, it was just American that was emphasized. Like in traditions we have around Thanksgiving, Christmas, the usual holidays where we all get together. There was a lot more of that kind of thing than the Japanese side." Asked about her experience with her cultural heritage, Bridget said,

> One moreso than the other. My dad is african american and my mom is Puerto Rican and my grandmother is straight from the island. My grandmother raised me, so I'd have to say that I've had more knowledge of Puerto Rican culture. My dad wasn't around, so my mother always instilled both in me, but I would have to say that—if you know your history, you know that Puerto Ricans are a mix of black and Spanish blood and of course the native population, so it's a mix of both and she's always taught me that.

On their respective campuses (Ivy and Big Ten), Jeff and Bridget maintained their biracial identities but were aware that they were not as steeped in the cultural heritages of their parents as were their peers who had grown up in monoracial households. As was the case for students choosing to assert Monoracial Identity, personal characteristics related to level of cultural knowledge were important factors in how students in this pattern were able to choose microsystems on campus and how the peer culture mesosystem interacted with identity choices.

Physical Appearance

Another personal characteristic in students' decision to identify in the Multiple Monoracial Identities pattern was related to *physical appearance*. Like the students quoted in the previous chapter, this group of students found that their appearance influenced others' first impressions and willingness to accept them fully into monoracial groups. For Summer, it was a disconnect between her "ambiguous, asian and white, maybe it's just a tan, but hard to tell" appearance and her Jewish last name,

So I wonder what people think when they first meet me, and a lot of people are confused and they hear my name and they think it's confusing. I don't know. Some people are really surprised when they find out my mom's Korean. But then looking at me some people think I'm totally Asian and eat with chopsticks all the time.

Ellen, Kate, and Bridget had two parents of color, and they were never confused for being white or just having a tan. Their monoracial appearances, however, operated in each case to conceal latina heritage. Of her experience at Rural Community College, Ellen said,

> I know I'm Mexican and black and native. But I look mostly just black. So it was kind of hard to get to know the other Mexican kids here, because they didn't know that I was, too. And they didn't automatically bring me into their group, I had to go up and tell them that I was one of them. The black students, though, they just thought I was one of them, so that was easier. And now with both groups, people know that I have more than just one thing in me.

Kate was of Chinese and Peruvian heritage. Before college, she identified mainly as asian, but she shifted her identity to include her latina heritage when she encountered sizable and well-organized networks of students of color at Ivy.

> It's really hard to even categorize myself sometimes as biracial because, all my life, because I look phenotypically asian and because I was always in school where the only minorities were asians, african americans, and latinos, and I could count them on one hand. So I basically went through most of my life just being asian, but there were weird things about me, like I spoke Spanish. I used to say, "I'm asian, with a twist."
>
> I'm latina. I speak Spanish, dance at [Spanish House], hang around with everyone else. But it's hard. I'm on the side, over here on the side. It's like I'm so illegitimate. Even though we share a lot of the same culture and language, and experiences and food and whatever. They're scratching their heads, they really are. They don't know what to do, because everything they've been taught and raised in tells them that someone who looks like me is not latina and I'm not legitimate. But my experiences with them over this year have helped. Almost to the point where this year I've asserted it so much that now it's "Oh, yeah! She's asian too—don't let her forget that!" (laugh) So now I'm just going back and forth. I totally need that room right now.

The complexity of latino/a or hispanic heritage and its role as a race or ethnicity in the United States is complicated and relates to colonialism, conquest, slave taking and trading, and nationalism. Bridget had come to terms with this complexity but was sometimes impatient with others who had not, who were not aware of the history leading to it, or who did not understand the role of physical appearance in masking it.

> You can definitely look at me and know—most people would just assume I'm black. And that goes back to knowing history. Like if you know a lot of latinos, you know that they're darker than a lot of blacks sometimes. And a lot of people don't know that. But in terms of [Latino Student Alliance, or LSA] and going to different events, well, this summer I stayed at Big Ten to work, and I met a lot of people, and it helped that I met them first and they were very accepting. They were like, "she's family" and stuff like that. Which is a lovely attitude to have. I love that. So once I went to LSA, [my latina identity] was a given. I knew a lot of the people there already and I was comfortable.
>
> In terms of meeting people off the street, a lot of people would just assume I'm black, and they do. And that, it kind of angers me, because you should never assume something like that. Being biracial, I would never assume somebody's race, I would always ask before anything. So that angers me a little bit that people don't ask. I would think that it goes both ways. A lot of white people would say, "She's just black" and stuff like that. I don't know. Just yesterday somebody asked me if I was biracial, and I was like, "Wow, that's funny that you're asking me that because no one usually asks, they just assume that you're just black." And he was like, "No, I can see your facial characteristics and—" and I was just impressed that they actually asked.

Bridget's appearance constitutes a developmentally instigative personal characteristic in that it prompts interactions with others in relation to her racial identities and the ways that they match or do not match how she looks. The same was true for Ellen and Kate as they entered latino/a student spaces with the appearance of outsiders. For all three, however, their appearance facilitated entry into the spaces of other monoracial student cultures (black for Ellen and Bridget, asian for Kate), an entrée not as easily available to mixed race students with white heritage or for those with "racially ambiguous" appearances who wished to associate with groups based on monoracial identity.

Developmentally Instigative Characteristics

Students' propensity to engage in exploration of racial identity and their ways of reacting to and interacting with their environments comprised some of the *developmentally instigative characteristics* that are key factors in the ecology model. Together with their level of cultural knowledge and physical appearance, these characteristics formed unique arrays of individual traits. These characteristics then influenced students' individual interpretations of and interactions with the college environment.

Like Dan, described in the previous chapter, several students in the Multiple Monoracial Identities pattern were inclined to explore identity issues on their own and in private. A variety of environmental prompts set off this exploration, though not every student would have responded the same way to the prompt. For example, Summer's law school application set her thinking about her college applications and the ways she had changed during the intervening four years.

> For law school, I wrote an essay about this whole racial identity thing. And it's weird because when I wrote my *college* essays, I thought, "Wow, I've really come to grips with it, I've really come to understand it." Because I had been so ashamed of it when I was younger and I just hated it. I wanted to be blond and have like blue eyes. I talked about how I blamed my mom a lot for that, and it was hard for me, and that I had come to really embrace and really appreciate it and be proud of it.
>
> It's just weird because I wrote that then and so much has changed since then, that I've come to understand it even more and appreciate it even more, that when writing these law school applications, I was talking about the whole diversity thing again. The question was like, "What can you bring to the environment, classroom, or something," and I said basically a cultural sensitivity and an appreciation and whatever, you know, that I think is really necessary in the classroom. It was weird because it had the same kind of idea, but yet I just realized I had learned so much and grown so much in that aspect, and I'd written both of my essays on that.

Whereas Dan's musings about race, described earlier, were linked to his monoracial Chinese identity, Summer incorporated her Chinese and her white identities. Indeed, from personal experience and observation of her "half-asian" friends, she concluded that many biracial students were disinclined to explore their asian culture in favor of adopting a white, "American" way of acting and identifying.

> I think everyone has such a different experience, but on the whole, most of us just feel like any other American kid, like I feel very American and I forget I don't look white. We all act like it, and I think there are very few half kids that end up going to the asian side, you know what I mean? And I don't really know why that is, but I think more of them in my experience, especially when they're younger, are just more inclined to reject that aspect of it because they want to be as American as everyone else, and then later on they sort of come to appreciate it, but really when it comes down to it, they're just as American as everyone else.
>
> That's totally my experience with all my half-asian friends. Aside from the little jokes here and there, the accents that our parents have, we're pretty much—I mean, we sound like everyone else, we act like everyone

else. It makes me kind of sad, because none of my friends have looked into it. I mean, I've definitely taken more steps than anyone else to explore that side of it, but I feel like most "halfs" here are just totally disinterested in learning about their asian side.

While Summer would not have used the term *developmentally instigative characteristics*, what she is describing is exactly that: students' propensity to engage one of their heritages. And whether or not she is accurate in her assessment of the biracial population at Catholic U, she has observed an important dynamic in their developmental ecologies.

A developmentally instigative inclination to self-label, to claim their own identities rather than accept the ones assigned to them by others, was a strong theme among students in the Multiple Monoracial Identities pattern. They resisted others' definitions of or limitations on the identities possible for mixed race individuals. Like Beth ("I explain that I am Mexican *and* anglo *and* more than that, too."), Ann is clear when she states her identity:

> I always described myself as half black and half white. I tell people I'm half African American and half white and I don't exclude either race. And I don't like to be called mulatto or mulatta. I don't like that word. And I don't like it when people just call me one race and not both of them. And I don't like the word mulatto.

Rhonda makes it clear that what she calls herself is up to her:

> I guess what matters is that I can be black *and* Italian and that that's okay. Like with my close friends, they get it and they know it's just Rhonda and that's how I am. But with other people who aren't my close friends, if they ask me I'll tell them, "Yep, I'm half and half—black and Italian. Like it or leave it." That's how I see it.

In addition to choosing his own racial labels, Benjamin decided to make a more personal claim to his heritage by changing the pronunciation of his last name from the Americanized version back to an Islander version.

> Actually, I just changed it. Cause in high school, like all my life it's been "[Americanized version of name]," but that's not the right way to say it. That's just the way that when my father came over to go to college, that's the way it looks, and he didn't really speak up about it or anything like that. So I told my mom, "When I go to college I'm going to start saying it the right way." I mean, no one else in the United States has my last name, so why not say it right?
>
> And I like it. I think it sounds better. And I think it does, in a way, make me realize my roots a little more. Like growing up in an all white town, mainly I identify with white people a lot. Like I can comfortably hang around with them and like that, but saying my name, just saying my last name with that kind of Islander sound makes me realize that I'm not white, but yet I still get along with them.

Benjamin's decision not only to name his identity but also to name himself—quite literally in the way his name is pronounced—illustrates yet another way in which individual characteristics influence identity. In the next section, I discuss the ways in which factors in the environment exert developmental presses on individual students.

MICROSYSTEMS

The immediate settings in which students operated—classrooms, performing groups, athletic teams, residence halls, campus jobs, families—interacted with their personal characteristics to promote or inhibit identity development and exploration. Beth's experience founding a hispanic student group at her junior college left indelible impressions on her identity that prompted her to seek a similar organization when she began at Rural University. Recognizing the cultural differences between two distinct family settings—her parents' and her grandmother's homes—helped Kimlien to understand her biracial heritage. Summer's study abroad year in Japan put her in multiple microsystems where she explored her asian heritage; she returned with a new appreciation for her mother's Korean homeland and culture. At home, in academic settings, friendship groups, and social or recreational microsystems, students developed in the Multiple Monoracial Identities pattern.

Family Microsystems

Family microsystems supported some of these students' identification with more than one heritage. Delores described the differences between her mother's african american family and her father's German family and how she understood herself as both black and German. In response to my question about how the families were different, she said

> I don't know, different senses of humor. It's understood in both places, but certain things are more funny in one than the other. I don't know how to explain it. But just everything. My dad's family isn't particularly white, either, though. He's from Germany. My dad was born in Germany, so it's extremely traditional German—like always completely German. And there's Mom, my mom's family, they're black and there's 12 aunts and uncles. They're like this hierarchy of people—it's a lot more chaos over there. But it's good. I'm comfortable both places.

Delores and her siblings all looked "pretty much mixed—definitely not white," yet they had very traditional German names (think Hans, Gretel, Dietrich). They turned this apparent contradiction into a family joke of sorts, teasing one brother especially badly for wearing his hair in dreadlocks, "Like some kind of Rasta-aryan!" The ability to share humor with both her black and German relatives, as well as with her mixed siblings, provided Delores with family microsystems where she could comfortably engage her cultural heritages while acknowledging her mixed identity as well. For students who lived at home during college or who, like Delores, lived away but were in frequent contact with home, family microsystems continued to exert developmental influences on collegiate identities.

Sibling relationships also formed a critical microsystem for the formulation of Florence's identity as black, native american, and white. The mixed race daughter of a black minister serving a predominantly white congregation, Florence was raised with modest financial means and felt that she lacked the pricey designer shoes or clothes necessary to be accepted by the black girls in her high school. "I didn't get accepted by the black people in my school. They saw me as acting white." She turned instead to an ethnically diverse group of girls who supported her precollege identity exploration that led to her comfort with her multiple heritages. She said, "In high school, I really got into my native american thing. And then, a couple years later, I was into my black thing and blah, blah, blah, blah, blah." What prompted her transition from exploring the "native american thing" to her "black thing" were "some discussions with my sisters and brothers—they all have different feelings about what they are." A family microsystem where multiple races were acknowledged, where cross-cultural relationships were common in her parents' work as minister and minister's partner, and where siblings supported Florence's identity exploration contributed to her identification with Multiple Monoracial Identities.

Alexandra linked her acquisition of cultural knowledge to her family microsystems, attributing her sense of cultural heritage to family celebrations of holidays and visits to distant relatives. She said,

> We celebrate Chinese New Year. And my mother's parents live on the west coast so we don't see them very often, but when we do we visit every Chinese restaurant in the city! And then we go see my father's parents, and my grandmother will cook traditional Spanish food. So they expose us to both sides, but it's not like I speak Spanish or Chinese, well very little. Mostly you smile and nod your head while they talk. Someone once asked why that was and I said it was because we speak English at home. And she asked, "Don't you lose your culture that way?" I said, ""No. I don't think that. I appreciate it, but I think I am more American. And I am not cheapening either side. I am not cheapening where I came from."

The presence of asian and hispanic culture in Alexandra's extended family provided important context for her identity as both Chinese and hispanic. She was also native american (her mother was Chinese and native american), though she was less engaged in that aspect of her heritage. Still, the family microsystem was an important one in her identity.

Academic Microsystems

Academic microsystems on campus formed important milieus for racial identity development and for the deployment of multiple racial identifications. Some academic microsystems were formed in classrooms, some were in group project settings, and some were in study abroad programs. In some cases, an academic assignment prompted independent exploration of identity or an academic decision, such as choosing courses or a major, became an opportunity to engage mixed race identity.

The immediate, face-to-face setting of college classrooms constituted important microsystems for some students in the Multiple Monoracial Identities pattern. At Rural Community College, Mina had often been quiet in class, "just taking it all in, not really talking much." But then, she said,

> So I took this class about race and ethnicity. It was a sociology class. And the teacher was saying that there are people who intermarry—marry outside their group. And this one guy was like, "That's not right. People shouldn't do that to their kids. They won't know what they are." And I said, "Well, my dad's South Asian and my mom's white. And I know what I am. I'm both." That was an interesting day in class.

Mina's "interesting day in class" led her to have conversations with her parents about their experiences in an interracial marriage and what they had thought life would be like for their mixed race children. A first-year anthropology course introduced Jeff to Japanese culture and society in ways that his grandparents and father had not, allowing him more fully to explore his Japanese heritage. He had been taking Japanese language classes since then. In another anthropology course, this one on multiraciality, Jeff was disappointed that the focus of the class was on interracial relationships, though "we had to do a presentation, which has been the best part of the class, because most people's presentations have been really concentrated on multiracial issues and what it's like to be more than one thing."

As discussed previously in the portrait of Summer and in the last chapter, study abroad experiences were powerful learning environments that immersed students in a new developmental ecology. Indeed, Summer was aware of the ways that study abroad programs were used by biracial Americans to explore their heritages. Unable to enroll in Korean language classes at Catholic U, she had taken up Japanese, which led to her decision to study in Japan.

> When I was in Korea, it was kind of sad, because all the Koreans were speaking Korean to me, and like I could only respond in Japanese. People in Japan would say things like, "What are you doing here? All the half-Japanese people are supposed to be here. You're supposed to be in Korea getting in touch with your roots." I'm like, "I know, I don't know how I ended up here."

The idea that "all the half-Japanese people" would end up in Japan made sense to Summer, although she still found that immersion in asian culture helped her better to understand her mother and thus her own heritage, "In that sense I learned more about Asian people. We'd be learning something in class and I'd think, 'Oh, that's totally my mom, that's totally Korean people, they're so like that.'" The physical shift from a campus-based developmental environment to one in another country created opportunities for identity exploration and definition.

For some students, choices of individual courses or academic majors created similar opportunities for identity exploration and definition in the U.S. campus setting. Some choices were purposeful, and others were somewhat serendipitous. B. J., for example, was a student athlete, and her academic advisor helped her choose courses. She ended up in a course related to one of her heritages—african american—somewhat by chance.

> I took a civil rights class—this is a fluke class. Because I was with my athletic counselor, and he was just picking classes, because it was the last day of picking courses. He was like, "What about this class?" I looked at it, and I thought, "one day a week, two and half hours, alright." So I said, "Oh, okay. I'll take this class," even though it didn't meet requirements or anything, but it still looked interesting. It is interesting. It's civil rights, black union laborers' movement, and stuff like that, so it's interesting. And it fills in some of the blanks where I didn't learn stuff from my dad or whatever.

Erika initially chose an international relations major as a way to use her dual identities to bridge cultures. She later amended her choice of major but maintained the central motivation to bridge cultures.

> I felt like I was a lot American, when I grew up in Japan. But now when I think about it, it was really in between, and I think it was really balanced. . . . I was going to be an international relations major, because I really wanted to do something in between Japan and the United States, because I grew up there but had a balance of both. So I wanted to do something in between, like teach Americans going to Japan how to act and how to be. But I don't really like the politics classes that I would have had to take as a requirement. So I think I'm going to major in Asian studies instead of that. I can still do the same thing when I'm done, I think.

Viewing herself as having a "balance of both" cultures enabled Erika to frame her academic and career goals around her identity. At Catholic U, Elektra made a similar decision, concentrating in international studies, with Europe and Asia as her areas of focus. Asked if she felt any of her academic work related to issues of identity as a biracial person, she replied, "I think that my concentration is pretty much about that. I'm European and I'm

Asian and I want to understand both origins." Academic microsystems, like the classes in Erika and Elektra's majors, created spaces to explore multiple facets of racial identity.

Social and Recreational Microsystems

Students' identification with multiple heritages was evident also in the social and recreational microsystems they chose. Students sought microsystems that supported different elements of their heritage and those that allowed them to express those different elements at the same time. Elektra had the same roommates for three years at Catholic U, and their room décor reflected their diverse heritages.

> I have two really close friends, and one's Irish and one's Portuguese. It's funny, because when I met them, I thought, "They totally identify with their culture." Irish flags everywhere, Irish this, Irish coffee, sweaters, just everything Irish! (laugh) And [my other friend], she's Portuguese, and she totally identifies with being Portuguese. She has the flags and everything. So I was saying, "Hey! I'm being squished out!" (laugh) And so I thought, "Well, I'll put up a Chinese flag and an American flag." Well, my father's German, so a German flag. I can never say I'm one or the other of any of them. And so we've had those flags up in our room every year.

Like Kimlien with her asian decorations, Elektra stakes a claim to her identities through her choice of residence hall décor, literally "planting a flag" to announce her multiple heritages.

B. J. was involved with the Filipino Society and Black Student Forum (BSF) at Catholic as a way to engage her identities; she also felt strongly connected to white culture because she was raised with a white stepfather. In fact, B. J. joined the BSF to immerse herself in black culture. She was also a student athlete and found an identity connection through the team. "And so the only black family experience I have is with my track coach and his daughter. We run together. So that's something that I really connected with. Running, but also being part of kind of a black family." In combination with her civil rights class and participation in BSF, the connection with her coach provided an important microsystem for understanding herself in the context of black culture. B. J. said, "I've just met so many different African Americans here, that I can see a side of me that I never had when I was at home. It was a learning experience for me, and I'm still learning."

In contrast, at Big Ten Benjamin found that although he attended one of the largest universities in the nation, the number of students sharing his Micronesian or Islander heritage was so small as to be largely invisible to him. Asked to what identity groups on campus he related, Benjamin replied,

> Like what group do I consider myself in, that type of thing? Well, half of me is Pacific Islander, Micronesian. So it's hard to relate to a group on campus

really because I couldn't find, like I spent the first semester looking, and still I'm trying to find another person from the Island. There were some guys from another fraternity practicing some kind of stick dance or something in one of the [residence hall] rooms, so I went in there, and it was mainly a Hispanic fraternity. But there was a guy from Guam in there, and he was the first one I met from the Islands. So that's one person out of like 35,000 or whatever. It's kind of limited. So I don't really have an identity—or a group that I identify with.

Pressed further about students he had met through the Asian Student Alliance, he said,

> No, they're mainly like Filipino or Korean, stuff like that or other asian. And I was talking, like I went to ASA, and I know a lot of people in there pretty well. I was talking to them and I was like, "Do you know how many Islanders there are on campus?" And this guy said, "There's you and there's a couple others. But not really a whole lot." A handful maybe.

Undeterred by the lack of a reference group of other Islander students at Big Ten, Benjamin pursued his own identity exploration, correcting the pronunciation of his last name and looking for academic courses in which he might be able to learn more about his father's culture.

In Benjamin's case, the lack of a microsystem with a specific connection to his Islander identity may have inhibited his identity development in this area, yet he persisted in maintaining identification with both his white and his Pacific Islander heritages. One way Benjamin pursued his white cultural identity was through joining a predominantly white residential fraternity at Big Ten. "My rush class," he said, " had the most diversity. There was me and an Indian kid and we were the second class to have anyone besides normal, just the usual white guys." With these "normal" guys Benjamin looked forward to being immersed in fraternity life and benefiting from the social networking he would be able to do. Although the fraternity constituted a white-identified microsystem, it was a place where Benjamin felt comfortable being himself as white and Islander.

Two other participants, Jeff (at Ivy) and Mark (at Big Ten) were also fraternity members. For Jeff in particular, the microsystem of the predominantly white fraternity created conflicts in other microsystems of students of color. The interactions among these microsystems formed the mesosystem of peer culture in which he negotiated his identity as asian, as white, and as hapa.

MESOSYSTEMS

When two or more microsystems interact, a mesosystem is created. The mixed race students in the study inhabited mesosystems at the intersections of academic and social settings, family and college systems, or multiple campus microsystems. Often, students in the Multiple Monoracial Identities pattern found support for more than one monoracial identification in the mesosystem, though some encountered obstacles to participation in student groups based on monoracial identity. Where mesosystems contained incongruous microsystems (i.e., microsystems sent conflicting messages about mixed race identity and the possibilities for identifying with more than one heritage), students in this pattern developed strategies to manage the incongruity while maintaining Multiple Monoracial Identities. Guided by their unique developmentally instigative characteristics and personal histories, students negotiated the varying racialized terrain of the six campuses. In this section, I describe some of the ways in which the mesosystem influenced students' identities.

Like Benjamin at Big Ten, Jeff joined a predominantly white fraternity at Ivy. Having been deeply involved in the Third World community on campus prior to pledging the fraternity, Jeff had two very different perspectives on campus life. Interviewed as a junior, Jeff had already had the opportunity to "scope out" campus life and peer cultures ("Freshman year a lot of my friends were part of the Third World Community and Spectrum.") and to form friendship groups ("I still have a lot of my friends that are from asian groups. Also, that year I spent a lot of time with my [residence hall floor], and so a lot of my friends are white."). Of his identity and his ability to connect with students from different peer cultures, he said,

> In college, identity-wise it's definitely different from home. I would definitely refer to myself as bi or multiracial, but those are, you know, white, mono-centric labels. I just see myself as I have these different backgrounds. It's also interesting because they're not necessarily different, completely different cultural backgrounds in a way, which is kind of a hard thing.
>
> Sometimes it's easy because in certain ways I can function well in the Ivy context, like my white friends can identify with my culture too because it's also theirs. Each person has a different background, so people understand that. In terms of minority or Third World communities, it's kind of hard, because I don't have necessarily as much of that Japanese culture side to identify with. Like I can identify with, through what my grandparents have said that, like how they've said stuff. And also how I look, it's interesting. People aren't sure what I am. (laugh)

The microsystems of white peer groups, the Third World community, and family interact with physical appearance to create a mesosystem that holds possible identities, which for Jeff include a bi- or multiracial label, white, and asian or perhaps specifically Japanese. Although Jeff holds biracial, white, and asian identities, he experiences Ivy as a place where white student culture is separate from asian student culture; he has his "white friends" and his friends from "asian groups," but he talks about them as separate entities.

After Jeff joined the predominantly white fraternity in his junior year the lines between white student culture and Third World student culture became much more sharply drawn. Time commitments forced him sometimes to choose between involvement with the fraternity and involvement with the Third World community.

> So the house is entirely white, and also a few of us that are minorities. I'm the East Asian, or *half* East Asian rep, I guess. But it's been good and bad. Like, in terms of its required activities, well any activities are hard to keep up with outside the house. So, a lot of activities that are important to me, I can't devote as much time to. So I've kind of missed out on things like Multiracial Heritage Week and things like that.
>
> I was [an assistant for the new students of color preorientation program] before I started doing pledge stuff this semester, and so that was another conflict. I became a lot closer with a lot of the [preorientation assistants] and Minority Peer Aides, who I've still kept in touch with and still hang out with, but the whole [fraternity] pledging process took a lot of time away from that—time that would have been devoted to that, so that was hard. But I made some good friends because of [preorientation], too. A lot of them are sophomores.

Although pledging activities took him away from activities in the Third World community, Jeff did what he could to make connections with incoming students of color and leaders in the community of students of color. The mesosystem formed at the intersection of the fraternity and the preorientation program created a degree of stress, but Jeff managed to maintain his sense of Multiple Monoracial Identities in both communities.

Jeff gave one more example of the peer mesosystem created by the fraternity and Third World microsystems. He began dating an african american woman, who was also "really active in Third World community activities." But then Jeff's girlfriend joined a predominantly white sorority, which caused "a lot of backlash" in the Third World student community. Jeff was pained by the situation, though he realized that his circumstance with the fraternity was somehow different.

> [My girlfriend] also joined a sorority, so that was for her, a hard decision, but parallel, on a very different level, because I have other parts of my identity—I'm part white, I'm able to step out and step into circles. For her, as soon as she mentioned that she was joining a sorority, there was like a lot of backlash from that. For me there was, but there wasn't. I guess it's sort of like people expect certain things, but they're not sure. They have differing viewpoints of where I fit in. So for me it was a hard thing, but for her, it was an extremely hard thing. People were like, "Why?" People were yelling at her.
>
> And it was hard on me, to go through that and realize I could understand it. But also I couldn't really say to her, "Our lives are the same." And

that was a really hard thing for me, because she's my closest friend on campus, and I can totally relate, but also I can't to a certain extent, I can't completely understand. It wasn't easy.

The pressure to be loyal to the Third World community was stronger for Jeff's girlfriend than it was for him, in part because mixed race Jeff was not held to the same standard as his ostensibly monoracial girlfriend. For the pair, the peer mesosystem held a complex array of messages about identity and group membership. I did not meet Jeff's girlfriend, but Jeff, at least, seemed to be persisting in his identity while living somewhat parallel lives in the Third World and fraternity-sorority subcultures, in spite of the conflicting messages circulating in the peer culture mesosystem.

As illustrated in Jeff's story, the ability to move among student groups in the peer culture mesosystem was an important factor in students' identity choices, as it was for the students in the Monoracial Identity pattern. But because they brought different personal histories and, as important, arrays of developmentally instigative traits to these same campus peer cultures, students in the Multiple Monoracial Identities pattern identified differently from the students described in the previous chapter. By and large, they experienced campus culture and the ease of moving among student subcultures similarly to the Monoracial Identity students; at four institutions (Big Ten, Rural University, Liberal Arts College, Rural Community College) it was relatively easy to move among groups, while at Ivy and Catholic U, the boundaries between student groups were rigid and well guarded. Students' reactions to these conditions in the mesosystem were influenced by their personal characteristics and histories.

The peer culture mesosystem at Rural University supported movement between identity-based groups, but there were microsystems where identity and identification were circumscribed by peer assumptions and larger cultural forces. For example, Beth said,

> What comes to mind is how Latin you are really. There was a situation, I was at a party and there was a Puerto Rican guy there and we were talking about a girl who was in the Hispanic Student Council. I said, "You know so-and-so? She is Puerto Rican." In a way I probably shouldn't have said that because she is not only Puerto Rican, she is african american. He looks at me and says, "She isn't Puerto Rican. She is black." I was like, "How can you say that? You know that she's president of Hispanic Council. So why would she want to be the president if she doesn't consider herself Hispanic?" And what it boils down to is that he was ashamed of people calling someone Puerto Rican who looked african american, because there is a stigma in Puerto Rico that if you have black blood in you, you are considered less than someone who doesn't.

> So it was really interesting because automatically he just wrote her off
> as "She is just black, she is not Puerto Rican." So I think that maybe if I am
> not there, they say, "She is really not Mexican and her mom is white." So
> who knows what happens if I am not there.

Beth's awareness that her identity may be judged by other students in the
larger context of cultural assumptions illustrates several features of the ecology model. First, she operated in multiple microsystems, which existed as
social settings even when she was not in them. Second, macrosystem factors
related to desirability of "black blood" and darker skin tone permeated cross-
culturally. Third, Beth's personal traits and history did not lead her to give up
her hispanic identity in the presence of peer attitudes about authenticity,
identity, and appearance. So within the peer culture mesosystem, Beth
encountered indirect messages about what it meant to be mixed race in the
context of hispanic student social settings.

At Big Ten, which was also characterized as a place where students could
move with relative ease among groups, Ann encountered resistance to her
claim of multiple racial identities. She said, "People can't really grasp that
somebody can identify with both sides and not just one. And not one only.
People say, 'Oh, well, she's black' or 'She's white.' I don't get that often, but
something along those lines." In defiance of peer expectations of monoracial
identity, Ann maintained her biracial, black and white, identity:

> I would prefer half-white, half-black, because I like people to know what my
> race and ethnicity is. I like people to know that. And I don't want anybody
> to get it confused. I'm not Puerto Rican. I'm not Dominican. Cause people
> always think that. I want them to know what I am. It's both.

In contrast, Alexandra found Catholic U to be a place where she could
exert her multiple racial identities in a peer culture that, if not entirely welcoming of students of color, created space for self-identification. She said,
"My father is hispanic and my mother is Chinese and native american, so I
like telling people that because it's cool. I like it. I'm not boring. I'm not just
one person." So in the context of an institution where the AHANA student
subculture was distinct from the mainstream, "white, jock-y" culture, Alexandra experienced the peer culture mesosystem as one in which her identification with Multiple Monoracial Identities was "cool" and "not boring."
Whereas this same peer culture led Jennifer to hold a private monoracial Chinese identity (as described in the previous chapter), Alexandra's personal
traits and history led her to interpret messages within the mesosystem as welcoming of her diversity and difference.

Even when peer microsystems were not welcoming of mixed race students' diversity, some of them persisted in exerting Multiple Monoracial

Identities. Like several of the students described in the previous chapter, Princess felt as though she did not conform to the cultural attitudes and behaviors expected in monoracial student communities. In her case, it was the community of black women with whom she failed to "make the grade."

> As far as friends in the black community, I do have a couple friends, like [name], who's of African descent, but technically Indian. I guess the white community just embraces me more because I was brought up more like them. Like I speak the way they do and I understand their cultural—like music and all that stuff. I never really shut myself off to any type of culture, but I found that the white community has embraced me more easily. . . .
>
> Growing up, I never knew what I was doing wrong. Like even now, there's a room of the girls that live over on the other side of the dorm, and I'm still intimidated because I don't fit in with the [urban] attitude. I'm not hardcore enough and I don't have the jewelry and the nails, and I don't dress that way, I don't speak that way, so I think it's always going to be an issue with me as far as the black community. Guys are fine! They're like "Hey, what's your name?" and blah, blah, blah. It's like, "Okay, I can handle them." But when it comes down to the black women, forget it.

Still, she said, "I do identify with being biracial. Like I don't just say, 'Yeah, I'm african american' or 'Yeah, I'm whatnot.' I actually have native american in my background also, so technically I'm native american, Romanian, and african american." In spite of her difficulty fitting in culturally with and being accepted by black women on campus, Princess persisted in identifying with her three heritage groups, whereas other students in her situation might react differently and have different developmental outcomes. Defying some messages in the peer culture mesosystem, she asserted her identity as she chose it rather than as others might have chosen it for her.

SUMMARY

Students in the Multiple Monoracial Identities pattern inhabited the same campuses as students in the Monoracial Identity pattern; indeed, they operated within the same peer culture, though individual micro- and mesosystems varied among participants. What accounts for the differences in how they identified? What would lead some students to identify with one heritage and others to identify with more than one? The answer lies substantially in the developmental characteristics, personal traits, and individual histories each student brought to campus. How students interpreted peer culture and interact with it varied, as did their levels of security and comfort with claiming multiple racial identities. In light of these personal traits and individual interpretations, the same number of students (twenty-seven) chose Monoracial Identity as chose Multiple Monoracial Identities. Overall, though, fifty students—divided evenly between these two patterns—chose a Multiracial Identity. In the next chapter, I describe the Multiracial Identity pattern, the students who chose it, and the environmental presses influencing this choice.

chapter six

I'm Mixed—Multiracial Identity

My racial identity, I would have to say, is multiracial. I am of the future. I believe there is going to come a day when a very, very large majority of everybody in the world is going to be mixed with more than one race. It's going to be multiracial for everybody. Everybody and their mother!

—Jack, Rural Community College

JACK AND THE COMPOSITE STUDENT, Kim, introduced in chapter 3, share the Multiracial Identity pattern with the majority (89 percent) of the study sample.[1] The terms they used to describe themselves varied substantially and included "biracial," "mixed," "mulatto," "multiracial," "multicultural," "hapa," "bicultural," "half-and-half," as well as combinations such as "half-white and half-black," "mixed black and caucasian," "biracial black," and "Amerasian or Eurasian." But some, most, or all of the time they identified not in the monoracial categories but as something new, something "on the border" (Rockquemore & Brunsma, 2002; Root, 1996; Wallace, 2001).

In this chapter, I describe trends within the Multiracial Identity pattern, as well as some characteristics and experiences shared across the fifty participants who identified in this pattern. I illustrate their experience with portraits of four students who hold a Multiracial Identity and then explore some of the ecological factors that contributed to students' identification in this pattern.

CHARACTERISTICS OF THIS PATTERN

A Multiracial Identity came with a wide array of self-labels, but in every case it represented a nonmonoracial construct. More than just being "both/and," like the Multiple Monoracial Identities students discussed in chapter 5, the students in the Multiracial Identity pattern identified some or all of the time outside the standard monoracial conception of race in the United States. Taking on a "border" identity (Root, 1996; Wallace, 2001), they asserted an identity beyond the category of "Other" they often encountered on institutional forms. To be hapa, biracial, multiracial, mixed, mestiza (some use more controversial terms such as *mutt* or *mulatto/a*) was to be of a new identity construction, one that was often self-generated and proudly claimed. Certainly, the majority (forty-two of fifty, or 84 percent) of these students sometimes also claimed one or more of their parents' heritages; they were "mixed black and Italian," "biracial, Filipina and white," or "hapa: half Japanese American, half white." But in each case, the notion of self as existing outside the monoracial paradigm was critical to personal identity.

TRENDS WITHIN THE PATTERN

Because of the sampling bias and consequently large percentage of students identifying in this pattern, it is difficult to draw conclusions from observed trends across gender, heritage, class year, and institution. It is interesting, however, to get some sense of the group of fifty and its characteristics. Students in this pattern represent 89 percent of the total sample. Only 75 percent of men, however, identified in this pattern, whereas 97 percent of women did so. Later in the chapter I will pose some potential explanations for this gender difference. In terms of parental heritage and multiracial identification, students across heritage combinations were all quite likely to identify as multiracial, though all students with one white and one black, Pacific Islander, or mixed parent identified in this pattern, and only two (40 percent) of students with one white and one latino/a parent did so. One hundred percent of the juniors identified in the pattern, with somewhat smaller proportions of the other class years. By institution, students were most likely at Rural University and Rural Community College (100 percent each) to identify as Multiracial, least likely at Liberal Arts and Big Ten (75 percent and 83 percent, respectively), with those at Ivy and Catholic (93 percent and 88 percent) in between. Two students (Dwayne at Rural Community College and Steve at Big Ten, both men with black and white heritages) identified exclusively in this pattern. The sample is too small to draw any firm conclusions from these differences, but getting a sense of the diversity of the group—and what trends lie within in it—is useful to understanding the context of the portraits that follow and the remainder of the chapter.

TABLE 6.1
Distribution of Students in the Multiracial Identity Pattern
by Gender, Heritage, Class Year, and Institution

		Total in sample	Identifying in this pattern
Gender	Men	20	15 (75%)
	Women	36	35 (97%)
Heritage	Two Parents of Color	12	10 (83%)
	One Asian & One White Parent	16	15 (94%)
	One Black & One White Parent	13	13 (100%)
	One Latino/a & One White Parent	5	2 (40%)
	One Pacific Islander & One White Parent	7	7 (100%)
	One Mixed & One White Parent	3	3 (100%)
Class Year	First Year	14	13 (93%)
	Sophomore	17	14 (82%)
	Junior	11	11 (100%)
	Senior	14	12 (86%)
Institution	Big Ten University	12	10 (83%)
	Catholic University	8	7 (88%)
	Ivy University	14	13 (93%)
	Liberal Arts College	8	6 (75%)
	Rural Community College	6	6 (100%)
	Rural University	8	8 (100%)
	TOTAL	56	50 (89%)

PORTRAITS OF STUDENTS WHO CHOSE THIS PATTERN

B. J.

I think a lot of people are amazed that I'm—when you tell them you're multiracial, they're like, "Oh really? What, what, what?" So I think it's pretty neat how people are still interested in what you are and stuff like that. I've just met so many different multiracial students, it's amazing.

B. J. was raised in Florida with her Filipino mother and white stepfather. She had less contact with her black father than she would have liked, leaving her "wondering about the other side of my family." She was immersed in Filipino culture through a performing arts group that did cultural dances and said she was "pretty much aware of that side of [her] heritage." Still, she said,

> I always wondered if it was wrong that I only identified with one side of my family. But it's not wrong, because of the fact that I'm easily accessed to that part of my heritage. So that's why I really identify with my Filipino culture.

At Catholic University, B. J. joined the Filipino Society and continued to give cultural dance performances, an activity that helped her feel "connected" during the transition to college. Of her experience in the performing group, she said, "We got close really fast. It was like a home."

As noted in the previous chapter, B. J. sought out opportunities in college to connect with african american people and culture, joining the Black Student Forum (BSF) at Catholic University as well as the Filipino Society. A student-athlete, she trained with her coach and his daughter, who were also black. Through BSF and the track team, B. J. said, "I've just met so many different African Americans here, that I can see a side of me that I never had when I was [at home]. It was a learning experience for me, and I'm still learning."

B. J. attended predominantly white Catholic schools from kindergarten through high school, and found the social transition to Catholic U relatively easy. She was disappointed, though, by the separation between Catholic's socially and politically identified AHANA community and the mainstream student culture.

> But so many people white people, basically, won't go to AHANA functions. The friends I have that are white, won't go to AHANA functions because they think it's not for them. Well, first of all, if they feel uncomfortable, that's the whole point of having cultural events, so different people, different cultures, can get together and not feel uncomfortable. It's stuff like that they don't understand. I don't understand why they think they just can't be a part of something just because they're white. I think they felt the same way some other people of color have been feeling, too.

In B. J.'s mind, this separation was based on "white students' perception" of campus cultures. As an example, she described a time in class when a white student wrote a paper arguing against multiculturalism and the AHANA student services Catholic U provided; B. J.'s response included the counterargument that AHANA services were not designed to exclude anyone, because "Why would the people who've been kept out try to keep anyone else out? What would they gain from that? Nothing." The exchange led her to reflect on her expectations for college:

And I thought people, when I came here, would be more mature. I think that's the basic word, mature. But I just realize a lot of people aren't exposed to so many things, and that's natural. That's how people live, and everyone doesn't have the same experience as I do, obviously.

B. J. believed that her views about race and her antiracist stance were rooted in her experience as a multiracial person.

And having a white stepdad, I don't know. I just can't really find any prejudice toward any part of me. I'm acceptant toward every part of life. I don't know how to explain it. I'll try. It's like because I love them so much and am exposed to his culture every day, whether we're talking about issues, or racial issues, or stuff that's going on in society, I get a lot of different perspectives. I know people say, "I'm not a racist, I'm not prejudiced," etc. But I can seriously say that I'm not. I'm not saying I have an excuse of my stepdad being white, my dad being black, my mom being asian. I can't say that's an excuse, but it's something I've experienced, and there's nothing I would be prejudiced toward because it's part of me.

The "different perspectives" that surrounded her, and her love for her family, provided a base from which B. J. understood cultures not as being all the same and therefore equally valuable, but equally valuable in all of their differences. Being multiracial formed the foundation for this understanding, which was enriched by her knowledge of Filipino, black, and white cultures.

Being multiracial was not without challenges in certain peer cultures on campus. B. J.'s older sister, attending another Catholic university, had warned her that she might not "click" with the "full african american girls right away."

She didn't want to sound petty, but she wanted to tell me the truth of how, when you get there, if you don't start clicking in with the full african american girls right away, it could be because of them, or they're the ones who are being petty, because you're not full african american descent, or you don't have the hair per se. And it is different. And she said just not to worry about it, it's not you, it would be them, because they're very cliquey. But then a lot of people are cliquey.

And it's true. I didn't really have this whole set of african american girls I was hanging out with. I don't have to. So sometimes—and I'm not saying all african american girls, of course not, because I do have female friends— but it was just sort of a sense and feeling, that when they're in a group, they'll know I'm half-black or something. And it was true. My sister had more experience with it, so she wanted to let me know about it.

At the time of the interview, however, B. J. hadn't encountered more than "just sort of a sense and feeling" that others were questioning her authenticity in the black community. "I haven't really gotten that much negative contact with it," she said. And the little bit she had gotten she attributed to her appearance and to her lack of cultural knowledge, "I think it's because I was-n't raised in an african american family, and the cultures that go with it. Maybe even more my features aren't so distinct as in african american girls. So they won't know exactly what I am." Still, B. J. persisted in participating in BSF *and* Filipino Society activities, as well as activities sponsored by other AHANA student organizations.

Motivated in part by her participation in these activities, B. J. was work-ing with another study participant (Phil) to start an organization for multira-cial students. A bit unsure how the group would be received in the AHANA student community and in the larger Catholic U climate, they nevertheless had researched multiracial groups at other New England institutions and were making plans to launch the group the following semester. B. J. and Phil were in fact successful, and an organization of multiracial students now thrives at Catholic U.

JONATHON

> Before, maybe in high school, the whole thing of self-determination, that was the driving force of exploration of a multiracial identity for me. And for a lot of people. That whole idea of self-determination, of being able to say, "Fuck you" to everyone who says, "Please check one only." And that's a lib-erating feeling, but as I've grown older I've learned more and talked more. I'm not some idealistic, well, I'd like to be idealistic, but sometimes I get cynical and old, instead of some starry-eyed, rainbow-eyed person running around saying this is gonna solve all our problems, because I know the real-ities. . . . It's self-determination, "They shouldn't tell us how we should iden-tify," but now it's more complicated than that. It's way more complicated than that.

Jonathon was the only child of an interracial Japanese American and white, Jewish couple. As a child in a West Coast city he thought being bira-cial was "normal."

> Growing up as a kid it was normal. It wasn't a big deal. It was taken for granted in my schools, friendship groups, friends of our family, relatives, that's just how it was. I started trying to formulate it as what it was and what it meant early on. I mean, with the whole Japanese American thing. I knew who I was. I knew what my dad was, I knew what my mom was, and I knew who I was. And that went from thinking that Japanese American meant half Japanese, half American—American meaning white—to real-izing that's not what American meant, to asking my dad and his fam-ily about their background, and turning it into Japanese American on my mom's side.

So like my father was from Jewish people from Austria-Hungary. And
I would do these things like, "Okay, the last name's German," so I put in
Germanic, because Austria-Hungary was more than just German-speaking
people, but I put in Germanic. And Grandpa used to talk about somebody
speaking Hungarian, so I put in the Hungarian part, and then the Jewish
part. And then my grandmother's family had somebody Irish, so I put that
in. If it had any bearing on me I would add it in. And it wasn't about white,
it was just about being accurate, I guess.

At Ivy University, "being accurate" for Jonathon largely meant identifying as
biracial, though he had not lost sight of his asian and Hungarian Jewish heritages. Active in the Third World student community, Jonathon worked hard
to maintain Spectrum, the bi- and multiracial student organization and to
ensure that there were spaces for mixed students within larger Third World
community events. Indeed, other students interviewed cited some of these
spaces—such as caucuses at the preorientation for students of color and
within the Minority Peer Aides (MPA) group—as important to their identity
development at Ivy.

Jonathon believed that separate spaces for multiracial students were
essential identity options, though not necessarily every mixed students'
choice. He believed "the whole MPA rhetoric about creating a legacy." He
said, "I *do* believe that, especially for multiracial people on this campus and
elsewhere. You know, creating a history and a community, or just an awareness." At one point, Jonathon's attempt to create public space for multiracial
students in the Third World community was met with resistance, and he was
accused of "trying to make the biracial black people 'hang multiracial' instead
of go to the black group." After being publicly confronted about the issue,
Jonathon was "just a wreck." But he persisted, he said,

> Because the point was exactly not to force a choice, not to tell the biracial
> people to go to the black group, go to the asian group, to the latino group,
> whatever. . . . It was to say, "*Here's* a space, this may be the first time you've
> ever been able to have this choice." I mean, we're not saying, "You have to
> go here." But it's an option, it's a time to explore. You may not have had this
> before, use it. And to make sure that people know that that space is there.
> Whether it's Spectrum, or whether it's just informal networks of friends. Just
> to make sure that that space is there—that's always been my thing—to
> make sure that that space is there.

The confrontation in the Third World community set off a period of identity
exploration for Jonathon. Before it, he felt he "was the one who could talk
the talk, knew the issues, could rattle off stuff, name names, drop names, cite
the books" about multiraciality; he said, "I *was* the well adjusted one. The one
who didn't have the problems other people had being mixed."

And then everything started falling apart. [And I started] learning *how much* of an impact being mixed and my family has had on me. That it may not have been the same kind of impact that it had on, say, a half-black, half-white person whose white parents got disowned by their family, but it still has defined who I am.

In exploring this definition of who he was, Jonathon came to the conclusion, "Normality equals good, right? But what's normal? For each side of the family, what's normal? What's normal is excelling at school and all this stuff. But more *symbolically*, what's normal? *Symbolically*, what's normal is being monoracial." The realization that he was somehow not "normal"—and that this might bother him—disturbed Jonathon. In spite of his substantial intellectual ability to reason about race, culture, and identity, he could not deny that he somehow felt "not normal" by a monoracial society's standards.

One of the ways that Jonathon processed the crisis precipitated by the confrontation with his peers was through writing. He had a history of writing about multiracial issues, including journalism and poetry in high school and college. He continued this writing with a senior thesis on "the construction and representation of multiraciality through Star Trek." His analysis included a racialized reinterpretation of Spock—who was half-human and half-Vulcan—as white (human, caring) and Japanese (stoic, unfeeling). Jonathon noted that although Spock identified as Vulcan, the other characters were forever trying to get him to act more human. Jonathon wondered, "Why didn't he identify as biracial? Why did he have to 'pass'?" The questions of biracial identity, passing, and pressure to identify as white resonated with Jonathon as he considered, and reconsidered, what it meant to him to be biracial at Ivy.

In addition to writing about biraciality, Jonathon had read extensively on the topic, and his reading informed his identity exploration. He cited Maria Root's (1996a) "Bill of Rights for Racially Mixed People,"

And that has that I have the right to identify differently from how my parents identify me, to identify differently from my siblings, to identify different from how other people expect me to identify. To identify differently over the course of my lifetime. And to come back to any number of different identifications. And so, I've sort of internalized that idea.

The idea of biracial identity as fluid and situational is the subject of the chapter on the Situational Identity pattern, but the centrality of the notion of fluidity and instability of identity to Jonathon's understanding of what it means to be biracial is important to understanding Jonathon and his identity. When he says he is biracial, he means, "All of it—biracial and Jewish and Japanese American, hapa, Amerasian, multiracial—all of it. That's what being biracial means."

MIKE

> Mixed kids have to think more about race. One of the students that I talked to for my paper said, "Yeah, by the time I was five, I knew the grownups were wrong. I knew that they were putting categories on kids. I know that's not right. So, I grew up knowing that authority never knew what it was doing really." It was the same for me. I've always known that authority didn't know what it was doing.

Mike grew up with more interactions with "authority" than many children; he was raised in foster families and eventually adopted as a teenager. Mike lived in Mexican neighborhoods in a midwestern metropolis with his biological parents for "a year or two," and although he was a foster child and then adopted, he had stayed in communication with his parents over the years. Mike always knew he was mixed, though he assumed he was white (his mother) and black (his father). A class discussion about ethnic neighborhoods prompted him to wonder why they had lived in Mexican areas, and shortly before I met him, Mike asked his mother, "Are you sure that you have no hispanic in you at all?" That was when he learned his mother had Puerto Rican heritage as well, though he said, "I guess that makes me Puerto Rican. I don't know whether it does or it doesn't."

Mike attended more than fifteen public schools before completing his high school degree at age sixteen. Academically talented, Mike took enough Advanced Placement classes to enter Rural University with advanced standing. His campus job doing laundry for an athletic team convinced him that although working with his hands could be profitable, he would much rather make a living with his brain, as a lawyer. He lived on campus and was active in residence hall government.

The frequency with which Mike changed schools before college helped him understand his mixed identity in the context of predominantly black, predominantly white, and racially mixed settings. Teased in an all-black neighborhood for being "high yellow," he also found that "white people don't accept me as easily as african american or hispanics do." But at Rural U, he "found that there are a lot more mixed kids that seem to hang together." Although there were "a lot more mixed kids," the campus was predominantly white, and Mike said, "We're able to identify each other because there are not very many of us on this campus, so when we do see each other, run into one another, it's always, 'Okay, great.'"

Mike's appearance marked him as outside the mainstream white and black communities on campus. Acutely aware of racial dynamics, Mike described how he benefited from and was denied privilege granted on the basis of white appearance.

> My friend Tom asked me, "Why is it that every time I see you you're around black girls?" I explained to him that I am by no means racist, but here's how

> it works. These are how the cards fell for me. I'm in a position—at least this is what I have been told—that black girls look at me and they say, "Well he has fine hair, a very pretty skin texture and a tone, and if I am with him and we have kids, my kids would be pretty." Whereas white people say, "Well, I already have all those things, fine hair, nice skin color and the texture. So, I don't need it and so I won't note that when I'm looking at him."

The sense Mike made of the situation fit his experience where desirability of friends and potential romantic partners aligned with the appearance of whiteness or the closest approximation of white features.

Mike was also prompted by "What are you?" questions to understand his racial identity as "mixed."

> Like coming to Rural U, especially at the beginning, everybody was like "What's your background? Do you speak Spanish? Are you really white? Are you really black? Are you multiracial, biracial?" I mean, it surprised me because I was like "Hey, wait a minute. You don't even know me yet."

Mike was consistent in his response that he was mixed, and he sought social settings that included black students and other biracial students with black heritage.

Outside of peer and social settings, Mike also encountered prompts to identify himself one way or another. Applying to college, he worried that he would be accused of lying on forms if he did not identify himself as mixed, though there was no way to do so on college and scholarship applications. Indeed, a conversation with his principal about the dilemma led to the principal's suggestion that Mike start a multiracial student organization at the high school so that students could connect with one another and share strategies for coping with social, personal, and academic questions about identity.

Mike was sensitive to the notion of mixed race people as somehow disadvantaged or "messed up." He replied to the posting about my study in part because he "wanted to make sure that you aren't just getting the messed up side—the people who hate their parents or themselves because they're not just one thing." He said,

> I think mixed kids are the most unique group of people. I'm not saying that we're better than anybody, I'm just saying that we're unique. And so, yeah, I heard about this research that you're conducting and I thought, "Well, if this is not an opportunity, then I don't think I'll ever get another one, so let's jump in and see where it goes." I would like to do it because I think biracial people bring a lot to the table and to society as a whole.

Moreover, Mike acknowledged the challenges of being outside the monoracial norm. Noticing an article on my desk entitled "Biracial Identity: Asset or Handicap" (Pinderhughes, 1995), he said,

"Asset or handicap?" "Asset or handicap?" Good, there's already a question mark there. It's an asset because I can speak Spanish and I'm schooled in a lot of different cultures. But I think it's a handicap as I'm not always comfortable with my own identity. Then again, that makes me get out and learn about other cultures, so that's an asset again.

Looking through other articles, he said, "Yeah. Here we go right here, mulatto, that would be me. And half-breed. I got that one growing up, too." He read, "'Mixed race persons have always had an ambiguous ethnic identity to resolve.' So we've had a problem all our lives then? I guess it's true, though. I've had problems all my life." Most recently, the news that his mother was of Puerto Rican heritage had thrown Mike a curve ball.

Now I would like to know for sure what I am, because I hope to meet some young lady that would have my kids some day and then I'll be able to tell them, "Hey, this is what your dad was." Without a question, I think that's like my biggest hurdle right now. I need to know what it is I *really* am.

The quest to find out what he really was prompted Mike to respond to my recruiting flyer. He was working on a paper about biraciality for a class, and when he saw the flyer he contacted me to see if I might have some resources for his project. He volunteered as a participant, and I shared bibliographies, articles, and books with him. When I told him that I planned to write about the experiences of mixed race students, he said, "That I want to see. Because I'm gonna publish—I'm going to publish something one day. Maybe about being mixed. Or maybe just about being Mike."

AUDREY

I think that for me, for a while, it was kind of hard for me to find a place where I felt that I was welcomed in. Because being a multiracial student, you really either have to find your own identity or confirm someone else's identity. . . . I think being multiracial has a lot to do with yourself, and how you want to live your life, and how you identify yourself. For me, I consider myself multiracial.

Audrey was born in Grenada and immigrated to the United States when she was five. She said, "My background is very diverse. My mom actually, is also biracial. She is Irish and her mother is African and Chinese. My dad is Scottish and English. So I'm quite a mix!" The family moved to mid-state New York, where Audrey attended predominantly white public schools prior to choosing Liberal Arts College for her higher education.

At Liberal Arts, Audrey was dual majoring in international relations and music, with a minor in theater, "or maybe I.R. with a dual minor in Music and in Theater." A sophomore when I met her, she had time yet to decide.

Audrey was deeply involved with an a cappella singing group, theater performances, and the campus Christian Fellowship. She identified as a Pentecostal Christian and relied on her peers to help her "not be tempted by the drinking and stuff on the weekends." Audrey found for the most part that it was easy to move among peer groups on campus, though she said, "There may be tension between races, but not between white and black or asian and whatever. Maybe differences between or conflicts between asians, or like african americans, but not really across the board."

Audrey believed that her Caribbean background influenced her way of understanding differences. "I think from being in Grenada, I really see things of culture, not necessarily of race. In America, it's totally switched around where race is more focused on, then the culture." To Audrey, the campus environment was best seen through a lens of culture rather than race. She said, "I think a lot of things that people consider race are more cultural differences than race differences. And I think they have a problem drawing the line between that." Nevertheless, Audrey understood how racial categories operated in the United States and the power that racial group membership had on and off campus.

> It was really weird for me coming here to America and seeing that people behaved very weirdly, and differently, and a lot of times, negatively, to people of a different race. I remember one time we went to this festival. And this man came up to my father and said, "What beautiful kids!" And my dad said, "Thank you." And the man looked at me and said, "Oh, is that your maid?" (laugh) And he was stunned like he couldn't believe, like I could be this white man's daughter! So it was kind of weird for a while.

Audrey made it through the "weirdness" of the transition but retained her strong emphasis on culture rather than racial categories.

Like B. J. and other women with black heritage who participated in the study, Audrey encountered some resistance from black students to her participation in the black student community, and she discussed this as a matter of intragroup bias.

> I really haven't had a big problem in african american communities, not necessarily at Liberal Arts, but just in general. There is a problem within different shades of colors within a group, and that's too bad because there is a lot that we can learn from each other. But it's hard to really try and forget those differences if people keep on bringing them up and making you feel self-conscious because your father is white and your mother is black.
>
> So for me, I even sometimes felt like an outcast from the black community. Not necessarily an outcast, but not necessarily part of the group. And then I felt the caucasian community could be more welcoming towards me because, especially like at Liberal Arts, people are more anxious to get

to know people of different backgrounds. And that's not to say that blacks don't do that. But I think that some of them have a tendency to think, "You don't know where I'm coming from because you're not of the same shade as I am." That shouldn't be a factor, but it is, and that's how some people think.

Audrey's experience of this phenomenon as not a "big problem" and her experience of the white community as being especially interested in welcoming her were somewhat unique among the sample. She attributed some of these experiences to her strong connections in the singing group, the Department of Music and Theater, and the Christian Fellowship; these tight knit groups were not based on culture *or* race and provided significant microsystems where the focus of activity was on other aspects of identity (e.g., performer, Christian).

When she did identify herself in terms of her race, Audrey identified primarily as multiracial. Like Jonathon, she viewed this identity as one that could include identification with specific heritage groups, although she generally chose not to delineate hers.

> I think that most multiracial people, and this is fine, they decide what they did to define themselves a certain way. Perhaps if they're mixed asian-white they want to identify themselves as asian. Which is fine! But just with me, I don't feel comfortable deciding which part of my identity that I'm going to emphasize. I'm both, and I really can't specify, I can't really say, "I'm totally going to be in the [Black Students Alliance]." It's hard to really say "Oh, I belong with this set or group of people," or "I belong with the other half of my friends," these other people. I don't like doing that. I don't like to choose. I wish there was a multiracial group on campus. I think I would probably feel I fit in more there than anything else.

And yet Audrey felt strongly that she "fit in" at Liberal Arts. She had very close relationships with peers and faculty; indeed, she was one of the very few students who spontaneously discussed faculty without being prompted to do so. Although there was no formal or informal multiracial space on campus, either through a student organization or informal student network, Audrey found other important microsystems that supported and even welcomed her multiracial identity.

THE ECOLOGY OF MULTIRACIAL IDENTITY

Although B. J., Jonathon, Mike, and Audrey are of different heritages, attend different institutions, and have very different interests, they share a common sense of identity. They are biracial, multiracial, or mixed. What leads a student to identify in this pattern? Interactions between personal characteristics and the environment strongly influence multiracial identification. Some students had not considered this identity until coming to college; others, like Jonathon, had already done significant exploration of the construction of multiracial identity before they finished high school. The concepts of 'peer culture' and 'space' play a role in this identification, as do developmentally instigative characteristics.

PERSONAL CHARACTERISTICS

As in the Monoracial Identity and Multiple Monoracial Identities patterns, personal characteristics played a major role in students' choice of the Multiracial Identity pattern. Operating outside the assumption of monoraciality, however, some different personal characteristics were salient in identification as mixed, biracial, or multiracial. Cultural knowledge, so important to students' ability to feel comfortable in monoracial identity spaces, played little role in Multiracial Identity, but appearance was still important, as were developmentally instigative characteristics related to self-labeling and persistence in identifying outside the monoracial norm. Family support for a mixed identity was important, and a characteristic related to students' ideas about race and mixed race emerged as important in students' multiracial identities.

Physical Appearance

Just as physical appearance influenced students' identification with a monoracial heritage, it influenced their identification as multiracial. For some students, it was a matter of looking too "ethnic" to identify as white, yet not solidly in any particular racial or ethnic group. Tim responded,

> I'd say I'm biracial or hispanic. Like I don't ever think of myself as just white, because I don't look that way. But I also don't look just hispanic, either. So people always ask. And I say I'm biracial, with hispanic and white. Most of the time that's what I say and how I feel.

Jeff said, "And also, how I look, it's interesting. People aren't sure what I am!" So he made a point to let them know he was hapa. Christina, too identified as mixed, "When people ask me what I am I identify as multiracial, for a number of reasons. The main reason is how I look." Eleanor, when explaining why she primarily identified as black, said,

> I'm a little shaky on that because I can identify myself as biracial, but walking down the street no one's gonna be like "Oh, there's that biracial girl." You know, they still could call me nigger, they still could be writing that on my dorm door [in reference to racist graffiti on her memo board in the residence hall]. Calling myself biracial didn't make me any different or any better, and in some sense, people hate me even more for that because, I whatever, like I unpurified the races or something.

Tim, Jeff, Christina, and Eleanor identified differently, but all were influenced by their appearance in coming to private and public identifications.

A number of students in the sample described how they could recognize another mixed student, and sometimes a shared recognition created a bond between them. Though sometimes leading to direct communication about mixed identity, often this was a tacit phenomenon. Summer met her boyfriend during her study abroad program in Japan.

> I met my boyfriend there who's half-Japanese and he goes to Brigham Young, and we just, I think right away had an immediate bond. He's like, "You're half, aren't you?" I was like, "Yeah, you're half too." He's like, "Yeah." You just notice. I'm always noticing people that are half, like rarely on TV do they have them, but if I'm walking down the street, I'll always mention it. And now my friends are like, "Hey, Summer, I think that girl's half." They know because of me, and they think it's cool, and so it's kind of weird.

Christina said that she would respond differently about her identity to someone who looked mixed rather than monoracial:

> For example, if I'd never met you before and you were looking at me like "God, what are you?" I probably wouldn't even answer your question, or I'd dismiss you. But if somebody that I know, specifically if another person that I know is mixed or I think looks mixed asks me, cause they're looking for a sense of like affirmation, it's a bond that we would have with one another, I would say, "I'm mixed, my mother's Indian-Jamaican and my father's white."

Phil was trying to start a group for mixed race students at Catholic University, and though he was a bit hesitant to approach them directly based solely on appearance, occasionally he would strike up a conversation. He said,

> I've seen a lot of people around here. I haven't actually walked up to them and said, "Hey, you're mixed!" but you can pretty much tell. So I've talked to some and we're like "there should be a group for that," and I've always kind of wanted to do something like this. But I've never really had enough people. Now there are.

At Ivy, Jeff and a hapa friend wished that they could recruit for Spectrum, the organization of multiracial students, by approaching people they saw. He joked during the interview, "I don't go to people, 'You look mixed,' but I think they do. We talk about this all the time. We're like, 'You should go [to Spectrum]. You really should go. We should talk about this. But we can't tell you to do that, you've got to find it for yourself.'"

Christina described a downside to the easy recognition and visual bond shared by mixed race students.

> How you look plays a huge, huge part of being mixed, about how you identify. If someone turns out looking very monoracially towards the ethnic side, it's much easier for them to identify [monoracially with that ethnicity]. And

the flip side of that is that the multiracial community might be more reti-
cent to accept them cause they don't look like typically mixed, you know.
Yeah, it gets scary when you think about identity politics reproducing itself
in the mixed community, but unfortunately it does.

These identity politics were in particular evidence at Christina's college, Ivy,
where multiracial students had worked hard to create their own space within
the Third World community. Later in the chapter I discuss the microsystem
comprised by Spectrum and how it operated to create a space within the
mesosystem of peer culture. For better or for worse, a belief that they could
recognize other mixed students was common among participants, and for the
most part it provided a sense of belonging, even if to a silent network of
mixed peers.

Gender

The role of gender as a personal characteristic in multiracial identification is
complex. As a social construction, gender is both a personal trait and an
environmentally sensitive identity influenced by sociocultural norms,
appearance, and individual interpretations of behavior and attitudes. I discuss
it here with other personal characteristics because it informs later discussions
of micro- and mesosystem influences on identity. In earlier chapters, gendered differences have appeared in students' ability to fit in with monoracial
student groups, particularly in relation to mixed black women and their
monoracial black female peers. Sociologist Kerry Ann Rockquemore (2002)
examined this phenomenon through a symbolic interactionist theoretical
framework, concluding:

> The definition of "Black" is becoming progressively more fluid and "bira-
> cial" is increasingly viewed as a legitimate category of self-identification. . . .
> Social experiences of race are fundamentally gendered because they occur
> within the cultural valuation of white-defined beauty and a patriarchal
> structure of mate selection. Because of the scarcity of marriageable Black
> men and the high probability that educated and affluent Black men will
> marry white women, the interpersonal tension between Black and biracial
> women currently runs high. That tension, at a time when multiracial peo-
> ple have identity options, has created a push factor for many biracial
> women, effectively driving them away from a Black identity and toward an
> exclusively biracial identity. (p. 498)

Although my data do not fully match those from which she drew these conclusions, the notion of gendered construction of mixed race identity did come
across among women of all heritage groups in my study.

   Students themselves offered a variety of experiences and explanations
related to gender and multiracial identity, positing sharper effects for women

than for men. Some of these experiences and explanations were rooted in women's experiences of being excluded from monoracial communities on campus. For example, in the previous chapter I noted that Princess said,

> I never knew what I was doing wrong. Like even now, there's a room of the girls that live over on the other side of the dorm, and I'm still intimidated because I don't fit in with the urban attitude. I'm not hardcore enough and I don't have the jewelry and the nails, and I don't dress that way, I don't speak that way. So I think it's always going to be an issue with me as far as the black community. Guys are fine! They're like, "Hey, what's your name?" and blah, blah, blah. It's like, "Okay, I can handle them." But when it comes down to the black women, forget it.

Like B. J., whose older sister warned her that she might not "click" with the "full african american girls" and Renee, who encountered difficulty with black women at Rural Community College (chapter 4), Princess experienced the tension described by Rockquemore vis-à-vis black and biracial women.

Discussion of gender differences and mixed identity extended beyond exclusion from particular monoracial communities and included students' awareness of the gendered nature of exotification of the bodies of women of color. In response to a question about the emphasis on appearances in identity, Clarice, who had taken a number of women's studies courses in addition to her premedical requirements, noted:

> I think a lot of it has to do with the fact that, well, all women of color, but especially asian women and a lot of times Indian women with darker skin and dark hair, I think we're exoticized *a lot*. I think men don't really experience that a lot. I think there's a sort of mark placed on black men within the Indian community and within the white community as well, but other than that I don't think that men are really "tagged," and women are. Like men will be like "Ooh, I really dig asian chicks" and stuff. I don't think all people do it, I just think there are some that really, like they're "Oh, you're so beautiful, you're so exotic" or whatever, and I don't really understand that. Because beautiful is one thing, but if someone says that you're exotic, are they dating you because they want to date you? Or are they dating you because they want to see what it's like to date somebody who's asian or whatever? So I think that's why it's different from women. And female appearance is always more important in this culture. It's unfortunate, but—.

She went on to describe the ways that mixed asian women could be particularly appealing to some white men because they represented both the exotic and the familiar, "and they're not afraid of what their [the men's] mothers will think if they bring home a light skinned asian woman."

The premium placed on attractiveness permeated some women's personal identification, in ways similar to those described in the section on appearance, but in particularly gendered ways. Christina observed,

> Issues of exotification have been really central to me and to my development, in the way that I've been accepted and the way that people have dealt with me and issues, specifically in terms of attractiveness, not in terms of whether or not I thought I was attractive, but the way that other people were always telling me how attractive I was, and being very conscious of that because I have light eyes and because of my hair, like the "You have good hair" type of thing, not in the Indian community, but that's not my community, kind of, but in terms of the black and Latino communities. . . .
>
> I'm a huge secret fan of like terrible magazines like *Vogue, Elle,* and *Glamour,* and I got (laugh) *Seventeen* when I was growing up and always, it was so interesting that the only models of color were very light, and clearly fitting into this quote "racially ambiguous" category. So definitely appearances, and women's appearances in particular, have been personally based in my development.

Christina participated in a number of campus activities centered on gender as well as race (e.g., an organization of asian women operating out of the women's center rather than the Third World student center), and she made a documentary film about exotification of mixed race women, drawing attention to the role of appearance in the gendered construction of racial identity.

To my initial surprise—a surprise revealing my own biases about male student athletes—Steve, who had black and white heritages and played football at Big Ten, made similar observations about gender and its role in Multiracial Identity, though a bit less directly. He said, "My story, compared to my sister's, is a lot different. She caught a lot of stuff growing up. She had a number of run-ins with discrimination and stuff, where I haven't had as much." Asked to elaborate on the differences between his story and his sister's, Steve said:

> Yeah, I think she had it a lot rougher. She had a lot of run-ins. Like, she's had money thrown at her, people following her, name calling, everything. She's been through all of it. She's a lot lighter skinned than me. There's this big stigma with women with really light skin and darker colored females—we actually talked about it in my class last year. So I don't know if people know about it a whole lot, but from what I've experienced, it does hold true. And some [black] females really do take back at that because they feel like [mixed women] think they're better than them and that. And it goes all the way back to slavery and stuff like that and being in the house and everything. And there's different stigmas about it and people just take into offense the different cultures for the wrong reasons. And then with caucasian females, I don't know if they portray [mixed women] as trying to be

white, or trying to pass as white, so from both ends [my sister's] caught stuff, but it's been more on the caucasian end.

I feel kind of bad, because half the stuff she went through, I'm like, "Man, that's just ridiculous." You can't even grow up without having somebody ridicule you because of what color you are? That's just ridiculous. And she's a very race sensitive person, so for her, this topic really goes to her heart because she's had experiences with it, whereas for me, I can just blow it off, cause it really doesn't make any different to me cause I could care less about what someone else thinks. They want to think negative or positive, that's on them. I'm still going to be who I am and I'm still going to like myself, so whatever. But with her, I think that's had a big, a big view on her ideals and the way she views things now. It really has affected her whole viewpoint on society and everything. And that's too bad, because that shouldn't have happened. A lot of things shouldn't have happened at all.

Steve conceded that some of his immunity from color-based "ridicule" might have been related to his physical size and athletic ability ("Well, yeah. Not too many people mess with me."), but these traits were clearly linked to his gender as well. Steve's analysis of gender and racial identity did not include the sophisticated language of exotification and identity construction, but he was describing the same phenomenon that Clarice and Christina were. Other men were less descriptive, but Mike noted, "Yeah, guys can get away with being mixed where it's harder for girls," and Tim said, "I guess some girls have it worse, being called names and stuff, but for me it's been mostly fine."

Focus groups (all gender mixed) on three campuses spontaneously raised the issue of gender and multiracial identity, with a consensus in each and among the three that women were more pressured than were men to identify in certain ways based on appearances. Skin tone, hair texture, and eye color were specifically cited as contributing to this effect. There was, however, no agreement about the extent of this effect on women's identities, with women weighing in that they felt "really influenced by how other girls accept me," "pretty much free from that now, but it wasn't always this way," and "sometimes I feel it more than others, it depends on who I'm with and how confident I'm feeling that day." These comments reflect a range of developmentally instigative traits related to individual proclivities and abilities to identify and self-define independent of others' opinions. Gender, like personal history and family, was a personal characteristic in interaction with these developmental traits.

Developmentally Instigative Characteristics

Developmentally instigative characteristics of students in the Multiracial Identity category were as varied as the fifty students themselves. One that they shared with the other six study participants was some curiosity about or interest in contributing to research about "bi- and multiracial college students," as my recruiting flyer, letters, announcements, and email messages indicated. Curiosity led many of them to ask about the study and my interest in it as well as about my appearance and identity (both white). When I asked them why they responded to the recruiting materials, many responded in terms of wanting to make sure that people heard their stories and that mixed race students would not be portrayed as maladjusted misfits. Several were social science majors and wanted to contribute to research, and others had done or were doing their own research on issues related to multiraciality and were interested in seeing what I could share with them from my own research. Students' motivation to engage with me in the study represents one developmentally instigative characteristic, but there were others.

As described in the previous chapter, the degree to which students in this identity pattern felt the need and ability to self-label was a characteristic that led to their Multiracial Identity. While it may be difficult for mixed race students to feel authentic in their claim to a monoracial identity, it may be just as difficult for them to claim an identity outside the monoracial norm that exists in U.S. society and on college campuses. Students in this pattern did not, as I stated earlier, agree on what that identity should be called. For Julia, "When I think of my minority-ness, I think of being biracial, rather than what it specifically is." Delores said, "I would say I have a multiracial identity. There's never been a time when I thought or when I answered someone just 'black' or 'white.' So I would definitely say multiracial identity." Julia and Delores's self-labels seem simple enough, but Sina varied hers a bit depending on the context:

> When I'm in the community of color, I talk about being biracial and how that seems to be the most valid, realistic category for me to put myself in because that's where my interests lie in the community of color at Ivy. But when I talk with someone who is Hawaiian, I'll say, "Hey, I'm hapa, part Samoan."

Stacey called herself a "multiracial bisexual feminist" of white and Filipina heritage. As a child, she had combined "American" (as a synonym for "white") and "Filipino" into "Ameripino," a term she still enjoyed privately.

Some terms were contentious, with different interpretations among the participants. Florence's father filled out multiple races on the census form, prompting her to do so as well.

> And it just seems to be more comfortable to me, not just to close myself off from all things and just focus on one thing, I like to think of myself as *everything*. A mutt. That's what I name myself. I'm a mutt. So that's what it is.

Florence was comfortable, even playful, calling herself a "mutt," but other students reacted strongly against the term. Stacey said,

> Oh, it makes me really angry. I get some people who say, "Oh, so you're a mutt." I got that the other day, and actually it was somebody I'm kind of friends with. And I said, "Well, you know, that's a really derogatory thing to say to me. First of all you shouldn't refer to somebody as a mutt. Second of all, it's really derogatory toward biracial and multiracial people."

The terms *mulatto* and *mulatta* drew similar mixed reactions from participants, with most finding the terms derogatory rather than empowering.

Many students recognized the many ways that mixed race people identified themselves, some like Jonathon citing Maria Root's (1996a) "Bill of Rights for Racially Mixed People." They also recognized that mixed people might identify differently in different situations and that situational identity was inherent in being multiracial. Kimlien described a student organization meeting where they discussed "how people identify themselves now and how they identified before. Like, before I identified as Vietnamese and French and now I identify as hapa." An inclination to claim a mixed, biracial, multiracial, or hapa label was an important developmental instigator for students in this identity pattern, and the ways that this inclination interacted with college micro- and mesosystems will become more clear later in the chapter.

Another important characteristic was students' inclination toward or avoidance of identity self-exploration. This trait led to students putting themselves in new settings, like Ellen, who joined a multicultural performance group at Rural Community College and learned that she could be accepted as Mexican, black, native american, *and* multiracial. This trait also led to students avoiding certain identity-based settings, like Dwayne, who shied away from all-black social events at Rural University, because, "I'm not a brother. They know it, I know it, and I'm cool with that. I'm mixed and I have my own group to hang with—some kids from different races, guys and girls."

David's identity journey was a conscious one, driven both by his desire to explore his heritage and by his need to be in a context where the majority of the population was not white. Like Summer and Dee Dee, he decided to study abroad, though he explained his decision as being about his identity rather than a particular academic focus.

> Last year to kind of explore my ethnic identity I went abroad. Also to kind of escape the racism—the daily psychological drain it is to be, at least for me, different. It was nice for me, I guess I passed [as Japanese]. Like people didn't stare at me on the street, so it was kind of nice.

David's year in Japan was part of a larger process of finding a space to be at home.

> Probably one of the bigger issues in my life is finding a place where I feel comfortable. Cause I found that in Japan. You'd think I wouldn't because I'm not Japanese, I'm hapa, but I was really, really more accepted there.

But, yeah, for the first time I could just think about the ordinary, everyday kinds of things. And now I come back and I start thinking about a job and my future here, and I'm a senior and that's natural, but also I don't have to worry about my existence any more, or justify an existence or fight to create a space for myself, because I felt like I found that, and I'm more settled and relaxed. So that's informed the way I've thought about race issues and identity.

It is certainly true that any student of color at a predominantly white university might want to study abroad in a country where he or she looks like most of the population. For David, though, there seemed to be a more existential question behind his decision to go abroad and his experiences there and when he returned. He had found "a space for [him]self" and was "more relaxed and settled," which created new ways for him to think about race and identity. David's developmentally instigative traits led him to study abroad, but at a deeper level, they also provided an impetus to explore identity and the meaning of being hapa in the United States. Like the inclination to self-label, the inclination to explore identity is a personal characteristic that interacts with the developmental ecology to promote or inhibit identity development in the five patterns.

Family Support

Family support is another important personal characteristic. Each of the fifty students in this identity pattern had a unique family background, and each family dealt with issues of bi- and multiraciality in a different way. Fundamentally, though, what the students shared was the experience of growing up mixed race in interracial families, no matter what the specific heritage combination or parental/sibling configuration. Even Mike, who grew up in foster homes and was adopted as a young teenager, shared this experience.

Most students (thirty-seven) had one white parent and one monoracial parent of color. For them, being mixed was about being different from each of their parents, but it was also about being a person of color with a white mother or father, a situation highlighted in Audrey's portrait when a stranger asked her white father if she was the family maid. Some parents addressed the issue directly with their mixed children. Julia said,

> When I was little, my parents were so worried about my sisters and me, about us fitting in. And as far back as I can remember, they were always telling us, "Hey, it's okay that you're biracial. You're friends might think it's weird or stuff like that, but it's really okay, because we love you."

Apparently the parental message sunk in, because Julia told the story of exploding in anger at being asked, "Are you biracial?" by another girl, only to have the other girl respond, "I am too!"

Other students addressed this issue directly with their parents. Eleanor interviewed her mother for a paper on "white mothers, black daughters, and raising the biracial child. She's been really supportive." Kayla discussed her identity with her mother but had a less supportive response to her choice of self-labels.

> She thinks it's kind of funny how I refer to myself as a mixed-race individual. Like the idea of being mixed she thinks of like a dog-breed term or something. . . . At Thanksgiving my cousin said, "I think I'm more of a mixed breed." And my mom said, "Oh there you go again with all that mixed stuff. Kayla talks about that all the time." And I said, "Well, I like that term because 'half' makes you wonder where's the other half, so I think mixed is more appropriate, and it's more accurate to like how people grow up and stuff." And she said some weird thing to me, I can't remember what it was. And I said, "Well, what did you think when you married dad?" And she said, "I thought, 'I'm a woman. He's a man. We'll have kids. They'll either be boys or girls.'" And I was like, "Mom, don't you think that's just a little naïve?" (laugh) And she was like, "No." But I think a lot of it has to do with the fact that a lot of her ideas about race came from the 60s.

Whether or not Kayla's mother was being "naïve" about having biracial children, Kayla found support for her mixed identity among others in her generation who shared her multiracial identity within the context of a family of Hindu Indians who married people of different backgrounds.

In a similar way, Mina's parents were supportive of her learning about both parts of her heritage, but they seemed to miss the point about a specifically biracial identity.

> My parents were pretty good about helping me be both. But they don't really understand that I'm also something different. I'm not like either of them, really. I talk about this with my little sister, and she calls herself Amerindian—like American and Indian together. I think that that's a little confusing with native american Indians, but I see her point. We're something different, something blended, something new.

Being "something new" was important to Mina's identity, and sharing the exploration of identity with her sister provided an important touchstone for Mina herself. While they would choose different self-labels, they both recognized something that their parents did not. B. J.'s description of how her older sister attempted to prepare her for the realities of campus life for african american mixed women seemed similar, in that a sibling who might have a very different appearance, experience, and orientation toward identity still was able to provide some perspective that monoracial parents cannot. Several other students like B. J., who had two monoracial parents of color, relied on siblings to help locate a multiracial identity option, though their experiences did not include the additional issue of being a person of color with a white parent.

Beyond identity and self-labeling, there was another aspect of family life that a number of students raised. It was the stereotype of interracial marriages as doomed to fail by a society not eager to lose the perception of crisp boundaries between races. Steve, one of the two students to identify only as multiracial (i.e., he did not identify in the other identity patterns), felt strongly about this issue. When I asked at the end of the interview, as I did as a standard practice, if there was anything I had not asked about that he thought I should know about him, his identity, or his experience before or at Big Ten, he said,

> Okay, one question I got all the time when I was growing up, I got it from a lot of teachers and stuff, too, they would always ask if my parents were still together. And I wondered if you'd ever come across that or anything.

As it happened, the majority of participants came from families with their biological parents still married to one another, a circumstance I considered unusual given divorce patterns in general.[2]

> I find that amazing. Cause I used to always get asked when I was little, and it didn't really hit me until I got older, and I'm thinking, "Why do people always ask *me?*" I see other mixed people and ask them if they get the same thing, if they've ever gotten that question and they're like, "Yeah, yeah, yeah." And I just find that awkward or weird. And so I started to think, "Alright, it's not supposed to work." Very interesting.

Steve managed not to internalize the message that Eleanor expressed ("I unpurified the races or something") and was annoyed by, rather than acquiescent to, the idea that his parents' marriage was "not supposed to work." Messages about interracial relationships and the consequently mixed race children were not always negative; there was some reporting of parents espousing the "rainbow baby" ethos of certain subcultures in the 1960s and 1970s. But Steve's concern that there is a stereotype that interracial marriages will not last was shared by many participants, including those who anticipated their own partnerships and marriages and wondered how they could possibly *not* be "interracial."

Ideas about Multiracial Identity

A personal characteristic that bears noting in this chapter relates to students' ideas about multiracial identity. What did each of them think it meant to be multiracial? Was it a positive, negative, or neutral identity choice? And what were the possibilities on campus for community building among mixed race students from different backgrounds? As with other personal characteristics, the fifty students in this identity pattern differed in their ideas about multiracial identity, though they each subscribed to it at least some of the time.

Students described multiracial identity in many positive terms, echoing the "Advantaged" standpoint described in chapter 1. At Rural Community College, Rhonda said:

> And being mixed is kind of fun, like being one and the other and then some. I kind of feel like I can bridge across from the white side to the black side, like maybe I can see things that other people can't because they can only look from their side.

B. J. found that her mixed identity provided a way to connect with other students:

> I think a lot of people are amazed when you tell them you're multiracial. They're like, "Oh really? What, what, what?" So I think it's pretty neat how people are still interested in what you are and stuff like that. I've just met so many different multiracial students, it's really amazing.

And Luz, a modern culture and media major at Ivy observed that "in terms of media and stuff, biracial people are really chic, they're becoming more and more stylish. You can read those things in so many ways, as empowerment or co-optation or exotification, or I guess it's kind of both." Although Luz was not sure whether being "really chic" was ultimately a good or bad thing for biracial people, she was clear that it was good to see more mixed people in the media.

Steve saw his "multicultural" identity as an entrée to educate other students, one potential element of an advantaged perspective.

> Mixed students, they pretty much form friends with everybody. I've never seen a clan of mixed people (laugh), never. They just hang out with any and everybody. That's one of the things about being multicultural, I guess cause you're different, people are interested in who you are and what you know. And so, it is sort of an attraction to a lot of people. Most people had never seen a lot of mixed people—or like any—and so they see me and, they'll ask, "Where are you from?" and everything and I tell them, and then they just ask different questions. And I have a lot of friends, they don't want to be or sound racist, so they'll ask me questions, cause they know I'm open about it and I'll give them my honest opinions, so they ask me stuff all the time. And I don't mind it. I'd rather have them do that than ignorantly go into a conversation or approach someone and say the wrong thing.

The idea that he could be helping his friends by teaching them something about race or racial differences was appealing to Steve, and he recognized his opportunity to help his friends not "be or sound racist." As a football player and strong student at Big Ten, Steve's idea that multiracial identity was a means to educate others put him in a position to influence a wide range of peers.

Although Steve had "never seen a clan of mixed people," certainly there were formal and informal groups of mixed race students on each campus except perhaps Liberal Arts, which may have lacked a critical mass. Ivy and Big Ten had formal student organizations at the time of the interviews, and Catholic was on the verge of starting one. No organizations existed or were on the horizon at Liberal Arts, Rural Community College, or Rural University. Nevertheless, informal peer groups and friendship groups of mixed students congregated everywhere but, apparently, Liberal Arts.

Two distinct philosophies emerged about such groupings. The first held that there was enough in common just in the experience of being mixed, no matter what the heritages, to justify forming and maintaining these groups. As he was working to start the group at Catholic University, Phil said,

> [My friend and I] were saying how we realize that being half-asian we'd probably had much different experiences as someone who is half-black. I don't know. But overall I think the same similar experiences we can relate to, if not the specifics of it, just whether you're half-asian or half-black or half-hispanic, just being involved with different ethnic groups, you're always scared that people aren't entirely accepting of you, like especially when you walk through the door and people look at you like, "Hey, you're not Chinese. You're not whatever." That sort of thing is going to happen to everyone. And no matter how they try to deal with it, or if they haven't had to deal with it, they've always had experiences that are similar. And then even if they haven't always felt like they were different. I don't know. It's kind of weird. Cause we're not minority, but we're not mainstream.

Phil acknowledged fundamental differences in experience but believed that what was held in common was greater than what was unique.

Sina represented the second philosophy about groups for multiracial people. She found that a Spectrum meeting at Ivy did not meet her all of her needs, "I'm frustrated because we don't really share like a common culture, you know? So that's a frustrating situation to be in." She ultimately decided it was a useful experience, saying, "But we do talk about like what we all go through being marginalized people or whatever. So it's really a good space." Balancing times to explore the commonalities of mixed experience and opportunities for exploration of unique issues for specific heritage groups ultimately seemed to satisfy most students.

Personal characteristics, appearance, propensity to explore mixed identity and its possibilities, and ideas about multiraciality were important ingredients in students' identification in the Multiracial Identity pattern. Where these identities were enacted was in the everyday spaces students occupied on campus. The presence of individuals claiming mixed identity in turn influenced those spaces. In the next sections, I discuss the micro- and mesosystems where these interactions occurred.

MICROSYSTEMS

Students engaged the Multiracial Identity pattern in a variety of campus microsystems, including academic, peer group, and social settings. In some cases, microsystems provided a means to explore and assert identity; in others they served as challenges to self-definition and the legitimacy of the multiracial label. The propensity to seek multiple microsystems or to choose a smaller number contributed to students' experiences, as did the other developmental characteristics they brought to those settings.

Academic Microsystems

Academic microsystems formed an important location of identity exploration, challenge, and support. Classes such as one Florence took on race and ethnicity at Big Ten became venues for developing ideas about race and multiraciality. Florence wrote, "In that class, we got into heated discussions, because it was so much diversity and everyone had a different view on life. I would say that whole class made me more aware about myself and others, especially about race." In some cases, students were challenged directly or indirectly by peers or instructors to defend or justify interracial relationships and multiracial people. Eleanor's teaching assistant told her class section that the TA's "parents were racist and that as a result she'd never see having interracial relationships." Dave was asked how his parents could stay together when "Iran and the U.S. hate each other so much—as if they are their whole countries!" LuLu had a professor who "just kind of said it wasn't right, like a 'people should stick with their own kind' type of thing." Amy, who identified as "a mixed, disabled lesbian," had a classmate who implied during a class discussion that Amy's disability was the result of her parents' interracial marriage. She said,

> So he just comes out and says that I'm the way I am because of my parents going against natural laws or whatever, and the professor just kind of nodded her head and then moved on. I couldn't believe it. I just couldn't believe it.

Asked how she responded to the incident, Amy replied, "I was so stunned, and then the time was gone, but I did manage to get my piece in later when she called on me. I just took it back to this guy's comment and said he was wrong." Mike and Samantha were not called on to defend themselves directly, but they both described times at Rural University when an instructor divided the class into groups based on race for a classroom activity. Samantha said:

> Being biracial can sometimes get hard in the black community. Like not just how you look, like lighter or with different hair, but also in feeling like you're really part of the group. There was one class I took on race in America and we were talking about slavery and race mixing and how most black

people now have bits of white and native american in them anyway. And the professor—now, I think this was a bad idea—put us into sides of the class by black and white. So I'm picking up my books to move to the "black" side of the room, cause I'm figuring that I can't really stay on the "white" side, and this girl says, "You don't go over here, you go over *there*."

I was just standing there, wondering what to do when the professor says, "Okay, I have another idea. Let's get in one line by skin color, like lightest to darkest." I thought that was a bad idea, too. But we did it and it turned out I wasn't the only biracial person there. Once we lined up, he had us talk about our families and then it turned out that not all the "black" kids had just black parents. There were four of us, and we got to be our own group for the discussion. So now we have a little biracial crew, and when we're at BSA parties or whatever we say, "Hi" and have this kind of connection.

Whether dividing students into groups based on racial identity or skin color is appropriate or pedagogically sound, a number of other students also described similar activities, most often in "diversity training" or orientation activities. Unless a group is designated for mixed students, some are left in the untenable position of having to choose one heritage over others in order to participate in classroom activities.

In addition to times when they had to defend their identity or choose monoracial identities for academic purposes, students described times when they were able to use their identity to educate others. Kimlien took great pride in having introduced a professor to a favorite book on asian identity.

I really liked the teacher, and I introduced him to a book called *Accidental Asian* by Eric Liu. I read it when I was in high school, like I just happened to pick it up, and I introduced him to it, and he's using it this semester in his class. And he said, "I wanted to thank you for introducing me to this book." I'm like, "Well, I thought this might help you." Cause the books he had chosen were good, but they didn't really deal with the kind of issues he wanted to touch on, and this book really did. It talked about the asian-ness and the american-ness and when it's the right time to act your asian-ness and when it's the right time to act american, I guess you could say, and he really liked it. And everyone, he said, liked it, cause you know how sometimes you get some people who like it and some people who hate it, and he said everyone liked it. And I was like, "It's a good book." (laugh) I only wish I would have written it!

Kimlien's experience of reading the book, giving it to her instructor, having him like it and use it in class, where other students liked it validated not only Kimlien's identity but also her sense of her place in the academic world. From the book—and her professor's reaction—she knew that her experiences of moving between "asian-ness" and "american-ness" (remember her dilemma in choosing an outfit for the Vietnamese New Year party) were not unique and that others could learn from them.

Kimlien's closing line ("I only wish I would have written it!") echoed a theme first raised by Christina. In terms of biraciality, Christina said, "I've studied it both academically and socially, especially in terms of my friends, and kind of rediscovered what community meant to me through that." At Ivy, Christina took the course Growing up Ethnic and Multicultural, started a multiracial Group Independent Study Project (GISP, like Kira's in Tagalog) and made a documentary film about multiracial women's identities. Her faculty advisor provided motivation and inspiration.

> She's very, very tough, has very high standards, and is incredibly tough. But to see what she's studied and how that's an accepted area of the academy and just to see how intelligent she is. I'm really, really impressed with her writing. She's so intelligent and she knows her shit, like backwards and forwards. And so now I'm feeling like, "Okay, this is something I could do in graduate school."

Christina's coursework and independent study helped her, as she said, "figure out my niche in terms of academics."

> I want to go to graduate school, I want to get my Ph.D., and I want to be a professor. . . . And what I want to study in grad school, it's definitely personally based. It's almost me giving validity to it through studying it academically. It is a real topic: look, this book is written and I'm going to write a book too! (laugh)

Kimlien and Christina, as well as Jonathon, Mike, and other students who voiced similar interests in writing about the multiracial experience were following the call of philosopher Naomi Zack (1995) to "write themselves into existence."

> To write about one's mixed race identity is as much to invent oneself or one's racial group, as to describe them. One invents oneself, on paper, as part of a theoretical inquiry, because outside of one's activities as an intellectual, that is, outside of the life of the mind, one has no secure racial existence. Mixed race is not recognized as an identity or form of culture by those individuals—the majority—who believe they are racially pure. (Zack, 1995, p. 296)

"Inventing themselves" intellectually occurred through large-scale academic projects such as Christina's documentary and Jonathon's senior thesis. It also occurred through coursework specific to multiracial identity taken by May, Dwayne, Jennifer, Jeff, Vincent, and Kate. Course assignments provided this venue for about half of the fifty students in the Multiracial Identity pattern, including one particularly colorful example given by Jennifer, who wrote a paper entitled "What's for Dinner?" based on multiracial identity and food-related epithets directed at mixed people, such as "Oreo Cookie" and "Milkshake." These inventions of the multiracial self provided students with an intellectual means to find and build community. Reading books by and about mixed people, writing their own narrative and research papers, and sharing them with others helped to locate multiracial people as legitimate members of the academy. Academic microsystems thus provided important developmental presses and opportunities for mixed race students.

Social, Recreational, and Cocurricular Microsystems

Nonacademic settings were also important sources of developmental impetus. Two kinds that were particularly relevant for students in the Multiracial Identity patterns were those that were purposefully created for mixed race students (such as Spectrum at Ivy or Hapa at Big Ten) and those that provided a student's first opportunity to identify as multiracial. Students discussed other microsystems, including roommates and friendship groups, where their multiracial identities were either challenged or supported. I describe many of these microsystems in the following section, in the context of the mesosystem of peer culture.

Participants at Ivy and Big Ten could join formal organizations of multiracial students—Spectrum and Hapa, respectively. They described these groups as places where they felt like they belonged and could choose to identify themselves on their own terms. For some students, these groups were springboards for involvement in other student organizations in the community of color, and they sometimes served as "safe spaces" when students had negative experiences with monoracial students of color or white students.

Spectrum meetings typically started with students introducing themselves, as they did in the composite portrait of Kim in chapter 3. There was a general ethos that any identification was acceptable, a circumstance I experienced when I attended meetings as an observer and was asked to identify myself. Jeff said,

> You don't necessarily have to identify, like say if you are bi or multiracial and, if you are, saying, "I identify as bi or multiracial." You can identify purely as whatever you are. Like at the beginning we go around the circle and it's like, "Who are you? What's your name? And how do you identify?" And it doesn't matter what you say. You can say, "I am a person."

The activity of self-labeling acted as a catalyst for self-examination for Luz, who said, "In [Spectrum] people ask, 'Do you identify as one race or the other or do you identify as biracial as a race category?' And I think maybe I'm starting to identify as biracial—or even just generic American or something—rather than Filipino or Irish or something." Hapa meetings at Big Ten, too, included opportunities for students to describe their identities and to discuss the issue of self-labeling and its politics on campus.

In addition to being a space to self-identify, Spectrum and Hapa were spaces that provided a sense of belonging, a place to connect with others whose individual experiences might be different, but who shared the experience of being mixed on an ostensibly monoracial campus in an ostensibly monoracial nation. Christina said,

> First semester, freshman year I started going to Spectrum meetings and it was really exciting to know that there was a whole community of people that shared my experience, that thought about being multiracial, that had experiences just like mine, people that I *looked* like.

Returning from Japan, David wrote an article in the student newspaper, which drew very angry responses from others. Spectrum became a refuge.

> And so when I face something as a multiracial person, like getting attacked for being multiracial, it's weird. I stop and think. And then I think, "Oh, I'm glad there's a place like Spectrum," because I'm like, "Oh yeah, I face issues as a multiracial person that a monoracial person wouldn't face," at least on a personal basis. So, that's part of the nice thing, that they've given me a little bit of that consciousness, a little bit of that comfort zone to step back into when I'm facing some issues like that.

The "comfort zone" of Spectrum extended into other activities within the Third World student organizational infrastructure, including a Multiracial Heritage Week, a designated multiracial student activities programmer (there were programmers for monoracial categories), and opportunities to represent multiracial students at activities fairs and other events for students of color. Asked what he would say about Ivy University to a mixed race prospective student, David said, "Partly because of Spectrum, I'd say Ivy is a place where there's a space for everyone. There's a place for you to be comfortable at Ivy with who you are. I think that's the best thing. It's a place to feel comfortable."

The infrastructure at Big Ten was not so well developed, but Hapa was represented on the Asian Student Alliance (ASA) executive board, which provided access to networking and leadership development opportunities in the broader community of students of color. Phillip and Kimlien were involved at the executive level of Hapa and ASA. Kimlien said, "It's great because I get to work with everyone from the different groups and learn what's going on with them, too." Like Spectrum, Hapa was "a place where you can be who you want to be, without people questioning you," according to Kimlien.

Just as participants had different ideas about what it meant to be multiracial and whether or not the commonalities outweighed differences in individual heritages, not all students felt like the mixed student organization microsystems were universally positive. Though she was involved in Spectrum leadership and active as a biracial student in the Third World community at Ivy, Kira had some concerns about the concept of a multiracial community as enacted in Spectrum. She felt that the group sometimes exerted pressure on members to identify as bi- or multiracial, which she had not done prior to coming to college.

> I don't know how it was brought up, but there was just a discussion of how you identify as bi- or multiracial, and I guess I was just listening to other people's stories. They were mostly stories from home, and I just felt like I couldn't really identify with them. I hadn't met people before who really identified with being biracial or multiracial. I had met people before who were half-asian or half-white or half-latina, but not identified with that term.
>
> And also I knew that I belonged there. Like there was no questioning that I was biracial. I mean, questions of legitimacy or things like that. And there were other people who felt out of place sometimes too, just in general. So I felt at that time that I needed to assert myself as saying, "Well, there are these two sides of me that are equally important." I guess I've drawn away from Spectrum, just sort of because I've felt like I've already reached that point and I needed it less.

The tension between students expressing the Multiracial Identity pattern and Kira's expression of the Multiple Monoracial Identities pattern led her to feel "out of place" at Spectrum and she "needed it less" to support her emergent biracial identity. This story echoes Christina's statement about identity politics among multiracial individuals and Jonathon's reaction to being accused of forcing people to "hang multiracial." Identity politics and the politics of identification were very real to mixed race students at Ivy.

Identity politics had not yet emerged within Hapa at Big Ten, although there was concern with maintaining the group as hapa only (i.e., not inviting, though welcoming, students of nonasian mixed heritages). The informal network of students that was moving toward forming a multiracial student organization at Catholic University was also comprised of hapa students who had, as Phil, Summer, and Vincent suggested, recognized one another based on appearances and maintained a social connection. At Catholic, there was no talk of limiting the group to hapa students only, and when the group did get recognized (a year after data collection there), students of different heritage groups were involved.

While internal identity politics are a downside to multiracial student organizations, they play an important role as microsystems in creating a physical and psychic space for bi- and multiracial identification. Indeed, students cited them and other college microsystems as specific prompts to identity development. Kayla said,

I guess the first big catalyst to my self-growth was probably [preorientation for students of color]. That's the first time I had officially been part of any sort of institution that was geared towards people of color. And it was the first time I identified as biracial, the first time I was surrounded by a group of biracial and multiracial individuals. I had met a few here and there, but not all of them really even identified that way and I don't think I would have necessarily felt a connection with someone who was also multiracial or biracial and not my same background until coming to Ivy, because I didn't construct my identity in that way.

Even microsystems that were not designed specifically for mixed students acted as venues for them to meet one another. Before college, LuLu had seldom identified with her Chinese heritage or even as a person of color, but at Rural University, she said, "I've kind of done the minority thing, like joining NSMAH, the National Society of Minorities and Hospitality. And through meeting other kids who aren't just one thing I've started to think of myself as biracial or maybe bicultural more than anything else." LuLu's experience is not uncommon among students of color who grow up in predominantly white environments and immerse themselves in an identity-based community on campus. What is different, however, is that the presence of other mixed students in a microsystem and her interactions with them instigated her identity development as a biracial person. LuLu's personal characteristics influenced her development in interaction with the NSMAH microsystem.

Rarely does one microsystem determine identity outcomes. According to the ecology model, it is the interactions within the microsystems, and then their interactions with other microsystems (in the broader context of sociocultural macrosystems) that ultimately shapes developmental trajectories. These multiple microsystem interactions form the mesosystem of daily life and campus peer culture. Just as the mesosystem was deeply influential in the identities of students in the Monoracial Identity and Multiple Monoracial Identities patterns, it is a key factor in Multiracial Identity.

MESOSYSTEMS

Although students on a single campus may share elements of the mesosystem (e.g., a common set of microsystems), each has a uniquely configured mesosystem, comprised of interactions among an array of microsystems. For the students in the Multiracial Identity pattern, mesosystems held both the possibility and the desirability of a multiracial identity. Microsystems of formal and informal networks of mixed race students were important factors, as were academic settings and the people in them. For example, at Big Ten, Phillip encountered a number of prompts to his identity development; coming from multiple microsystems, these prompts gelled in the mesosystem as support for the development of his hapa identity.

Phillip transferred to Big Ten halfway through his first year of college. Living in a residence hall, he encountered a Minority Aide, who gave him information about Asian Student Alliance (ASA) and Filipino Alliance (FA) meetings. He said, "I had never been involved with anything asian diverse like that before, so I decided to go. And I enjoyed it and continued to go and got involved. I became an executive board member in both organizations the next fall." During his first year on campus, he noticed that there were

> A lot more hapas on campus who didn't come to ASA or FA, or their respective ethnic group meetings. So I thought maybe they weren't coming because they didn't feel welcomed or they didn't feel accepted, because sometimes I felt that way at FA, like I didn't understand the jokes a lot of the times and if people were speaking the language I didn't really understand it. So I thought maybe we should have a group for people like me, other people out there.

The residence hall microsystem led to involvement in the monoracial/monoethnic student organizations, which prompted a sense of belonging ("I enjoyed it and got involved") yet also prompted a sense of being different as a mixed race student.

The involvement of faculty/staff advisors was a significant prompt for Phillip's identity development and his campus involvement. Asked about how he came to identify as hapa after considering himself only Pilipino,[3] Phillip said,

> Through Doug Tingson [a pseudonym]. Last spring he was our advisor. So last spring I went to go see him. And he asked if I, cause I was telling him these feelings, like I wasn't feeling welcomed or I wasn't feeling that connected to everyone else, and he said, "Have you heard of the term hapa?" And there's the national Hapa Issues Forum, and he told me to go to that website, and I went to the website and learned a little bit more about it and stuff. I found out that all these famous people were hapa and I had no idea. So that's where I found out about it.

Phillip then had a name for his sense of mixed identity, and having thus come to call himself "hapa" he set out to form a student organization. Again, the influence of an advisor was evident in his development.

> I started Hapa last semester. It kind of got started in the spring with help from one of our FA advisors, Peter Yamamoto, he's in the [administrative] office and was a student here before that. He helped me with the constitution and just getting things started with that. And we registered it in the fall. I'm considered the founder because it's basically my thing and I've been, it's been basically my thing this whole year. Peter had always wanted to do it, but he had never gotten a chance to, so I did that.

Phillip's micro- and mesosystems expanded to include Doug and Peter, as well as student peers. Through the advisors, Phillip encountered developmental presses on which he acted, leading to a new self-defined identity and the founding of a student organization. But there were more identity-related elements in Phillip's environment.

Once formed, Hapa got "a lot of positive response from the community." Phillip said, "The APA community on campus thought it was a great thing to have. The response from other hapas was not that good. There were just some people that didn't care. They didn't feel the need or didn't want to come out. They were too busy or whatever." The first meeting of Hapa drew about thirty people, of whom Phillip estimated five were hapa; the others came to support the organization. Phillip and the other leaders persevered through the year and held a number of meetings, events, and activities, including a half-day conference about mixed identity called "Which Box Should I Check?" Hapa continued to receive support from the asian student community, which Phillip attributed to a belief that "everyone's a little hapa in some ways, just from being asian american, they have two cultures there, so lot of our topics they have a lot of feedback on too, about issues that do relate to them." The asian student community's acceptance of and support for Hapa affirmed Phillip's sense of his own hapa identity as part of a larger community of people of color and, in particular, asian americans.

The mesosystem that supported Phillip's identity development extended into the classroom as well. Doug, who was a graduate student and instructor, helped Phillip and other students set up an independent study class (like Ivy University's GISPs) on Filipinos and Filipino Americans that "we all take— or that most of us take to learn more about Pilipinos and where we come from and our culture." Phillip took a class on race and ethnicity with a Korean teaching assistant; the focus was largely on asian americans, creating another microsystem that supported Phillip's panasian identity. Phillip recalled one assignment particularly meaningful.

> The TA opened the class up to where people could speak on their own backgrounds—their racial and ethnic backgrounds. I had like 10 minutes to speak and I talked about being Pilipino and being hapa at the same time. And people had a lot of questions, and I really did feel like I educated people a lot. Like I didn't even know what hapa meant last year, so you know, I think people found out. It was a good way to do it.

Of course, as Phillip's environment was influencing him, he was also exerting an influence on it. Other students in his section of the course may have taken away new ideas about race and identity from Phillip's presentation and answers to their questions.

I provide these parts of Phillip's story as an example of the power of the mesosystem to influence Multiracial Identity. As his relationships and interactions unfolded across microsystems, Phillip was exposed to new ideas about race, culture, and identity. He took in some of these ideas and made them his own; he then acted on his environment by creating a space for hapa students at Big Ten, by joining an independent study group on Filipinos, and by talking about his identity in the race and ethnicity course. Extracurricular, social, and academic microsystems connect in the mesosystem to create a rich environment for Phillip's identity to develop.

The mesosystem of peer culture was not, however, universally supportive of Multiracial Identity. Study participants encountered negative reactions to asserting a mixed identity or just to the idea that they *were* mixed. At Ivy, a forum sponsored by Spectrum on the topic of interracial dating deteriorated into an attack on multiracial people. According to Kayla, "There was a lot of antagonism there. People were accusing other people of trying to quote 'escape their blackness' by identifying as biracial." Around the same time an article appeared in a campus-based african american newspaper; Sina described it and her reaction to it:

> Basically they were saying that the biracial category shouldn't exist because it was undermining other groups, specifically african american, and they didn't see any future for it in progressive politics. And also that biracial people are the result of relationships that are based on racism, so there shouldn't be interracial relationships. And reading that it was just like, "Boom! Boom!" or whatever. I get really frustrated with that. It's like saying some blond people are results of rape and they shouldn't exist, or since there's racism in relationships then they shouldn't date or whatever. It's literally throwing the baby out with the bath water. (laugh)

Through the peer culture mesosystem, Kayla and Sina were exposed to direct and indirect challenges to their chosen multiracial identities. Kayla experienced her peers' "antagonism," and Sina experienced these challenges as abrupt—"Boom! Boom!"—and confrontational, even when they came through written accounts.

Eleanor experienced a more gentle, though no less direct, message about the desirability of a biracial identity. During her first year at Ivy, she went with friends to an interracial dating forum.

> It was really important to me to have these black female friends, because I never really had black women who accepted me on the same level. So they were talking, and I'm sitting there with my two friends, and they're saying you needed two black parents to have a black child. That's what people had decided. And I was, you know, sitting there and I looked at them and they were like, "Oh, except you."

Eleanor went on to describe how disappointed she was that black women at an elite institution would not accept her as black. "And I had always had that from white students so then to get it from black students at Ivy, I was very hurt by all that, I had a fallout with those women." During Eleanor's first year the "Oh, except you" phenomenon propelled her to identify strongly with the black community, and she excelled in leadership and involvement in a number of activities for black students and black women in particular, causing her to say that she was seen by some on campus as a "closeted biracial," a term that did not fit with her self-definition as a biracial black woman.

Julia interpreted anti-interracial dating discussions as part of a larger culture in which monoracial students of color privileged their own needs over those of mixed students. In the context of the Third World community at Ivy, she said,

> A lot of times I feel like we're kind of pushed aside. Like thought of as, like we're just trying to find an excuse to be special and to have a special biracial community. And you're allowed, they'll say, "Yeah, it's okay for you to be that, but our issues and our needs come first." And okay, no one's going to argue. You can be black or you can be asian, all these kinds of things, and of course there's nothing wrong with that and if you say there is, you're a racist. But being biracial or multiracial, there's kind of moral value judgments in there about interracial dating and things like that. So it's like a totally separate thing.

The notion of multiracial identity as "a totally separate thing," distinct from monoracial identity because of the historically fraught nature of interracial relationships in the United States, highlighted the connections among microsystem interactions within particular organizations, mesosystem interactions among peer microsystems, and macrosystem factors related to the sociohistorical context of mixed race and interracial relationships in the late twentieth century.

The conflation of interracial relationships with biraciality was a common theme at Ivy, though it was not as common in the peer culture at the other institutions. Asked directly about this phenomenon, students replied that they did not think there was an "issue" with interracial dating, though they often did not know many people who were dating people of other races. Moreover, several students described their own dating relationships and the reactions they received from peers. Reactions ranged from neutral or positive (Ellen: "No, nobody says anything, and John fits right in with my black and Mexican friends.") to hostile (Clarice: "I brought my [white] boyfriend to an Indian students' party and people were just nasty to us."). A number of students commented on the necessity of "interracial" dating for mixed students, with Ellen noting, "If I sit around waiting for someone who's mixed just like me, I'm never going to get a date!" Responding to the prompt "Write about a time when you were aware of being multiracial," Kayla wrote:

In that terrible moment standing before the western wall in Jerusalem when [my boyfriend] suddenly informed me that being half-Jewish is an impossibility and demanded to know what I REALLY was. And I fell out of love with him forever.

For most participants, however, having a mixed identity was not a major factor in forming intimate relationships with monoracial individuals, though some noted that monoracial students were not always interested in being involved with individuals outside their own monoracial groups and, consequently, with mixed race students.

The peer culture mesosystem thus contained direct and indirect messages to students about the desirability of mixed race identity. Mixed students picked up the messages, both positive and negative, and were guided by individual traits to respond in various ways. For example, in response to the concern that increasing numbers of people identifying as multiracial would reduce the number of individuals counted as monoracial people of color, Julia said simply, "I don't feel like someone else should tell me what my identity should be just for your own political reasons." Though the peer culture mesosystem was unambiguous in its promonoracial messages, Julia resisted and remained strongly identified as biracial.

SUMMARY

Claiming multiracial, biracial, mixed, or hapa identity depended on the complex interaction of personal traits, microsystems, mesosystems, and larger environmental factors. The presence of a public multiracial space, either formal or informal, was both a prompt to identification in the Multiracial Identity pattern and an environmental resource (support) for identification in other patterns. These students—the overwhelming majority of a sample self-selected as "bi- or multiracial"—identified all, some, or part of the time in this pattern, an identity made available largely through sociocultural factors operating in the late twentieth and early twenty-first centuries. In the next chapter, I describe another pattern made available largely through sociocultural and intellectual factors as well. The notion of identity construction, and thus the choice to opt out of U.S. racial classifications or to deconstruct racial identity categories, emerged during most of the participants' lifetimes to become part of the intellectual landscape on their campuses.

chapter seven

I Don't Check Any Boxes—
Extraracial Identity

I just identify myself as being Jamaican, and then people say,
"[B]ut are you Black, what are you?" I just say "Jamaican." I am
what I am. I don't get into the specifics. Of course, applications all
say to check the little black box, but I don't really identify myself
as anything. I hate being called african american. I'm not American,
and granted way down the line I'm of African descent, but I don't
really identify with it or anything.

—Marisa

THIRTEEN STUDY PARTICIPANTS identified at times in the Extraracial
Identity pattern. Representing the least common identity pattern, these
students were like Jared, the composite portrait in chapter 3, in that at
least some of the time, they resisted identifying in U.S. racial categories
or with race-dependent terms such as *multiracial, biracial,* or even *hapa*.
This identity pattern was a tenuous one to hold in a world that relies
heavily on racial categories for social sense making. Students in this pattern called themselves by a variety of terms, including "hapa, biracial, or
multiracial," "mixed, mixed race, or multiracial," "none of the above,"
"Grenadan," "other," "just mixed," "of the human race," and as cited
above, "Jamaican."

In this chapter I describe the Extraracial Identity pattern, the students in
it, and the environmental influences that led some of them to this pattern. I
feature portraits of three students in this pattern to illustrate the complexity
of identifying outside the racialized norm of U.S. campuses.

CHARACTERISTICS OF THIS PATTERN

The thirteen students in the Extraracial Identity pattern were those who some or most of the time chose not to identify along the lines of U.S. racial categories as well as those who did not subscribe to the construction of racialized identities. Kilson (2001) called this a "raceless" identity, and Rockquemore and Brunsma (2002) called this a "transcendent" identity; in all three studies, a relatively small percentage of participants fit this identity pattern (23 percent in mine, 19 percent in Kilson's, and 13 percent in Rockquemore & Brunsma's). Differences among research samples and data collection and interpretation techniques explain much of the variation across the study findings; what is important to note, however, is that fewer students fit this identity pattern than any other. Also important is that no students identified exclusively in this pattern; they all identified in at least one other. Given the ubiquity of racial construction in the United States and on college campuses, it is not surprising that the majority of participants in these studies of racial identity do not see Extraracial Identity as either a viable or desirable identity pattern; attention to individual traits and peer culture is especially important in examining this identity pattern to see how some students came to identify this way.

TRENDS WITHIN THE PATTERN

Differences occurred in the Extraracial Identity pattern by gender, heritage combinations, class year, and institution. Only two men (10 percent) identified in this pattern, yet eleven women (31 percent) did so. The tendency for women to identify in more identity patterns than men (discussed in chapter 3) combined with the fact that every student in the Extraracial Identity pattern identified in at least one additional pattern could explain the greater number of women in this pattern than men; if being in this pattern meant also being in one—or more than one—additional pattern, then women were more likely than men to be here.

In terms of racial heritage, students with two parents of color or one white parent and one Pacific Islander parent were most likely (42 percent and 43 percent, respectively) to identify in this pattern, while students with one black and one white parent (8 percent) or one asian and one white parent (13 percent) were least likely to do so. This finding supports Rockquemore and Brunsma's (2002) findings for their black-white study population and may highlight the power of black-white race relations in the United States; to be mixed black and white does not necessarily lead to a conclusion that opting out of or deconstructing categories is possible or desirable.

Within this pattern, sharp distinctions arose by class year. Only one of fourteen first-year students (7 percent) fit this identity pattern, yet 45 percent

TABLE 7.1
Distribution of Students in the Extraracial Identity Pattern
by Gender, Heritage, Class Year, and Institution

		Total in sample	Identifying in this pattern
Gender	Men	20	2 (10%)
	Women	36	11 (31%)
Heritage	Two Parents of Color	12	5 (42%)
	One Asian & One White Parent	16	2 (13%)
	One Black & One White Parent	13	1 (8%)
	One Latino/a & One White Parent	5	1 (20%)
	One Pacific Islander & One White Parent	7	3 (43%)
	One Mixed & One White Parent	3	1 (33%)
Class Year	First Year	14	1 (7%)
	Sophomore	17	3 (18%)
	Junior	11	5 (45%)
	Senior	14	4 (29%)
Institution	Big Ten University	12	1 (8%)
	Catholic University	8	1 (13%)
	Ivy University	14	7 (50%)
	Liberal Arts College	8	2 (25%)
	Rural Community College	6	1 (17%)
	Rural University	8	1 (13%)
	TOTAL	56	13 (23%)

of juniors and 29 percent of seniors did so. Eighteen percent of students who were sophomores or in their second year of community college were in this pattern, filling the gap between first-year students and juniors. Finally, there were also distinctions by institution. Big Ten, Rural University, and Catholic University (8 percent, 13 percent, and 13 percent) had the smallest proportions of students in this pattern; Rural Community College and Liberal Arts had about the expected number (17 percent and 25 percent); but at Ivy, seven of fourteen (50 percent) students fit this identity pattern. These findings by class year and institution support the idea that exposure to academic and peer culture in college prompts new ways of thinking about race, culture, identity, and identity construction, an idea that will be more fully developed later in discussions of micro- and mesosystems.

PORTRAITS OF STUDENTS WHO CHOSE THIS PATTERN

AMY

> I guess since I'm outside *all* the boxes, for everything, I just started looking at what the boxes do, who they're for, and how you can get trapped by them. And I don't want to get trapped by someone else's boxes, so I won't do it. I won't play the game.

Amy came to Rural University from her small hometown in an isolated area of the southern Midwest. Her mother, who was white, had raised her alone after she separated from Amy's father, who was black. Amy had paraplegia and used a wheelchair, a circumstance that had not slowed her down as she prepared to finish a senior thesis and graduate with honors in her dual majors of English literature and education. When we first met, she had been admitted to a graduate program in education and planned to begin classes immediately after completing her bachelor's degree, "Yep, I graduate on Friday and start school again on Monday."

Amy described painful childhood experiences when others, usually adults, insinuated that her disability was the result of the "unnatural" pairing of her interracial parents. A church school teacher quoted Bible verses about "how damnation and hell and punishment on earth awaited those who violated the will of God, and how people shouldn't marry people who were different colors." A grade school classmate said that her mother told her that Amy was "crippled" by her parents' "going against God."

> Going against God? What kind of God would take out on a kid for what their parents did? And if we're all made in his image, then that means different colors and abilities, too. But if you really want to talk about going against God, then you have to know that I'm a "crippled lesbian kid of a crazy white woman and a black man." (laugh)

Amy joked about her identity as she imagined she was seen through the eyes of the conservative rural Christians among whom she was raised, resisting the notion that her physical ability or sexual orientation resulted from her mixed heritage.

Amy came out as lesbian after she entered college, though she described parallel processes between her racial identity and her sexual orientation identity.

> It was easier in some ways to come out and call myself lesbian or dyke or whatever because I already didn't fit into some image of what you're sup-

posed to be. I mean, once you're mixed and in a chair, what the hell? Who cares if you're a lesbian, too?

I've always been different—always been aware of the world not fitting into nice neat boxes. When I was in high school, I finally figured out it wasn't the world that was too messy, it was the boxes that were the problem. Like, I stopped checking off the race boxes and I stopped checking off the "single" or "married" boxes, too, because what if I'm not either? If I have a girlfriend, I'm not single and I'm not married. So in both ways I knew that the world was too messy and it was time to lose the boxes.

Asked what "losing the boxes" meant, Amy said, "Well, it's simple. I don't check the boxes and I don't make boxes for other people to check. I don't buy into the system that says the boxes are more important than the people in them." For Amy, the "system" she rejected was one that classified individuals based on their race, ability, and sexual orientation.

Although Amy rejected the classification system, she did say that she would describe herself as a "mixeddykeinachair, that's one word." The conflation of the labels *mixed, dyke,* and *in a chair* situated Amy not fully outside the constructions of race, sexuality, and ability. She described times when she would identify as mixed race, "usually depending on who I'm with. Like if it's good friends who are also mixed, then, yeah, I want to connect with them on that." The connection with others who shared her experience mattered to Amy, as did connections with other lesbian or gay students and students with disabilities. As a whole, though, Amy felt "one of a kind," asking, "How many other ones like me are there here, anyway?"

Amy described ways that Rural University helped her learn how to be "one of a kind" and outside the boxes. She took a course on disability studies that exposed her to ideas related to the construction of ability and disability in society, the media, and literature. She said:

And then I had a language for talking about not just my ability, but also about being mixed and about being lesbian. I realized that other people had been thinking about—and talking about and writing about—the same things as me. About how the ways we see ourselves and other people are affected by the scripts we carry in our heads about who we think they should be, mostly just based on how they look. Also about how we can consciously undo those scripts and quote-unquote "deconstruct" the categories of race, gender, ability, whatever. So I started writing more about that, and thinking about myself in relation to it.

Through the language of disability studies and postmodernism, Amy gained a tool to facilitate her approach to analyzing her lived experience. She *knew* she did not fit into the designated boxes, and she *knew* that she wanted to get rid of the boxes and what they represented, but before she took the course she lacked the cognitive tools and language that helped her to break out of the boxes and begin to dismantle the boxes themselves.

CHRISTINA

> The thing about multiracial identity is that it's such a strange construct on it's own. There are no set rules to go by, which is kind of the exciting thing about multiracial identity. And it has inherent in it almost counter-hegemonic possibilities, cause it challenges traditional paradigms of race. For example like when you talk about stereotypes—well there are, actually there are stereotypes about multiracial people, but not as deeply ingrained, that type of thing—so that you can work out your identity a lot more.

Christina was a first-generation college student. Her father, a white man, was a mechanic; her mother, an Indian woman whom Christina and some family members believed also had Jamaican heritage, was a secretary for a major international nongovernmental agency that paid a substantial portion of private school and college tuition for dependents of employees. Before coming to Ivy, Christina attended an "elite and elitist" all-girls school, "the kind of place that when you drive in has rolling hills and tennis courts and horses that the girls board when they stay there." Christina estimated the proportion of students of color at her prep school at about 30 percent, similar to that of Ivy, but she said that half to two-thirds of that 30 percent were international, "which gives a very different sense of race, like they don't go off with the same binary construction of black and white, or whatever it is, that we have in America." Early exposure to this alternative approach to differences in culture and appearance may have contributed to Christina's awareness that U.S. racial categories are constructed rather than fixed biological realities.

In high school, Christina was deeply involved in community service and activism but "not with race issues at all." Keeping with this approach, Christina elected not to attend the preorientation for students of color, saying that at the time she assumed it would be "separatist," she had been "scared because [she'd] never been in a huge minority community" and because she "didn't know if there was going to be a multiracial group there, which would have changed things entirely."

But when she discovered Spectrum among the many student organizations on campus, Christina joined because, as I quoted her in chapter 6, "It was really exciting to know that there was a whole community of people that shared my experience, that thought about being multiracial, that had experiences just like mine, people that I *looked* like." She started a GISP on multiraciality, made a documentary film about multiracial women's identities, was a founder of Ivy's Multiracial Heritage Week (akin to Black History or

Latino Heritage Months), and was the first student programmer for multiracial issues at the Third World Center (there were student programmers for the monoracial groups: black, asian, native american, latino). Of her activities, Christina said, "I have this whole huge resume doing multiracial stuff." As described in the previous chapter, Christina found multiracial role models among multiracial peers and faculty and concentrated her academic energy on multiracial issues; she was also involved with women's communities on campus through both the Third World Center and the Women's Center. The intersection of racial and gender constructions as played out in the exotification of mixed race women's bodies became one of Christina's central intellectual and political concerns.

In the course of exploring multiracial identity, Christina came to the paradoxical reality that multiraciality exists within the confines of racial constructions while drawing attention to the artificiality of those constructs. While believing in the "counter-hegemonic possibilities" of mixed race, she also

> discovered what it means to be multiracial within a community of color. It makes me really uncomfortable when people talk about multiraciality as this thing existing completely outside other races, cause that's something that I think is very destructive, because it's not the real world.

Simultaneously acknowledging the construction of race (and hence the ability to deconstruct it) and the reality of living in a socially constructed, racialized world, Christina struck the central paradox of mixed race identities and the complexity of the Extraracial Identity pattern.

Christina was adept at countering the rigidity of the social constructions, in part through her own identifications. She described working outdoors and living in a latino neighborhood for two summers, an experience that led to an unusual congruence between her appearance and her setting.

> At Ivy a lot of people thought that I was white and Jewish, more like white ethnic, and that bums be out because I don't see that. I feel more attractive in the summer. I change drastically different colors in the summer. I'm like two different people entirely. And I feel that I look like I feel in the summer. Especially the last two summers living in the South Bronx, in the Fordham Road area, which has a huge latino community. Cause that's the way that I look.
>
> It's very exciting to be accepted on a face value level and not looked at like, "What are you?" and as the exotic other, since everyone looks like that. These last two summers living in the Bronx is one of the first times I felt like I'd found a sort of visible community. I feel really different in the winter. Not so much that I'd go to a tanning booth (laugh), but I feel like I'm happy once I have some color, some sun on my skin!

She later said, "Just the way that I construct myself as being, as looking, Puerto Rican, as looking black and white, even though I know *what* I am. Because I'm *constructing* myself I don't have an issue with that." So although her Indian mother would consider identifying as Puerto Rican or part black "a slight, like I was identifying 'down,'" Christina was comfortable enough with the explicit, intellectual process of identity construction to follow her appearance to identities other than those of her heritages.

Asked how she came to her own identity construction, Christina said, "When I'm identifying myself I think about the way that I interact with people who ask who I am and what I stand for, and in the negotiation of how I look versus what I am." In other words, the active construction of identity was based on appearances ("how I look"), heritage ("what I am"), the negotiation between them, and the context of the identification ("the way that I interact with people who ask who I am"). The ability and inclination to deconstruct racial categories enabled Christina to reconstruct her identity in different ways at different times, a key feature not only of the Extraracial Identity pattern but also of the Situational Identity pattern described in the following chapter.

MARISA

> I'd moved from Jamaica to Boston when I was ten. In Jamaica everybody's the same, and there are different shades, and you have white, you have black, you have Indian, but it's interracial. So you never really have to describe yourself and who you are. But now I have to check off these charts, and what am I? I remember having to deal with "other," put down "other," and I was like, "Other of what? I'll just put black." It was like I felt trapped, the American side was kind of putting you in this cubicle, this is what you identified as, and so I felt really limited, not really being able to be myself.

Marisa's heritage included Indian, Afro-Caribbean, and white, and she called herself "Jamaican, multiracial, or black." From the time she was ten until she went to Liberal Arts College, Marisa lived with her family in Boston and then in a predominantly white Boston suburb. She described adjusting to the American notion of race as a teenager, but when she came to Liberal Arts, she said, "It was like I started again, having to deal with people. Well, not really 'deal,' but work to be accepted." Although she knew that Liberal Arts had a small population of students of color, Marisa was attracted to its strong reputation in the sciences; Marisa eventually chose dual majors in English and Hispanic studies over her original pre-medical curriculum.

Marisa was active in the community of students of color at Liberal Arts, though she sometimes struggled to find her place in it. She wrote:

> I became part of the Black Students Association on campus and also started
> networking with the other groups, like the Asian group, the Hispanic group,
> because at the same time although I identified with the Black students, I
> really didn't feel I completely fit in.

It was Marisa who relayed the scenario described in chapter 4 about a black
student looking around the room during a BSA meeting to decide who was
"black enough" to belong to the organization. Other than that extreme
example of students separating based on monoracial criteria, Marisa described
a more general sense of not belonging. She said:

> I never really feel that I completely belong. Sometimes I have to put myself
> in the mentality that "you're just here to go to school and don't worry about
> it." I don't feel like it's my school, just like how I couldn't call it my high
> school. I'm just a student and I really don't have any connections outside of
> academics with the school.

Marisa's statement that she "doesn't feel like it's [her] school" presents a powerful counterexample to the rhetoric of diversity and inclusivity prevalent in
both official Liberal Arts College publications and in the campus ethos of
openness to difference and multiculturalism.

Marisa's sense of not belonging extended to the classroom as well. Early
in her academic career, she had the unpleasant experience of being tokenized
by a professor who asked her to provide "the African American point of
view." He said, "What do you think about the African Americans? Marisa,
would you like to speak?" She responded, "No, I do not want to speak. I am
not African American, and anyway why do I need to be the voice for everybody?" In this example, Marisa's professor assumed she was african american
and further assumed that she could—and would be willing to—provide the
african american viewpoint. Marisa's response indicated both her rejection of
an african american identity and her awareness of the professor's tokenizing
her. Marisa developed a strategy to cope with this phenomenon, which she
encountered in other classes as well.

> I now speak to professors after class, "Please don't do that. Do not put me
> on display. I do not appreciate that." And that's a strain. But through the
> years I've grown accustomed to being the only [person of color] in class, and
> I speak up when I feel the need to speak up, without them putting me on
> the spot and telling me when to speak.

Marisa attributed the attempts at tokenizing her in part to the overall lack of
diversity at Liberal Arts, and she attributed her resistance in part to her
strongly held belief that race was an American social construction "having
nothing to do with who I am."

Because she wanted to be in a more diverse learning community where
she might feel more like she belonged, Marisa seriously considered transferring

to another college. In particular, she considered Spelman, a historically black women's college. She reconsidered this plan, however, when she realized, "It's no different, just that I'll have people who look more like me, but I'll probably deal with the same issues of not fitting in." After considering other small private colleges, she decided to stay at Liberal Arts, change from premedical to English and Hispanic studies majors, and make the best of it. She cited professors as critical in her decision not to transfer, demonstrating the power of individual connections with faculty in influencing student retention. Once she decided to stay and "make the most of it," Marisa embraced her roles as a campus leader and as a journalist on and off campus. "I just became a voice not only for the study body, but for multicultural students."

Marisa also decided to study abroad in Costa Rica, an opportunity she described as "a remarkable experience." In contrast to her experiences of traveling in Jamaica as a young adult, where childhood jokes about being a "coolie" (i.e., being mixed with Indian) had been transformed into insults directed toward her as a woman of mixed heritage, Marisa's experience in Costa Rica was one of acceptance.

> Although my hair is different, and skin color, and my features are different from theirs, I fit in completely. I felt so accepted. There wasn't anyplace else I could think of that I fit in so well, that people were so accepting of me. They were very inviting. They were just so laid back, and it was like nobody was competing about the skin color. They referred to themselves as the lighter skin and the dark skin, and then you have a shade darker. But it wasn't like it really mattered all that much.
>
> It was just the best experience, being able to travel and being able to get along with everybody—well, not get along with everybody, but feel comfortable around everybody. They took my features as something unique, but very appealing. Versus here, in the United Sates, there's so much a big push on beauty and what is really considered beautiful, which usually means closest to white. There, I really didn't run into a problem. People were accepting, whether you were beautiful or not. People were just very nice to you, no matter what you looked like.

Like David studying abroad in Japan, Marisa found a place where she felt accepted in ways that she was not in the United States.

On Marisa's return to the United States after four months away, she determined to extend her experiences more fully into the campus latino culture. Her time in Costa Rica convinced her that participation in culture was different from racial or ethnic identification within that group.

> So I think I came back here with more enthusiasm, more excitement for meeting people, and more of a passion for the Latino culture. I think what

I figured out is that you don't have to be from a particular culture to really fit in, to identify, and that's a big thing for me. Wow, I wasn't even Latino, but [Costa Ricans] accepted me as if I were.

The idea of identifying with a cultural group not one's own challenges the racialized—and specifically monoracial—climate of college campuses and larger U.S. culture; in that sense, Marisa was "opting out" of or resisting the racialized norm at Liberal Arts. And although she squarely retained her objection to being labeled "african american," after her experience in Costa Rica, she said, she "relaxed some about what other people think." She said,

I don't know, I've just learned to accept it. It's like, "Okay, if they call me black, it's okay. I know what I am." It's not as if I'm afraid of being put in that category. I just feel that if I'm also a mix of everything else, other things, then why should one dominate the others?

Marisa's "Jamaican, multiracial, or black" identification cut across identity patterns, though she maintained a strong inclination to opt out of U.S. racial categories, no matter what others might make of her.

THE ECOLOGY OF THE
EXTRARACIAL IDENTITY PATTERN

Amy, Christina, and Marisa identified some of the time in the Extraracial Identity pattern. Their ways of arriving at this pattern, describing it, and enacting it were substantially different, yet they shared the experience of making their way on three very different campuses—Rural University, Ivy University, and Liberal Arts College—to similar identity outcomes. They resisted institutional, social, and peer influences to identify in monoracial categories or in the border identity of bi- or multiracial. And while they could not sustain such an identity at all times, they seemed to exercise some agency in choosing when and where they would identify in one of the other patterns. Discussion of personal characteristics and environmental influences on the thirteen students in this identity pattern illuminates some of the ways in which these students approached the challenge of stepping outside the system to assert an "unboxed" identity.

PERSONAL CHARACTERISTICS

The thirteen students occupying this identity pattern displayed a range of personal traits and backgrounds in terms of family, international experiences, gender and sexuality, and developmentally instigative characteristics such as ways of thinking about race and identity. In this section, I describe and illustrate some of the personal traits that led students to interact with their environments in ways that supported engagement of the Extraracial Identity pattern.

Family Support

For the most part, families were not a source of new or different thinking about race and identity. Some parents displayed dismay at their children's adoption of specific identities, whether they be monoracial (Kayla: "In a conversation about being asian american, my own mother turned to me and said, 'You're NOT Indian, you're half-Indian.'"), multiracial (Ellen: "My father hates it when I say I'm mixed. He'd prefer I passed as just black, like he does."), or outside of racial categories (Amy: "I make my mother nuts when I talk about not being a race. I think she thinks it's impossible and that you *have* to have a race, you can't not."). These parental reactions contributed to some students' assertion of an Extraracial Identity. Ellen said,

> So to help my dad understand why it's okay to say, "mixed," I had to explain to him about how, really, race is just a way of categorizing people that goes back in history and that we got stuck with. When I was able to tell him about how the categories aren't based on anything biological, even though he still didn't really agree with me, he could understand better how come I say "mixed" rather than "Mexican, native american, and black." "Mixed" gets away from those things and kind of makes a space apart from race, where the first thing you think isn't "race" necessarily, but maybe you think, "Oh, 'mixed.' Ellen is mixed. What's that about? Who is she?" But my dad still hates it when I say I'm mixed. (laugh)

The opportunity to explain the concept of racial construction to her father created a way for Ellen to think about who she was—and whom she wanted others to think she was—apart from, or outside of, constructed racial categories. Although her father did not directly introduce Ellen to new ways of thinking about race and identity, he provided an environment in which she could put forward her new ideas in this realm.

Another significant contribution families made to students' thinking about race, culture, and identity was in the form of international experiences during childhood. A substantial number of the total group of participants (nine of fifty-six) had spent part or most of their childhood outside the United States. Four of the nine (Audrey, Luz, Marisa, and Sina) identified in the Extraracial Identity pattern. Kira had traveled to visit family in the Philippines, and an additional two students in this identity pattern had (Dee Dee and Jeff) participated in study abroad programs before joining the study. So over half of the students in this pattern (seven of thirteen) had been immersed in cultures outside the U.S. for substantial periods of time. Luz, who attended international schools in Africa and Asia, said, "I'm just beginning to realize the way I've been brought up, which is really different from everyone else, in disregarding the dominant way of thinking about race." Less direct, but demonstrating her own disregard for "the dominant way of thinking about race," Audrey described her experience of Grenada, a country she left when she was ten:

> But I come from a background where on the island, the big deal is not really racial. There are many different races there, like Indian and Asian, and there are a lot of people there from Scotland and Ireland during the potato famine when a lot of people came over. . . . I think a lot of things that people consider race are more cultural differences than race differences. And I think they have a problem drawing the line between that.

Marisa, as quoted at the opening of the chapter, simply called herself "Jamaican," relying on her family background and early childhood experiences to guide her through the maze of racial identification on campus and more broadly in the United States. Knowledge, whether direct or indirect, of racial construction in the United States came to some students through exposure to other countries and cultures where people were classified by different criteria (sometimes skin color, but just as often class or religion); the theme of international experience will arise again in my discussion of personally held ideas about race and identity, as well as during discussion of academic microsystems.

Gender and Sexual Orientation

Ideas about and experiences of gender and sexuality also constituted personal characteristics that influenced students' location in the Extraracial Identity pattern. More than in other patterns, students in this pattern made explicit links among racial, gender, and sexual orientation identity construction. An awareness of social construction of identity permeated some interviews, like those with Luz, who said,

> I'm not that attached to those identities and, in my own idealistic mind, everything's kind of fluid, and I don't know, everything's—well, these categories of black and white, and homo and hetero, and male and female, are kind of part of a discourse that I'm not involved with. I mean, of course I am, I definitely am, but I don't have that much sense of a stake in it. So I don't know, there's kind of like the personal and then there's the political realm. I want to become more aware, but I'm definitely not there yet at all.

Luz was interested in moving her "personal" and "idealistic" notion that race, sexuality, and sex (or gender) are fluid into the more "political realm" of campus discourse. This private/public dichotomy, which appeared also in the Multiracial Identity pattern, also persisted throughout the Extraracial Identitypattern. What is possible on an individual, personal level is not always tenable in the public landscape of racialized college campuses.

Other students made explicit connections between race and sexual orientation constructions. Jeff described a joint program of Spectrum and the bisexual student organization at Ivy:

> It wasn't a talk, it was a study break between the groups. So that was also interesting, identity-wise, in terms of seeing the parallels and differences there. I guess being of different backgrounds puts you in a context where identity becomes an issue. I guess that's true for all of us, but it's also true that it's something you consciously think about it—something I've constantly thought of, whether I knew terms for it or not, it's always there. I guess it's interesting to see the parallels with how we think about race and how we think about other identities.

The conscious effort to bring together groups that existed outside the mono-racial and hetero/homosexual norms provided a way for Jeff to think about socially constructed identities, as he said, "in terms of seeing the parallels and differences" between them. Kayla expanded on Jeff's observation:

> Sometimes I think bisexual people must feel the same frustration, because I have heard on countless occasions the sentiment from heterosexuals that although they can understand and accept homosexuality, bisexuality is completely beyond their comprehension and is more apt to be thought of as "wrong." Because after all, how can you possibly be attracted to *both* sexes?

Sina, who identified as "queer," made additional connections among the constructions of race, gender, and sexuality. She described the meaning of girls' and women's long hair in Samoa, where she lived for part of her childhood, linking gendered and sexualized identities in the context of one of her cultural heritages.

> When I was in Samoa I cut my hair off, which was the beginnings of coming out, you know. (laugh) And that's really bad in Samoa. Like basically parents do that to their daughters when they're really bad, just awful. So I went around and people thought I'd done something horrendous. Which if some of them knew I was coming out as queer, they'd probably have thought so, but that wasn't it at all. I just cut my hair off. So I started thinking more about how gender operates in Samoa, and how Samoan culture operates in terms of my identity, and how I construct myself as a queer biracial woman who is white and Samoan of Chinese descent. Or sometimes some or all or none of those things.

This self-aware construction of identity was common among students in this identity pattern, and as the three quotes illustrate, students saw connections among identity constructs, both theoretically (Jeff and Kayla) and in practice (Sina).

Developmentally Instigative Characteristics

Developmentally instigative characteristics of students in the Extraracial Identity pattern included their inclination to self-label or to resist labels and their openness to consider and re-consider ideas about the nature of race and multiraciality. Although the ability to self-label was important to most students in the identity patterns previously discussed, students in the Extraracial Identity pattern displayed a range of approaches to the importance of self-determination. For example, Clarice was not terribly concerned about self-labeling, in part because she saw herself outside the standard racial categories:

> It's been shown that there's more variation within a certain "race"—it's been shown that 94% of variation is within that race and 6% is between, or something like that. And after hearing that, I'm like, "It doesn't make sense." Race is something that exists in our minds. So does it matter that I'm half this and half that? No it really doesn't. For some people it *really* matters. And I think the people it matters most for are the people that are one thing or the other, which makes me glad that I'm biracial.

Kayla combined a propensity to self-label with her understanding of racial construction:

> I was saying that if you accept race as a social construction, that gives us even more legitimacy in the freedom to choose what you want to identify as, because there's no biological thing tying you to one or the other background. Because a lot of people are, "Well, you are what you look," or some people think like that.

The portrait of Christina illustrates a similar approach to self-labeling, with Christina constructing herself as latina during summers in the South Bronx, in spite of a heritage that included white, Indian, and perhaps Jamaican ancestry. Alexandra took a less intellectual but more firm stance on self-labeling. She decided not to identify in any racial categories as a result of being

> aware of the silliness of it all. . . . Those forms! If I checked the boxes I would be checking all of them. And that's just ridiculous to me. Who cares? And what does it mean, anyway, that I check black, white, hispanic, and native? What are they going to do with me? Report me as .25 of a person in each group? So I don't check anything. I leave it blank. If they want to know, they can come ask me to my face and I'll tell them what I think about the boxes.

The boxes—referring to the common practice of asking individuals to identify themselves in one race only[1] on institutional and governmental forms—were a common theme throughout data collection, and students in this identity pattern cited them frequently as an example of "the silliness" of racial categorization and the omnipresence of such forms. Dee Dee was skeptical of the boxes and the uses to which racial data would be put, though she acknowledged that the ability to self-identify was important.

> Sometimes I feel like it doesn't matter, just about the box—it's just, "Whatever, does it really matter?" There's so many other important things to worry about than this (laugh). And other times I think, "Yeah, well, people should be able to self-determine." I think one way to settle that would be just to put down culture (laugh) instead of race. Because it's already been established that the human race exists but not in racial categories based on physical characteristics. But if they put culture down, I'd be like, "Oh, I'll check this" or whatever. But then later on, behind the scenes, if they wanted to group all the white people, all the black people, you know, that's fine! (laugh)

Interviewed prior to a decision about whether or not to include a "multiracial" option as a separate category on the 2000 census, Jonathon also displayed skepticism for how data collected in a multiracial category would be used.

> If you're going to use the data for something, you have to know what you're doing. And to use the term "multiracial community" I still think is a misnomer, but because of the way we speak, the dialogue we make, in order to speak we have to use those terms. (laugh) But if we have to do that, we have to know how they're going to use those statistics.

A strong proponent of self-labeling (see his portrait in chapter 6), Jonathon also recognized the complexity of reifying racial constructions through the use of the term *multiracial* for the purposes of official records and data collection. "It's problematic because the existence of people of mixed race refutes the notion of race. But the word 'multiracial' still has the word race in it. How do we fight a concept by referring to it with the word?"

As an individual characteristic, the propensity to self-label or the desire to do so prompted several of these students into the Extraracial Identity pattern. Finding no one monoracial category that fit their self-description, students learned early—often in childhood—that there was, as Ellen said, "something wrong with the category system. It just didn't work the way they said it was supposed to." In college, the continued need to "check one box only" or to answer "What are you?" questions interacted with individuals' desire to self-label, prompting some to defy categorization or to deny the validity of the categories. To declare oneself outside the boxes ("I'm Jamaican") or to get rid of the boxes altogether ("Race doesn't exist, therefore I won't identify that way") is as much a self-determination as checking a monoracial or multiracial box.

Another important individual characteristic influencing student identification in this pattern was personally held ideas about race, mixed race, and identity, just as these ideas influenced students in the Multiracial Identity pattern. To hold an Extraracial Identity required a belief that this was an option. Examples given thus far illustrate the many ways in which students in this pattern conceived of "race" and, therefore, their ability to see nontraditional ways of approaching race and racial identity. Christina and Luz described the fluidity of racial identity, Amy and Alexandra refused to check the boxes, and Marisa and Dee Dee focused on culture rather than race. The three approaches were different, but they all relied on individuals' propensity to think, literally, "outside the box."

Thinking outside the box in a world predicated on the existence of boxes, however, was not an easy position to sustain. The idea that "race isn't real" contrasted sharply with the experience of nearly all study participants—a lived experience that included being a person of color on a predominantly white campus in a predominantly white nation. Students' ability to persist through the tension of this paradoxical meeting of race theory and racialized reality was another important developmentally instigative trait demonstrated by students holding this identity pattern. In describing this tension, Jonathon said,

> See the thing is, I can talk the talk. I can do the whole refutation of race as a biological concept, it's a social construct da-da-da-da-da-da-da, you know. But living in this world I have to acknowledge that it has social ramifications and social realities. . . . I've read the literature. I know the arguments and it's appealing, the deconstruction of race and Naomi Zack's "philosophy of anti-race." And the anthropologists who say race doesn't exist, but I don't know what it will be like, cause I just don't know how to get there. Because it's gonna take some time. I don't buy the "rainbow baby" version of saving the world, because the mere existence of people like me is not the answer. Inter-marriage and having kids like me does not equal destruction of race. As a concept it has power. . . . I know on an intellectual, academic, Ivy level that race is a social construct and doesn't really exist, but well, go tell that to somebody living in [the urban area surrounding campus].

Amy said, "Yeah, I can deconstruct race and disability all night, but the next morning when I wake up, I'm still brown in a white world, sitting in a [wheel]chair." And although Christina cited the "almost counter-hegemonic possibilities" of multiraciality, she still contended with issues of exotification of mixed race women in the media and popular culture. In the following sections on environmental features of the developmental ecology, the ways in which students maintained their balance in this paradox of theory and reality will become more clear.

MICROSYSTEMS

Critical campus microsystems related to holding an Extraracial Identity pattern occurred in academic, social, and peer contexts. Exposure to the idea of social construction of race and to the intellectual and cognitive tools to deconstruct it, as well as the support to do so, was a common element among the stories of the thirteen students in this pattern. Students spoke about direct prompts ("I took a course on deconstructing race") and indirect supports ("It's the way all my friends think") to developing and maintaining this identity.

Among the six campuses the environment, and micro- and mesosystems in particular, differed sharply in this regard. Students at Ivy described significantly more campus-based challenges and supports that influenced identification in this pattern. Remember that seven—over half—of the thirteen students in this pattern were from Ivy. These seven represented 50 percent of the participants from Ivy, whereas only 14 percent of all students at the other five institutions combined held an Extraracial Identity. Although with a small sample size it is difficult to generalize in any substantive way, Ivy students described more microsystem interactions supporting this identity pattern than did students at the other campuses, leading me to postulate, as I have elsewhere (Renn, 2000, 2003; Renn & Arnold, 2003), that the academic and peer environment of a campus can perhaps have a greater influence on this identity pattern than on others. The more students are exposed to postmodern theory and supported in their exploration of Extraracial Identity, the more likely they are to do so.

Academic Microsystems

Intellectual and course-related microsystems were central to a number of students' position in the Extraracial Identity pattern. Academic systems seem to have served three major functions. First, they exposed students to the idea of social constructions. Second, they provided tools for students to deconstruct race and language to describe this process. Third, they sometimes acted in a similar way to parents' negative reactions to self-labels, creating unpleasant situations from which students emerged more committed to dismantling or disengaging racial categories for self-identification.

Some students described academic courses where they were directly exposed to the tenets and tools of social constructionism. Jeff said, "This semester I'm taking that anthropology course about deconstructing racial discourse and deconstructing interracial relationships." Kira, too, took a course that dealt directly with racial construction, leading her to further exploration in other settings:

> I took a course last year, the actual title was "Race, Gender, and Class in the U.S." We didn't really talk about issues of biraciality there, but that had a great influence on my views on the race dialogue on campus and how race gets constructed in different ways at different times for different reasons.

Christina's coursework and GISP addressed racial construction, as did Jonathon's senior thesis on *Star Trek* and, less directly, some of Luz's art assignments. Luz described her dual majors of religious history and art/art semiotics:

> They're kind of diametrically opposed. In my mind I have this division between religious studies, which is kind of like reality, and art semiotics, being where I could take apart social constructions and kind of play with this new language. And reveal various oppressions and stuff, but it's also its own kind of BS in a way. . . . In my art I've been bringing up stuff recently, it's kind of cool, sort of semi-conscious or subconscious, bringing up issues of culture and inscrutability and cultural borders and that kind of thing.

Students were thus exposed to postmodern theory and deconstruction of socially constructed categories.

Beyond having been merely exposed to theory, students demonstrated their acquisition of language and cognitive skills related to deconstructing categories. Some students were aware at a metacognitive level of this acquisition. In discussing art and identity, Luz said, "Yeah, you could put it in cheesy art semiotics terms, like 'signifier for this or that.'" Commenting on the "cheesiness" of theoretical jargon marked Luz as self-consciously aware of her use of the tools of postmodern theory to explain herself and her work. Jonathon, too, was aware of his knowledge of postmodern theory and methods ("I can do the whole refutation of race as a biological concept, it's a social construct da-da-da-da-da-da-da, you know"). Amy's disability studies course gave her cognitive tools—and a community of other supportive thinkers—to articulate her long-held understanding that categories of race, gender, sexuality, and ability were socially constructed ("And then I had a language for talking about not just my ability, but also about being mixed and about being lesbian").

While academic microsystems positively supported students' exploration of Extraracial Identity, they could also provide a negative stimulus to exploration of racial construction. Of a classroom discussion, Ellen wrote,

> I just couldn't believe people were saying these ignorant things [about slavery and slaveholding]. I was so angry I didn't say anything that day, but I went home and thought about it and figured out how to say what I wanted to say about it. In our next class I explained that what we call race is not based in biology, it's based in categories that we made up and put people in based on how they looked and where they came from.

The scenario, while not necessarily supportive of Ellen's identity, caused her to articulate her beliefs about the social construction of race, creating an intellectual space for her to follow the Extraracial Identity pattern.

Kayla felt silenced by an assignment that she felt reinforced the rigidity of racial categories. In an email to a friend (shared with me during the data collection process), she wrote:

> I'm trying to write my final paper for Judaic Studies and it bites my butt. I
> hate writing about stuff like this (i.e. the problems of intermarriage and
> assimilation and the future of American Judaism) because it threatens my
> identity, my sense of belonging. Sometimes I feel like the only place I will
> ever truly feel at home is at Ivy. I don't want to minimize the importance of
> my identity in my future, with my future friends, bosses, colleagues, partner
> (hopefully), children etc etc. Why do people have to be so stupid and binary
> in their limited conception of the way things are? I hate this paper. And I
> hate the fact that I have no way of standing up for myself in it, for my dad's
> right to marry out, my right to have been born. I have to write an analyti-
> cal, unemotional representation of several recognized viewpoints. Well,
> when the hell are people going to recognize MY viewpoint??? I just feel so
> helpless—and silent.

A student not invested in the instability of racial and ethnic categories might
have written the paper without experiencing the existential angst that Kayla
described. But this unsubtle developmental nudge in the context of her
Judaic studies microsystem prompted Kayla to think about her own identity
and, in expressing those thoughts to a friend, to seek support for herself and
her viewpoint. The interaction of the microsystem (via the final paper assignment) and Kayla's individual traits (propensity to resist binary definitions of
identity) prompted feelings of isolation and frustration, out of which she
crafted an articulation of her resistance and of her awareness of being silenced
in the process. Although this articulation did not explicitly create space for a
nontraditional identity, as Amy's may have, it demonstrated Kayla's resilience
in the face of a significant challenge to the legitimacy of her claim to Extraracial Identity.

Social and Recreational Microsystems

Outside the classroom and academic microsystems, students encountered
social and recreational microsystems that influenced their identities as well.
Sina discovered that students at Spectrum meetings welcomed her not only
as she opted out of racial categories but also as she challenged the heterosexual norm.

> I started going to Spectrum meetings and finding out it was okay to be queer,
> too. That's another reason why I go there—it's such a nice atmosphere. Peo-
> ple are receptive, and I made a lot of my friends through it.

In her first year at Ivy, Kayla attended the opening convocation of Multiracial Heritage Week, where she received the message "Race isn't real, but
racism is."

> Naomi Zack was our Convocation speaker my freshman year. And she's a
> philosopher, and she was basically saying, "Okay, race isn't real, so do some-

thing about it. Change your world view." But we were like, "Maybe some anthropologists accept this, intellectuals accept this, but it's not like you can go to the community at large on this." . . . I think we have to deal (laugh) with the fact that socially race is real, and it affects our social interactions. And even if race isn't real, culture is real, and upbringing is real, and environment is real. I don't know. I go back and forth on this a lot.

Kayla left the convocation stimulated to think more about the paradox of race theory existing in a racialized reality. Certainly not all activities or events on any campus prompt such introspection, but the opportunities for mixed race undergraduates at Ivy to participate in student led microsystems dealing directly with multiracial issues and identity did seem significant in creating a space for participants to operate in the Extraracial Identity pattern. More than any single microsystem, though, the interactions between and among microsystems that created an intellectual and social peer culture mesosystem challenged and supported students' identification in this pattern.

MESOSYSTEMS

Students at every institution and in every identity pattern described the ways that college in general was a place where race and racial identity got more attention than in their previous educational and social environments. The omnipresence of dialogue, programs, and emphasis on race was cited as both a negative and a positive factor, with students reacting strongly on both sides. The overarching effect, however, was that it was nearly impossible to avoid the topic on campus and that, for many mixed race students, immersion in such a race conscious environment provided prompts to identity development and encouraged consideration of new and different ways of thinking about race and racial identity. Interactions across microsystems formed a powerful mesosystem of which race was a nearly inescapable part, for better or for worse. Students having an Extraracial Identity interacted with the mesosystem in a variety of ways, some of which supported this identification and some of which challenged it.

For some students, the constant presence of racial dialogue in the mesosystem created an opportunity for a passive position of Extraracial Identity. At Big Ten, Bob said,

> More people come out about what they are, like being gay or talking more about their race and being more comfortable with their ethnic background. And people seem more open here than they do at home. It's more comfortable here because more people are open, so everybody, if somebody's open, it just starts comfort, so "They're open, so I'll be open," and you feel safe and comfortable talking about it.

Asked where this openness occurred, Bob said, "In the dorm, like with my roommates, and in classes sometimes. Also in clubs and activities, with wanting more diverse students." For Bob, part of feeling "safe and comfortable talking about it" included talking about the idea that he did not "believe in the way races get divided." Though he did not actively pursue deconstruction of racial categories or public identification outside them, he privately held a position of opting out of categories. The "open" and "comfortable" atmosphere Bob experienced in the mesosystem provided this identity option.

Just as Christina discussed her "huge resume of doing multiracial stuff" academically and as a student leader, Sina made explicit connections between race theories learned in class, social networks she joined on campus, and the general campus culture regarding discussion of race and racial construction.

> I feel like theory is pretty central to my racial identity. I really like to deal with it. Right now, race is right on top. My freshman year, I was coming out to myself and that was what was important. And I sort of noticed race, like, "Why aren't I taking Asian Studies? Why aren't I taking African philosophy?" But I didn't at all open it up. . . . I finally got into race stuff because a lot of people here talk about it. A lot.

Messages in Sina's mesosystem prompted her to seek microsystems directly related to race and culture, which provided her with more of the theory that was "pretty central to [her] racial identity." She attributed her identity development directly to peer culture, even when that peer culture was contentious or unsupportive of how she chose to identify.

> I think Ivy's completely changed how I think about race. And that's totally due to the atmosphere. I think that's probably it. I think also, experiencing the kind of people, like just watching groups interact and having to be articulate and advocate for yourself. That's something I've really been struggling with, just watching people. In terms of getting upset about something and feeling like I've got the backup to say, "Hey, this is wrong." And again everybody being involved in things they care about. And that's totally Ivy. Totally being with your groups and (laugh) talking to them constantly and doing all this stuff. So that's what's influenced me I think.

Alexandra found the emphasis on race at Catholic University something of an annoyance. On this predominantly white campus, frequent "What are you?" encounters—either verbal or nonverbal—created more emphasis on her racial identity than she might have liked.

> Race seems to be more important here than it was before, and you are more aware of it. As far as the way people will look at you. You know, "You're 20% this, 30% that." It's more at the forefront of my thought when people meet me. Of course they're going to see that, cause that's the physical outside, but it's one of the things that even if I didn't talk about it, it would automati-

cally be that when they meet me. So I think of that a lot, and I thought that was interesting. Race seemed more important in a lot of ways, which got me thinking about why and what that meant and how the exact amount of each thing that I am shouldn't matter. And then that the categories shouldn't really matter—or be there at all.

Preferring to opt out of categories, Alexandra dealt fairly constantly with the question of "what she was." Alexandra grew up in New York City, in a family of nine children. Racial and ethnic diversity—and an abundance of mixed race peers in and outside her family—had been taken as a matter of course prior to coming to college. The increased emphasis across the mesosystem on race and racial categories at Catholic U prompted Alexandra to identify privately, and sometimes publicly, outside of monoracial or even multiracial categories.

More specifically, the peer mesosystem influenced students' thinking about the concept of 'deconstructing' race. For example, in the mesosystem formed between peer and family interactions, Luz contrasted her ideas about race with those outside Ivy:

> You know, it's kind of scary—this discussion is going on here and not out there and well, where else is it going on? (laugh) The way people think here is awesome, you know, it's wonderful, but when I go home and talk about "the construction of race and blah-blah-blah" (laugh) and "race does not exist" (laugh) people are just—, well, it's completely absurd to their reality.

Kira also contrasted external microsystems with the internal peer mesosystem:

> Like the race stuff here, I guess I personally am frustrated with the way it's being conducted. Sometimes the frustration doesn't have to do with the issues it has to do with the fact that people are quick to label other people. And I feel the need to really talk about these things and what other options to identifying this way or that way might be. But in other ways, sometimes I'm really glad to go home, because even though I know it's really important to talk about race so that people come to a better understanding of each other, sometimes it's nice to just go home and have people not talk about race. And then it's good to come back here where people can talk about "deconstructing this" and "constructing that."

The incongruence between racial discourse at home and at school heightened Kira's awareness of the postmodern theory in circulation in the peer mesosystem at college, which was not present for her in the outside world. Kayla also noted the ways that the college mesosystem specifically prompted her to think about social constructions:

> My views of race, and gender and homophobia and heterosexism—I hadn't even heard the word heterosexism before here. And compared to the other

people I was around when I was in high school, I saw a lot, but I didn't really see it that much, like the complicated structures of those things. I didn't realize how much we internalize a lot of stuff from just being here—being part of these discussions in different places, in different communities.

Unlike the students at Ivy University, Amy, Ellen, Alexandra, Audrey, Marisa, and Bob found themselves on campuses where postmodern discourse was a feature of some academic microsystems, but rarely (or never) a matter raised in the peer mesosystem. Their decisions to adopt an Extraracial Identity were not well reinforced in the mesosystem, though they did find support through independent reading and some private conversations. For example, Ellen said, "There are some great sites on the Internet where you can read all about this, and there are people talking about how race isn't biologically real and questioning why we have to be in these set categories." Bob expressed interest in taking classes that would address race, mixed race, and racial constructions, and Amy found reinforcement for opting out of categories through her disability studies coursework.

I suspect that if more students had been exposed to social constructionism in their coursework, and if other campuses featured peer cultures that supported exploration beyond identifying in monoracial or multiracial categories, additional study participants would have engaged this identity pattern. The curriculum, cocurriculum, and mesosystem formed by the interaction of microsystems within them appear to be key elements in how students understand and choose this identity pattern, if they know it is an option at all. At the one campus (Ivy) where postmodern theory permeated the ethos of peer culture, half of the participants fit this pattern. I do not argue for an exclusively postmodern approach to racial identity, but I suggest that exposure to postmodern theory and peer support for active exploration of an identity not predicated on rigid categories (of race, gender, sexuality, ability, etc.) provides students an important alternative to mono- or multiracial identification. And while it is a difficult identity to sustain in a society that is predicated on the existence of monoracial and, increasingly, multiracial categories, the cognitive challenge of the Extraracial Identity pattern is one that undergraduates at a range of institutions—not only elite private research universities—should have the opportunity to negotiate.

SUMMARY

Extraracial Identity is not especially common among mixed race college students. Yet it remains an important alternative for identification outside the ubiquitous system of racial classification in the United States and on college campuses. Just as campuses provide venues for the exploration of Monoracial Identity through courses and activities related to specific cultures, they can provide venues for taking up the cognitive and emotional challenges of learning to live in a world where "race isn't real, but racism is." Managing this apparent paradox provides students opportunities to challenge dominant paradigms and to explore postmodern ideas in the midst of distinctly modernist institutions. All students in this identity pattern also held other identities at times, a sensible strategy for managing the paradox depending on context and situation. In the next chapter, I discuss the phenomenon of the Situational Identity pattern and the ways in which students from all identity patterns engaged it on campus.

chapter eight

It Depends—Situational Identity

But the fact of the matter is, sometimes I identify as asian american, sometimes I identify as latina, sometimes I identify as biracial. That's really cool, too, because there are just certain situations, like, I totally identify differently in different situations.

—Kate

LIKE THE COMPOSITE STUDENT Lena introduced in chapter 3, Kate engaged a Situational Identity pattern. In some settings she identified as latina, in some as asian, in others as biracial. The Situational Identity pattern held thirty-four of the fifty-six study participants (61 percent). By nature of the fact that in this pattern students identified differently in different contexts, the labels they used to describe themselves were many: "biracial, mixed, black," "mixed or chicano," "multiracial," "half white, half Filipino," "biracial or hapa yonsei," "mixed, biracial, or half asian," "half Indian, half white." When asked how they identified themselves, they also responded, "It depends," "It differs," and "Well, that's a complicated question."

In this chapter, I describe characteristics of the Situational Identity pattern and trends among the students who identified in this pattern. I offer four portraits of students to illustrate the complexity of this pattern and discuss some of the personal traits and ecological conditions influencing Situational Identity.

CHARACTERISTICS OF THIS PATTERN

The Situational Identity pattern was comprised of those students who identified in more than one of the other four patterns (Monoracial Identity, Multiple Monoracial Identities, Multiracial Identity, Extraracial Identity).

Situational Identity involved the conscious or unconscious shifting of racial identification—or a shift to the Extraracial Identity pattern—depending on the context in which students found themselves. Wallace (2001) referred to this identity pattern as "Shifting Gears," Kilson (2001) called a similar pattern "Multiple Descriptors," and Rockquemore and Brunsma (2002) designated it as a "Protean Identity." Principal characteristics of this pattern are that individuals considered identity fluid and contextual and that they foregrounded different identities at different times.

I did not determine a minimum or maximum duration for an identity shift to consider it situational rather than a fundamental change in identity pattern; a student's identity might shift several times in the course of a day (from one microsystem to another), in a week (going from school to home for a weekend), or in some longer period of time (a semester abroad). All of these could be considered Situational Identity if they involved a context-dependent alteration of self-identification. Students who were in a Monoracial or Multiple Monoracial Identity pattern and held a private identity as bi- or multiracial (Multiracial Identity pattern) but who did not identify as such outside the context of the research project were not considered to belong in the Situational Identity pattern; similarly, students who publicly identified as multiracial but who privately identified with one or more of their monoracial heritage groups were not included in the Situational Identity pattern. Situational Identity involved some kind of *public* deployment of multiple identity patterns.

TRENDS WITHIN THE PATTERN

With a few exceptional tendencies that I will describe, there were relatively few trends in the Situational Identity pattern by gender, heritage, class year, or institution. Women were more likely than men to identify in this pattern (72 percent and 40 percent, respectively). The gender difference may be related to men's greater propensity to identify in just one pattern (eight of the twenty men did so; none of the women did); a man who identified in only one pattern was, by definition, ineligible to fit the Situational Identity pattern. Therefore, fewer men than women could potentially be in this pattern. Students with two parents of color were far more likely (eleven of twelve, or 92 percent) to engage Situational Identity than were students with one white parent and one parent of color. No students with one latino/a parent and one white parent engaged Situational Identity, though two of them strongly held a Monoracial Identity while maintaining a private, less dominant biracial identity. Across class years, no strong trends appeared in the Situational Identity pattern. Two institutions stood out in this pattern; Ivy had a much higher percentage (86 percent) and Liberal Arts a much lower percentage (25 percent) of students in this pattern than the other four schools. Elements of the peer culture at these institutions, which I discuss later in the chapter, are likely involved in these observed differences.

TABLE 8.1
Distribution of Students in the Situational Identity Pattern
by Gender, Heritage, Class Year, and Institution

		Total in sample	Identifying in this pattern
Gender	Men	20	8 (40%)
	Women	36	26 (72%)
Heritage	Two Parents of Color	12	11 (92%)
	One Asian & One White Parent	16	9 (56%)
	One Black & One White Parent	13	7 (54%)
	One Latino/a & One White Parent	5	0
	One Pacific Islander & One White Parent	7	5 (71%)
	One Mixed & One White Parent	3	2 (67%)
Class Year	First Year	14	9 (64%)
	Sophomore	17	9 (53%)
	Junior	11	8 (73%)
	Senior	14	8 (57%)
Institution	Big Ten University	12	6 (50%)
	Catholic University	8	5 (63%)
	Ivy University	14	12 (86%)
	Liberal Arts College	8	2 (25%)
	Rural Community College	6	4 (67%)
	Rural University	8	5 (65%)
	TOTAL	56	34 (61%)

PORTRAITS OF STUDENTS WHO CHOSE THIS PATTERN

PHILLIP

If somebody asks what am I? Well, right now I identify as—if it's some-body who I kind of know—I'll say I'm hapa. And then I'll clarify. I'll say I'm hapa and then I'll say Pilipino and white. If I don't know them as well, it depends. I might say just Pilipino or Pilipino and white. It depends.

Phillip grew up in a liberal university town in the northern Midwest. His mother was Filipina and his father was white, "mostly German, but mixes of other Europeans, too, so I can't say he's German, so I say white." Phillip began his college career at a private university in Florida and transferred to Big Ten halfway through his first year. When we met, he was finishing his sophomore year at Big Ten and had completed his transition to the new environment. Indeed, he had fully immersed himself in campus life, taking on leadership positions in student organizations and the residence halls.

Phillip remembered how he identified prior to coming to Big Ten:

> In high school, I was half-Filipino. Because I didn't look like everyone else. But in elementary I just considered myself white. On the exams, on the achievement tests or whatever, I would check caucasian and everything like that. It wasn't until about 5th grade, when I went to the Philippines with my mom, that's probably when I started saying half-Filipino.
>
> Down in Florida, I identified myself more as latino, just because all of my friends there were latino. My roommate was from Ecuador, everyone around me, there were so many Spanish speaking people, who would come up to me speaking Spanish, because of the way I look. So I was like, "Okay." I didn't really identify as latino, but I felt more attached to that culture, to that life and so on.

Since arriving at Big Ten, however, he had encountered a number of microsystems that influenced his self-label. An advisor introduced him to the term *hapa*, and an instructor helped him deepen his understanding of Filipino intellectual, political, and cultural history (a description of the advisor and instructor's roles in Phillip's identity development are included in chapter 6 in the section on mesosystems). Other students, too, had an influence on Phillip's self-labeling:

> About the "half"—I stopped using half this semester, just because another hapa said, "I'm not a half a person, so I'm not going to say half." So I just started using just hapa and then Filipino and white instead of just saying I'm half-Filipino. . . .
>
> Even over the last summer or sometimes, I just considered myself Pilipino. Like since coming to FA (Filipino Alliance) meetings, all of my friends were Pilipino and asian and stuff, so I just considered myself Pilipino. I had to remember that I had another side, and so then I started using hapa a little more and other people around me, like [name] and Kimlien were using hapa too, so I thought, "Maybe it's cool to use 'hapa.' Other people are using it, and the more I use it the more people will be educated about it." So I started using that a little bit more.

By the spring of his sophomore year at Big Ten, Phillip strongly held two identities: as Pilipino (the Monoracial Identity pattern) and as hapa (the

Multiracial Identity pattern). His campus activities and coursework reflected this dual identification. He was a founding officer of Hapa, the organization of mixed asian students at Big Ten, and he was active in FA and in the umbrella Asian Student Alliance (ASA). He worked in the residence halls as a Minority Aide, providing support and advice on issues related to students of color in general and asian students in particular. Of this role, he said, "It's been good, just being able to be an APA [Asian Pacific American] Aide as a hapa, because it shows there are hapa people who do relate to being APA." He was taking a group independent study on Filipinos and Filipino Americans and enjoyed other courses related to asian americans.

Phillip's ability and inclination to identify situationally as hapa (multiracial) or Pilipino (monoracial) worked well for him on campus. He was able to explore and identify with his Filipino heritage, immersing himself in that student community and providing a strong foundation for claiming a Filipino identity in his interactions with students outside that community as well. In interacting particularly with white students in his role as a Minority Aide, his Filipino identity was highly salient ("Most of them just see me as Filipino and don't see the other part."). In this context he was subject to tokenizing by well-meaning fellow staff members.

> It's kind of tough sometimes, because the hall directors and others will ask me about different programs they can put on for APA Heritage Month, for which they did nothing. So sometimes it's all put on me to come up with stuff. But I'm all for trying to educate people, 'cause it's my job to educate everyone else, like the [resident advisors] and stuff, about issues and that's been fine. We haven't really had that many issues.

Phillip seemed comfortable taking up the role of educating others from an APA perspective. He planned to continue as a Minority Aide in his junior year as well.

In other contexts, however, Phillip preferred to foreground his hapa identity. He formed Hapa because he "felt there was a need in the community" for a space for mixed asian students to come together.

> I thought there were a lot more hapas on campus who didn't come to ASA or FA, or their respective ethnic group meetings. I thought maybe they weren't coming because they didn't feel welcomed or they didn't feel accepted, because sometimes I felt that way at FA. Sometimes I didn't understand the jokes—a lot of the times—and if people were speaking the language, I didn't really understand it. So I thought maybe we should have a group for people like me, other people out there.

Hapa held weekly meetings where students discussed issues related to being mixed and asian, and the group sponsored a conference titled "What Box Should I Check?" on multiracial issues.

It was so cool at the conference. There were other people, mixed, multiracial, who weren't hapa—like some were black and white—who had the
same kind of latino identity thing. And it was so cool to find out that other
people went through that, that other people had the same identity issues
that I did.

Phillip's leadership role in Hapa and the conference provided a very public
forum for engaging his hapa identity within the context of the APA community at Big Ten.

Phillip's identity shifted depending on whether he was in a predominantly white environment (the residence hall), an APA environment (with
ASA), or a multiracial environment (Hapa). Different elements of it, such as
his "asian-ness," his "Pilipino-ness," or his "hapa-ness" were more or less
salient depending on cues from the immediate microsystem.

MINA

I'm South Asian and I'm white, but I'm more than that, too. And so if I'm
with my cousins I might be more Indian, but with my friends it's usually
more white. And being mixed is another thing, which there aren't many of
us here [at Rural Community College], but which is, I think, something
that's going to be bigger and bigger in the future.

Mina's father was South Asian and her mother was white (Scottish,
Dutch, and English). Mina herself identified "different ways," with her
South Asian and white heritages, her sense of herself as mixed, and her
growing knowledge that "there's something beyond race, beyond what we've
decided to call 'race' in this country." She came to Rural Community College with the goal of transferring to Rural University or another public four-
year institution for a degree in medical technology. Coming from an almost
entirely white community ("We were one of like three or four families that
weren't all white"), Mina found the relative diversity of RCC both refresh-
ing and challenging.

It's funny, because you'd think it would just be, "Wow—this is great. All
these diverse people." But sometimes it's more, "God, I don't want to talk
about it anymore." I just want to be me without having to explain that
South Asians have been in this country for years and no, I don't want to
be the one to speak for all asians—cause you know how they do that—
they want you to tell everyone quote-unquote "how asians think about
this or that."
    And then, too, people expect me to be friends with other students of
color, no matter what they are, just because we're all not white. And I don't
know them all. I don't even like them all! (laugh) But I guess it's better than
being with all white kids again, like high school. Yeah, it's better than that.

Mina felt that because she had been "with all white kids" in high school but also had spent significant amounts of time with her South Asian extended family during the summers growing up, she was "comfortable with both parts of myself. Like I know how to be white and that feels okay, and I know how to be South Asian, and that also feels okay." She also said, "Unless I'm dressed traditionally and wearing a bindi, I pretty much look like a white girl with a good tan. Maybe hispanic to some people, like I get that sometimes, but a lot of the time people don't really know unless I tell them." She enjoyed this ability to "fit into all kinds of groups, depending on where I am and how I feel." Asked when and why she might choose to identify with her different heritage groups, Mina said,

> Well, usually it's more about being like the people I'm around. So if I'm around my cousins and their [South Asian] friends, I'll be more South Asian, like in how I dress and how I talk—even my nickname with them is that way. And at school, like I don't know any South Asians there, then it depends on the situation. With close friends [who are all white], it doesn't really matter. They just know me as Mina and we don't talk about what race we are. We like the same music and movies and stuff—which is probably what you'd call stereotypically white, I guess, certainly not South Asian at all. But if I'm in class and something comes up where someone says something against asians or against other races, then I feel more like I'm not white—more like I'm asian. And then I'll usually say something—which surprises some of them since they didn't know I was asian to begin with.
>
> Sometimes it's in a positive way, too. Like I was in a cultural show we did with the multicultural office here at RCC. Different groups did performances, and there was food from different restaurants, and I got my sister to come do a dance with me. It was really cool, cause my friends here had never seen anything like that, anyone like me. That was fun.

So the opportunity to identify with other South Asians, to express cultural pride, or to oppose antiasian or racist comments made Mina's South Asian heritage more salient, while the chance to relax with friends and enjoy "stereotypically white" youth culture made her white identity more salient. She thus identified in the Multiple Monoracial Identities pattern.

Mina was also aware of herself as being multiracial, which she described as "something different, something blended, something new." Her sister called herself "Amerindian" to represent this blend, but Mina called herself "mixed" or "biracial." Some of her cousins were also biracial, and she said that she liked that because

> there are things our parents don't understand about us and what it's like to be half-white and half-Indian, so when we're together we talk about it and what it means for the future, like who *we* might marry and what *our* kids will look like and be like.

The microsystem formed by the cousins during annual summer visits became a multiracial community of sorts for Mina, where she felt comfortable mixing her white and South Asian heritages, being "something new," and not having to explain the complexity of those positions. At RCC, too, she sometimes identified as mixed, "when it makes sense, like when people are talking about interracial dating and how it might not be a good idea, and I say, 'Hey, don't worry so much about the kids—we turned out just fine!' (laugh)."

Mina also at times engaged the Extraracial Identity pattern. When discussing the future of race in the United States, she said,

> I think it's going to get less and less important whether you're in this group or that one. We already know that the groups aren't really rooted in anything genetic, like it's about culture and origins and stuff, but not about your genes.

Asked if and how this knowledge influenced the way she self-identified, Mina said,

> There have been times when I know that I'm Indian, and times that I know that I'm white, and times that I know that I'm mixed. More and more, I have times that I know that it's just categories someone made up to put people in. And when I'm thinking like that, then I don't really want to be in any of them—more like I want to be in all of them, like "the human race" or whatever, or maybe in none of them, like "no races." . . . So maybe that's where we're all going. No races.

Mina's ability to shift among Multiple Monoracial Identities, Multiracial Identity, and Extraracial Identity patterns placed her in the Situational Identity pattern. Her identity was fluid and contextual, though by no means amorphous or unformed. Microsystems at home, in extended family, and at RCC called forth different aspects of her racial identity, including the growing knowledge that race was constructed and therefore could be deconstructed.

KATE

> There's this comfort level you have being biracial and also the freedom that you have that you've never had before, and you can identify how you want and people don't put that on you, people just kind of let you be.

Kate wrote, "Now, my background is Asian/latina or chinese peruvian. I look EXTREMELY asian and not really ambiguous." She identified as asian, latina, and biracial. Before college, she attended predominantly white schools, where she identified as "asian, with a twist," mainly because of her appearance. She was raised, however, speaking English and Spanish in a bicultural household. The strong bicultural foundation prepared her to feel culturally at home in latina and asian communities in college.

Identity is very fluid, it depends on what situation I'm in. If I'm at a [Mexican Students Association] thing, well then it's latina—or if I'm sitting at an [Asian Students Association] meeting, well you know (laugh) I'll identify differently at that point. That's the thing, like people who think with biraciality you have to have just one, like you can't have both. But my parents have very fully passed down both cultures to me, and I pick and choose, things I value, and in that sense, not all values, but I feel very cool both places.

Kate arrived at Ivy University prepared to participate in activities within the Third World student community, beginning with the preorientation program for students of color. It was during this event that she was first exposed to the notion of a separate, biracial identity. At one point during the program, students were asked to form groups based on their racial identity, with spaces set aside for the various monoracial groups as well as for bi- or multiracial students. Of this experience, Kate wrote:

A defining moment would be the first time I identified as biracial. It was at [pre-orientation] and I had been to both the Asian and Latino groups but felt uncomfortable there. I decided to go off with the biracial group and as we were talking about our histories and personal struggles, we all realized what an amazing bond we all have with each other. For many of us, it was the first time we realized there were other people like me who have gone through the same things as I have. The idea of community and complete acceptance was INCREDIBLE and NEW!! I felt for once I didn't have to explain my "unusual" circumstances, defend myself, or have my legitimacy questioned. I could just be me and not half this, half that, mixed up, weird, interesting, etc. It meant so much to me because for the first time I could be accepted on my terms and not society's and allow both of my cultures to coexist to other people.

So from Kate's entry to college, literally within her first day on campus, she discovered a new way to identify and microsystems based on biracial or multiracial identity within the Third World community.

Kate embraced this new biracial identity and student community, saying, "With biraciality there's nothing definite, there's no definition of it, but you know, it's not like non-biracial people aren't cool (laugh), like 'Oh, you're a whole! Get out of here!'" Spectrum was in need of a cochairperson midyear, and Kate stepped up to the challenge, even though she was in her first year at Ivy. Like Phillip, she found that leadership of the group provided a certain visibility with other students of color on campus. Unlike him, she also felt the visibility somewhat constraining.

I kind of feel like, cause everyone's gotten to know me as "the Spectrum girl," right now if I identified as anything different than biracial everybody'd be like, "What?!?" So also it could be weird cause it would upset everybody if I stepped out of that arena. It'd be "What?" So right now I think I identify as biracial because I can't do anything else right now, but I think once I step out of the spotlight I'll be able to.

Leadership in the biracial community and the visibility she garnered as "the Spectrum girl" meant that identifying with one or both of her heritage groups was more difficult.

At the same time as it was more difficult to identify as asian or latina, Kate strongly wished to do so. Her bicultural background had prepared her for it, and she wanted to immerse herself in those student communities. Because she looked "extremely asian" she struggled somewhat to be accepted in the latina community at Ivy U. She said that when she went to the latina group during the preorientation program, "I'm sitting there in the room and thinking, 'No, this isn't quite me.' I feel like everyone's staring at me thinking 'Who is this asian woman?'" After she became strongly identified with the biracial community, she realized, "This [asian] part of me has been marginalized and this [latina] part has been marginalized. So all year I've been really pushing, 'Okay, I'm biracial—and do you remember that I'm latina?'" By the end of the year, she had made substantial inroads in the latino community. She wrote about an important time in her identity at Ivy:

> For most of this year, I have been definitely an outsider, kind of strange to most Latinos. I look asian but spoke Spanish, danced salsa just like them and used the same swear words. Many latinos have a hard enough time with black latinos, what were they going to do with an Asian Latina? Anyway, after becoming active and present at Latino forums, events, etc. people are actually taking a second thought at who belongs to which groups and I believe are beginning to see me as kind of part of their community, but they're not totally sure yet. So anyway, as I walk into Latino Seniors Night on Friday, people greet me in Spanish (very bonding), the other Peruvians there call me fellow countryperson (in Spanish) and Dean [X] and Professor [Y] (the big people of the Latino community) ask me to sit with them. It was nice. As a biracial person there is always a struggle to fit in and be included. My legitimacy I am sure is still being questioned on certain levels, but this was the first time that I felt somewhat comfortable or welcomed at a Latino event. I always feel like I stick out like a sore thumb, but as time is passing and people see me more, it seems as though people are getting used to the idea of my dual identity and my "latina"-ness. It means so much to me to have some acceptance in the community because it is such a large part of me and it seems slowly I am.

Interviewed shortly after this event, Kate said of her biracial/asian/latina identity, "So now I'm going back and forth, and I totally need that room right now."

THE ECOLOGY OF SITUATIONAL IDENTITY

Phillip, Mina, and Kate are very different individuals. They have different heritages, come from different geographic regions, and attended different colleges. Yet they shared a need to identify themselves in more than one way. Depending on the setting, they identified with one or more of their monoracial heritages or as biracial, multiracial, hapa, or mixed. In each case the college environment provided specific prompts to identity and to situational identification. Personal characteristics, microsystems, and peer culture mesosystems played important roles in the shifting identities of these students and the thirty-one others in the Situational Identity pattern.

PERSONAL CHARACTERISTICS

Situational Identity is necessarily influenced by a number of personal characteristics that were components in the other four identity patterns: cultural knowledge, physical appearance, gender and sexuality, ideas about race and identity, and developmentally instigative characteristics related to self-determination, propensity to resist externally imposed identities, and willingness to persist in identity independent of countermessages from various peer microsystems. Rather than describe again examples of how each of these characteristics influenced students' decisions about *which* identity patterns to engage within the Situational Identity pattern, I focus on examples of these characteristics as they relate specifically to the issue of holding multiple identities and shifting among them depending on the context. In this section, the characteristics I describe in relation to Situational Identity include ideas about race and Situational Identity and developmentally instigative characteristics such as self-labeling, propensity to explore the possibility of Situational Identity, and desire to resist a norm of stable, uniform identification across contexts.

Ideas about Race and Identity

Students' ideas about race and identity were important elements in this identity pattern. In order to engage in the Situational Identity pattern, students had to believe—even if they could not clearly articulate—that holding different identities in different situations was possible and, perhaps, desirable. Inherent in the thinking of several students in this pattern was the notion that being mixed race conveys the benefit of being able to identify differently depending on the context. For example, Benjamin said,

> I was thinking again about what category I fall into. I don't know. I feel kind of like a chameleon or something. . . . I think it's an advantage, cause I've been able to move around freely and not worry about a lot of the stereotypes that come along with—the wrong stereotypes—that come along with belonging to a certain race group.

In a similar vein, Kate believed,

> Biracial people tend to be more open to certain things because your conceptions of race aren't set. You tend to be more accepting of things, and there's a certain outlook that a lot of biracial people have towards race, because that's how we grew up. It's really amazing, cause it gives you the room to take more than one [identity].

Eleanor, however, felt that the fluidity of being biracial was a mixed blessing. While being black and white provided opportunities to identify as either black or biracial, the choice was sometimes a "lonely" one. After she attended the preorientation for students of color at Ivy, she started asking her parents more questions about race and identity.

> [Preorientation] was also a powerful experience for my family, who didn't quite have the answers to the "Who am I?" "Where do I belong?" "Why didn't you teach or tell me?" questions I started to ask them. I realized that I was the only one who could answer these questions. Actually, I'm still figuring some of them out. I know that identity is a very fluid and life-evolving concept, and I'm definitely on the road. But sometimes as a mixed woman, this road can be really lonely.

Although Eleanor found the road lonely, she also knew that it provided her with options other people did not have. Eleanor's realization, "It can be good, too, when you see that there's more than just one way to be," provided a foundation from which she could consider her racial identity as context dependent. Kira, too, found the fluidity of being mixed race positive and negative, saying, "Sometimes I think it's good, because I can at least superficially kind of fit into all kinds of different environments, but sometimes it leaves me nowhere, with no set place to be. And that's discomforting."

Amy also held ideas about race and identity that influenced her decisions about Situational Identity. She sometimes identified as mixed but preferred the Extraracial Identity pattern. She took an instrumental approach to identity, placing personal identification in the context of larger sociohistorical forces.

> And even though I don't buy into the boxes, there are just some times when you have to stake a claim to an identity. The world's not going to change if we all just say, "Hell no, I won't check your boxes." We have to be able to say, "No, I don't believe in these categories, but there's injustice going on and it's happening to me and it's time to make it stop." So sometimes, for political reasons, I'll do it. Like going to a march or a rally or something. They need to see how many of us there are, and that we're not all the same, and that we're not going to go away.

Amy chose sometimes to interrupt her resistance to categorization by race, sexuality, or ability in order to join with a community of others in a larger struggle for social justice.

Developmentally Instigative Characterstics

Amy's position was based in her ideas about race and identity and intersected with a key developmentally instigative characteristic, the drive to determine one's own identity. Within this characteristic, the belief in the right to self-determine in ways that might change depending on the context is one key to Situational Identity. As illustrated in other chapters, Jonathon's desire to name himself was as strong as it was dependent on context.

> What do I say I am? It depends on the situation. I mean, it varies. It's varied over time and it's varied over situations. I can identify as multiracial, biracial, multiracial Asian American, Hapa, Amerasian, Eurasian, Asian American, multiracial Japanese Jewish American, Japanese Jewish American, Japanese European American. At one point in elementary school it was Japanese, Germanic, Austro-Hungarian, Jewish, Irish American. (laugh) That was probably fifth grade, for a little while. In the beginning it was Japanese American because I thought American meant "white," so that took care of that. Then I figured out that that meant "Mom." Now I probably most consistently, well for shorthand, I use multiracial, but I also agree that's a problematic term.

While most other students were not so adamant or detailed in their self-descriptions, some were equally clear. Samantha said, "No one else gets to decide what I am, no matter where I am. I might be biracial over here, and black over there, but it's not theirs to decide. It's mine." May put it bluntly, "[My identity] depends on who I'm with, but it's *always* up to me." A propensity toward self-determination influenced students' identities across settings.

A propensity to resist the societal and campus norm of maintaining a singular racial identity across contexts also influenced students in the Situational Identity pattern; students did not conform to the choose-one-only ethos that permeated official and peer cultures at these institutions. I discussed some of this nonconformity in chapter 5 (Multiple Monoracial Identities) and in chapter 6 (Multiracial Identity), but it bears repeating here because an individual tendency to resist the environmental press for unilateral identity is central to the idea of Situational Identity. In the course of data collection, I attended a student forum on interracial dating sponsored by Spectrum at Ivy University; to the frustration of several mixed race students present, the forum disintegrated into an attack on biracial people and their identity choices. Of the event, Kayla said:

> People could not understand how we wouldn't be sure about our identity, like how it would be different in different occasions, or if you have different choices you put down something in a different way, just because sometimes you feel like you have an option that's right and sometimes you have to compromise and sometimes you just don't want to write down anything.

Kayla's monoracial peers made clear their lack of understanding of the fluidity of multiracial identity; Kayla persisted in identifying situationally but recognized the animosity she faced from monoracial students. More often, the pressure from peers to identify unilaterally is more subtle, of the "Why can't you just make up your mind?" variety discussed in the focus groups at Catholic U and Liberal Arts. "People just don't get it. We're not being wishy-washy. It's really different depending on where I am," said one participant.

While appearance, gender, cultural knowledge, and family were key personal factors in monoracial and multiracial identifications, they were not so directly related to students' adoption of Situational Identity itself (though they did influence which identities students would choose in different situations). Instead the ideas students held about the fluidity of race and identity and developmentally instigative traits (self-determination, resistance to external pressure to identify unilaterally) were influential factors in Situational Identity. Situational Identity, of course, was enacted within micro- and mesosystems. In the next sections, I describe features of these environments that promoted or inhibited engagement of the Situational Identity pattern.

MICROSYSTEMS

Some microsystems were more supportive than others of students' shifting identities according to context, and moving between incongruent microsystems often served as a prompt for students to shift identifications. Unlike the four other identity patterns, academic microsystems played a small role in the Situational Identity pattern; social and recreational microsystems played a more significant role. A few students (Jonathon, Kayla, Amy) described specific courses or course assignments that led to the belief that situational identity was possible and desirable. For the most part, however, messages about Situational Identity—and the positive and negative consequences of engaging it—came through nonacademic microsystems.

Nonacademic Microsystems

Comfort Level and Familiarity with Individuals in a Social Context. Within the area of social, recreational, and cocurricular microsystems, several students said that how they publicly claimed their identity depended on their comfort level and familiarity with individuals in a certain context. The effect of this comfort level varied across participants; individuals reacted differently to similar situations, making them more or less likely to identify with particular monoracial groups, as multiracial, or outside racial categories. Kira said:

> I guess the fact is that how I identify does change with my environment, who I'm with, not even the race of the person that I'm with, but my comfort level. If I'm comfortable, if I'm friends with the person, I don't think about my race. But if I'm uncomfortable, then I feel that the other half of my race—the one that they're not—stands out more. I think because of my level of comfort, I see myself as different, and then I associate that with race because that encompasses so many things.

The more comfortable Kira was, the less likely she was to think about her racial identity; the less comfortable she was, the more likely she was to identify with her heritage that corresponds to being different from the people in a setting.

However, Beth was more likely to identify with her multiple heritages when she was more familiar with individuals in her immediate settings. She described how she identified publicly when asked a "What are you?" question.

> I'll say that I am half hispanic and the other half is a mixture of a lot of things. My mom was born here and that is usually what I say, if I know them well enough and we have time and they are not getting bored, because a lot of people just don't care. They want to know why I am not dark. Why I have blond hair. Why I am articulate and don't have an accent and dark skin. If they are my good friends they want to sometimes know why I have the identity that I do. So then I get into "Well, my grandfather is an Austrian Jew and my mom's mom got married, but because of the interracial relationship they got divorced. So that is all that stuff that went on on that side. Then my grandma came over before the depression and my dad was born here too, so I don't speak Spanish." They want to know why I don't speak Spanish. So I kind of get into more detail depending how my relationship is with the other person.

I wondered about the connection between how Beth described herself in different contexts and how she understood her identity in those contexts. She said,

> Around good friends, people who know me and know my story, then I feel like I'm all there—all of my parts. But around people I don't know well, usually it's more like I'm hispanic. That's how I feel, especially when it's mostly white people. But if it's mostly hispanics, and I don't know them, then I'm more aware that I'm part anglo, part Jewish. With my good friends, it's all there, being biracial, hispanic, anglo, Jewish. With people I don't know as much, it depends on the situation and what they are.

The salience of Beth's various heritages and her biracial identity shifted according to both her comfort level with those in the immediate setting and to their racial and ethnic backgrounds. With closer friends, "all of her parts" were present; with those she knew less well, she experienced herself as different, as had Kira.

Dichotomous Microsystems. In addition to being influenced by their comfort level within a microsystem, students discussed ways in which they shifted identities between dichotomous microsystems that prompted (and perhaps required) particular identities. Because these microsystems did not interact, they did not form a mesosystem environment, and some students were sharply aware of traveling between two microsystems that called for different identities. Vincent, who lived in a number of different countries while growing up with his [white] Swiss father and his Chinese mother, described how his identity shifted from location to location, including between two campus-based friendship groups.

> When I'm in Asia and when among asians, they always consider me as white. When I'm here, they always consider me as asian. So I'm grateful for the fact that I can go both ways. And I'm surprised at how easy it is—like I can go over and hang out with either group. And the problem is that I start having two groups of friends that I can't bring together. One night I wanted to spend some time with *this* friend, and *that* friend also wants to spend time, and I said, "Well, why don't we all go together?" And it's not that I think something bad is going to come out of it, it's just that it's very awkward.

So although going "both ways" was easy for Vincent himself, bringing both groups together was more challenging. Erika spoke of similar experiences with friendship groups at Liberal Arts:

> I had a roommate who was an American. She was totally this "All American" girl. All my friends were Japanese, but I hung out with my roommate at the same time. So I went back and forth being like an American[1] and being Japanese. All my Japanese friends didn't really hang out with Americans, and I was half American, so I just went back and forth. I never had just one group of friends or just one friend. It was kind of back and forth I guess.

The "back and forth" nature of Vincent and Erika's identifications with their dual heritage groups captures the essence of a dichotomized Multiple Monoracial Identities pattern; they each also identified at times as biracial, adding a third element to their Situational Identity.

Monoracial Microsystems. The composition of some monoracial microsystems called on Situational Identity in a variety of ways, depending perhaps on students' individual characteristics and developmental inclinations. For example, some microsystems influenced students to identify with the group that was dominant in that setting; and others made students more aware of their differences from the dominant group. Regarding the former, Sapo said, "In a group of minorities, I tend to be on the minority side. But in a group of Irish people, I'd say I'm more Irish." Regarding the latter, several student quotes in previous chapters illustrate the challenges for multiracial students in mono-racial settings.

Mixed women with black heritage expressed particular challenges in this area. Their stories form the basis of many of the quotes I just mentioned. The Situational Identity pattern offered a partial resolution of this tension for some women. Of her sometimes fraught relationship with other black students at Liberal Arts, Marisa said:

> Sometimes I wonder, "Do they think they're too good to say hi?" Sometimes you start questioning yourself, "Am I lacking in some area? Why aren't they friendly with me?" So I keep my personal identity as Jamaican or mixed on the down low when I'm around them, because I just don't want them to feel like they can't or shouldn't associate with me. I think of it more when I'm with them, but I talk about it less.

For Delores identity was context dependent, but she was as likely to identify as black when she was in a group of black students as in a group of white students.

> My identity? It's like the moment, actually, how I feel at that moment, but for the most part I do feel "mixed." My comfort level in both places really is fine. Some days I'm more comfortable in one place than the other, just because there are differences. A lot of times I do feel more black though, because when you're around a lot of white people you still are black, but when you're around blacks, you're just one of them.

Bridget found acceptance on her multicultural dance team, which had a majority of black dancers. Because she maintained her mixed african american and Puerto Rican identity when she was with them, they came to rely on her for specific cultural knowledge.

> I just incorporate both [identities] into anything that I do. So that's something that they can always see, that all of my teammates always know. And when it comes down to doing a little salsa, they'll always look at me like, "What comes next?" (laugh), and then I'm a little more identified as Puerto Rican. So that's interesting. It's in me, so I incorporate it, no matter where I am and what I'm doing.

Within the microsystem of the dance team, Bridget could experience her identity as black, Puerto Rican, and biracial. Specific situations in that setting prompted her to shift her identity at times to benefit the group's artistic performance.

Microsystems That Were Explicitly or Tacitly Formed around Mixed Race Identity. Venues like Spectrum, Hapa, the emerging student group at Catholic University, and informal networks of mixed students on some campuses also supported students in the Situational Identity pattern. Kate described her joy at discovering a biracial space at the preorientation at Ivy and how she learned that there was no one way to identify. Through Spectrum meetings, Jeff learned that a fluid identity was an option.

> In Spectrum you don't necessarily have to identify, it's not necessarily about, like say if you are bi or multiracial and, if you are, saying, "I identify as bi or multiracial." You can identify purely as whatever you are. Like at the beginning we go around the circle and it's like, "Who are you? What's your name? And how do you identify?" And it doesn't matter what you say. You can say, "I am a person." Or you can answer differently on different weeks—sometimes even at the same meeting! (laugh)

Summer's enjoyment of the informal group of "half-asians" at Catholic helped her learn that there were a variety of ways she could identify at different times, and leading Hapa at Big Ten helped Kimlien and Phillip practice Situational Identity as they moved between the mixed race group and the larger asian student community.

Predominantly White Microsystems. It is important to remember that the six campuses in the study were predominantly white and located in predominantly white communities. So when students were not in microsystems comprised of students of color (monoracial or mixed), they were in what amounted to a mainstream white culture that presumed monoraciality as the standard identity. The incongruence in the mesosystem between the presumption of monoraciality in white mainstream microsystems and messages received from monoracial or multiracial microsystems brought some students' attention to the situational nature of their racial identities.

May and Rhonda were two students who experienced this phenomenon in their mesosystems. May ran track at Rural University, where the vast majority of the other runners were black; she lived in a residence hall that reflected the campus population, which was 81 percent white. She said,

> Sometimes, like when I'm with the team, I'm more aware that I'm mixed. There are a lot of black girls on the team, and only two of us are mixed. But in the dorm, it's really more just black. No one really makes a difference between me and the other black girls, even though they [the black students] know I'm mixed. But because everyone thinks I'm just black, that's more of how I am there. It's not as important being mixed.

The track team microsystem elicited May's mixed race identity, whereas the residence hall setting elicited her black identity. Her identity was context dependent, with the predominantly white and monoracial campus culture prompting her to focus on her black identity. Rhonda, who worked off campus at a local mall in a predominantly white community, experienced a similar phenomenon when she was immersed in the local white populace.

> At school, where there are more african americans, I think more about being mixed than I do when I'm at work, where it's like they couldn't care if I was 99% white and only 1% black. I'm just black there. And I work it like a sister! (laugh) They gonna call me black? I'll show them black! (laugh)

Rural Community College, though predominantly white, was more racially diverse than its surrounding community, and Rhonda, because she was at a nonresidential institution, was immersed in the surrounding community the way residential students would be immersed in campus culture. The mesosystem created by the interaction of the work and school settings brought her attention to the possibility of "working" identity differently in different settings.

Monoracial and multiracial settings exerted a range of environmental presses on mixed race students, influencing their identities in a range of situations. Students' individual characteristics interacted with these microsystems to determine what identities students saw as possible and, among these, which were most desirable at that time, place, and setting. Possibility and desirability were in turn largely determined by the influence of mesosystems, in which students received messages about race, identity, and community that were congruent, incongruent, or a combination of both. In the next section, I discuss the influence of the mesosystem in Situational Identity.

Mesosystems

More than in the other identity patterns, mesosystems are central to the Situational Identity pattern. As microsystems interact to create mesosystems, they also create the occasions for the identity shifts that mark Situational Identity. While it is true that an individual microsystem may evoke different identities at different times (as Bridget experienced with the dance team), more often it is the case that as microsystems interact in the mesosystem, students become aware of the situational nature of their identities. In this section I describe some of the ways that the mesosystem became the milieu in which Situational Identity was made manifest in participants' experiences, as well as the ways that mesosystems supported the intellectual and personal exploration of Situational Identity in college.

The Situational Identity pattern often became clear when students described challenges negotiating a unitary identity in disparate settings. For example, Jeff was involved in Spectrum, wanted to be more active in the asian student community, and had joined a predominantly white fraternity.

He believed that asian students did not view him as having an authentic or legitimate claim to asian identity; when he was among them, he felt paradoxically more asian than when he was in the fraternity (because he was identifying with asian culture) and less (because he was aware of his white heritage). When he was with his fraternity, the situation was similar, but for opposite reasons—he felt more white (identifying with the mainstream, white, U.S. culture in which he grew up) and he felt more asian (because he was different from other men in the organization).

Jeff was aware of the incongruence of the messages he received in the mesosystem created by the interaction of these two microsystems; he was also aware that he could engage in a sort of "identity management" in order to create space for him to identify as he wished in different situations. One of Jeff's active identity management strategies involved how he told students where he lived. At Ivy University, fraternities lived in university residence halls that also housed nonfraternity students. He said,

> I get a very different reaction if I say, "Yeah, I'm living in [Lyon Hall]," versus "I'm living in [Alpha Beta]." And yeah, I kind of judge it based on who I'm talking to. Like some people, I say to them, "I live in [Lyon]." It depends on the context. And if I'm in a group where the majority of people I really know well, I say, "Yeah, I'm joining [Alpha Beta]." To other people I might go, "Yeah, I live in [Lyon]." So, it kind of, well, it changes a bit depending on what I want them to know about me.

Asked what the different responses would tell people about him, he said, "If I say [Alpha Beta] then they'll just think I'm being more with my white side. If I say [Lyon], they don't know and can't assume anything about who I am." So Jeff tended to tell students of color the name of the building rather than the name of the fraternity, in an effort not to diminish himself as a "sell out to their eyes."

Jeff also joined the Asian Student Association and become active in the Minority Peer Aide program, considered the gold standard of authenticity in the Third World community. He said,

> A lot of people know who I am now, and I really feel like I belong right now, which allows me to branch more toward my asian side, because I don't feel like people would question my authenticity as a Third World student. And even if they did, I'm definitely more confident, so it wouldn't matter. And also Spectrum has kind of helped me find that place, that confidence.

On a campus where membership in the Third World community was carefully bounded by peer culture, joining a white fraternity was seen as evidence of inauthenticity; engaging a Situational Identity required active management of first impressions and attention to what activities could mark him as an insider. Jeff maintained a consciousness of different identity contexts and what different identities meant in those contexts, even as he was developing the self-confidence and support network to resist some of the messages of the peer mesosystem that might imply that he was not "asian enough."

Sina, too, operated in multiple, interacting microsystems and was aware of the ways she identified differently across them. I asked her how she described herself. She said,

> It depends on who I'm talking to. When I was talking to college admissions, I'd talk about being biracial, talk about being Samoan, living in Samoa, living in Saudi, and sort of the perspective that gave me on American culture and diversity, and about race relations and just like pluralism and stuff.
>
> I'm very opportunistic about how I define myself. Like there are some times when I'm with mostly white people when I'll use it as self-examination where I say what it means to be white. I'm white, or people think I'm white and I have that privilege, you know, and I can carry on my life that way and I take advantage of that. But I feel I'm also really excluded. My sister and I talk about how I'm really excluded from Samoan culture, because my [Samoan] mom didn't feel like teaching her children Samoan and my [white] dad who wanted to bring us up American. So my sister and I, we're really not *Samoan* Samoan. So sometimes I identify as having white privilege, and how that also excludes me from Samoans and sometimes from people of color.
>
> And when I'm in the community of color, I talk about being biracial and how that seems to be the most valid, realistic category for me to put myself in because that's where my interests lie in the community of color at Ivy. But when I talk with someone who is Hawaiian, I'm like, "Hey! I'm Samoan!" (laugh)

Asked if her self-definitions related to her identity, she said, "Yeah, it's not just about the label, though that's important. It's about how I'm able to be and be with a community and if I feel like I'm part of it or if I just feel outside it and different." Sina was aware that she identified differently depending on whether she was talking to an admissions counselor, discussing race and identity with white students, or being in the community of color generally or with other Pacific Islanders in particular. The mesosystem formed by these campus microsystems offered opportunities for Sina to identify in multiple identity patterns, and it also drew her attention to the fact that she shifted primary identities depending on the situation.

Other students also found that college presented opportunities to explore different identities and to shift identities according to context. Erika specifically sought opportunities to identify with different groups.

> I feel like I have more expectations of myself [than my parents have for me], because I'm half American, and I have all these things inside of me.

So I want to be everything. I don't just want to be stuck into one thing. That's why I can't hang out with my—just my Japanese friends, because I felt there was more that I should be doing. So I went back and forth, and I could never be just—I could never just belong to one. And I want to keep myself like that, flexible. I like that kind of flexibility. So I don't really have just one group of friends. I don't just belong to one group. I don't want to be stuck.

Erika took advantage of the range of student organizations and informal social networks at Liberal Arts to find identity-based groups with Japanese international and Japanese American students, asian students in general, Hawai'ian students ("They're like me—part asian and part American"), and white students. Similarly, Dan sought opportunities to explore different identities and identity shifts. Reflecting on his identity during his first three semesters of college, Dan said,

I guess I used to say biracial asian american, and I think since coming to Ivy my asian american identity has definitely been moved more forward, but still I really recognize that I'm biracial. . . . I'd use "Chinese" if it was more asian americans, because it's more differentiated, and if I'm with them [asian americans], then I feel more differentiated, too.

Asked what caused his asian american identity to be "moved more forward," Dan said,

Just all the groups and people, times that I've been able to identify differently and see what that's like. People accepting—or not accepting—that that's how I identified. All the groups, really, seeing how I feel different in all the groups, even though I know I'm really the same person in all of them, but just having different parts moved forward in some of them.

The variety of identity-based formal and informal groups in the peer mesosystems provided students like Erika and Dan places to try on new identities and to practice moving among identity choices.

SUMMARY

Engaging in the Situational Identity pattern required, at a minimum, that students identify in more than one of the four other identity patterns. For some students, Situational Identity was something they just did; for others, it was something to think about and to enact purposefully. In either case, the outcome was similar: students shifted between or among identities as their personal characteristics interacted with influences encountered in their environments.

It is not enough, though, to know how and perhaps why students chose different identities in different contexts. It is important to consider what these identity choices—and the campus conditions that make them possible and desirable—could mean for educational practice as an increasing number of mixed race students come to college. In the next chapter, I discuss the implications suggested by an ecological analysis of mixed race student identities.

chapter nine

From Patterns to Practice—
What Mixed Race Identity Patterns
Mean for Educational Practice

PERHAPS THE MOST IMPORTANT finding of this study is that, for mixed race students, achieving a singular racial identity outcome is not necessarily reasonable or desirable. The fifty-six participants in this study demonstrated a range of identifications within an array of identity patterns and various combinations of these patterns. Interactions among individual characteristics and ecological factors resulted in different identity outcomes for each student. It is important to understand the ways in which mixed race college students identify themselves; it is even more important to use this knowledge to reconsider higher education practice, policy, scholarship, and theory in relation to race, mixed race, and identity on campus. In this chapter I take up these issues in light of my study findings.

HIGHER EDUCATION PRACTICE AND POLICY

The finding that mixed race students identify in a variety of ways holds implications for higher education practice and policy, which until now have been largely predicated on a philosophy of one body, one race. Bearing in mind that 4.0 percent of all census respondents under age eighteen and 7.7 percent of all respondents indicating hispanic/latino ethnicity claimed more than one racial category, at least a two-fold increase over previous generations, what does it mean for the curriculum and co-curriculum that an increasing number of students coming to college will be mixed race? How might institutions prepare for and respond to this change? I suggest changes in institutional administrative practice, approaches to campus peer cultures and curricula, and national policy, to support a more fluid construction of race and racial identity on campus.

INSTITUTIONAL ADMINISTRATIVE PRACTICE

At the level of institutional administrative practice, strategies might include assessment, changes in policies, programs and services, and attention to elements of structural diversity.

Assessment

Assessment efforts should include both a population assessment to determine numbers of mixed students and how they identify and evaluation of campus climate vis-à-vis mixed race issues. Knowing how many students had more than one racial heritage and how these students chose to identify could serve as a baseline for tracking the growth of this population and their outcomes (including retention to graduation) as well as provide important information for making decisions related to the provision of programs and services.

Given the fluid nature of racial identity evident in the study sample and in other studies involving mixed race college students (Kilson, 2001; Rockquemore & Brunsma, 2002; Wallace, 2001), it might seem challenging to get students to, as a colleague of mine once put it, "stand still and let us count them." I suggest that this is not as impossible a process as it might at first seem. Although the collection of racial data by institutions is not uniform, even within public university systems in some states (Renn & Lunceford, 2002), it would be relatively easy to standardize an annual collection of racial and ethnic data that asked students (a) how they identified and (b) what their racial heritage(s) were. Such a method is not perfect. It fails to address concerns of students such as Alexandra ("Those forms! The silliness!") and others concerned about "the boxes," but it provides more information than asking once, at application, for students to "choose one box only." The implementation of OMB Directive 15 (1997) will ensure that students have the option to indicate more than one heritage, but it will not require institutions to ask students how they actually identify themselves, nor will it require them to use data on multiple heritage respondents for any internal purposes. A bi- or triennial qualitative survey of a random sample of students could supplement an annual online survey of heritages, providing more accurate information about the ways students identified in various situations.

At a minimum, institutions should collect and report data on the number of students who come from more than one heritage group; ideally a more in-depth process would provide information on how these students identify. This process could be politically touchy, as indicated by Kayla's report of student animosity regarding biracial students identifying—or not—as black, but it is important in understanding the status of mixed students in higher education.

In addition to figuring out how many students come from more than one racial heritage, assessing the campus climate for mixed race students would provide information for making decisions about necessary changes in programs, services, and policy and for creating a baseline against which future climate assessments could be measured. I recommend consideration of both structural features and student attitudes and satisfaction. For these purposes, considering mixed race students as a unique constituency (i.e., assuming they take up the Multiracial Identity pattern) is probably most simple, though not without the danger of oversimplification. Setting aside for now these concerns about oversimplification, a climate assessment for multiracial students might ask, for example:

1. Are programs and services available for monoracial groups equally available to multiracial students? For example, if there is a staff person for asian student concerns, is there someone for mixed student concerns? If not, why?
2. Do multiracial students have equal access to resources such as scholarships, student organizations (meeting space, activities fee funding, campus services), and support?
3. If the institution measures student satisfaction, are multiracial students as satisfied with their campus experience overall and in specific areas (curriculum, cocurriculum, etc.) as other students and, in particular, students of color who are ostensibly monoracial?
4. In what ways do outcomes (e.g., retention, academic achievement, graduation rates, other measures of student learning and development) vary for multiracial students compared to the population as a whole and monoracial students?

Of course, these measures assume that such information is available for the campus population as a whole. While I more generally recommend that institutions conduct ongoing assessment of a variety of variables (student learning, satisfaction, outcomes), here I suggest that whatever information is known about the student population overall should also be analyzed including multiracial students as a constituent group.

In addition, careful examination of existing programs and services for their level of accessibility (both measured and as perceived by multiracial students) is in order. Do multiracial students know that programs and services are equally available to them as to "whole" students of color? What are their experiences when accessing these programs and services? Does accessing these resources require them to claim an identity pattern (such as Monoracial Identity) to which they do not subscribe? How many eligible students decline available resources because they would rather forego resources than shift identity patterns? Answers to these and other climate-related questions could serve as data to undergird changes in campus policy or practice, or simply changes in how resources are presented to students.

Institutional Policy, Programs, and Services

In terms of institutional policy, programs, and services, the findings of this study suggest a number of measures, which should be further supported by institutional assessment before adoption on campus. I have already discussed the importance of changing racial and ethnic data collection to comply with the revisions to Directive 15 (see Renn & Lunceford, 2002, for a detailed analysis of the status of federal and institutional data collection) and to assess the prevalence of mixed heritages among the student population. But the means of racial and ethnic data collection are themselves prompts to mixed race identity awareness, if not development. Students were sharply aware of the need to revise data collection and interpreted the common institutional practice of the "check boxes" as either an inclusive or exclusive message. They were also aware that data were used in ways that they could not control once they checked the boxes. (Julia: "A lot of college applications say 'Check One,' and I felt happy that I could check two for Ivy, but then I found out they didn't use it anyway. They just put me with the minority group.")

I do not see a viable way around asking students how they identify, nor do I recommend that we abandon the practice altogether. It remains critically important to understand differences by racial category in higher education access, persistence, and outcomes. What I suggest is that institutions adopt at least a two-step question about racial identity, part of which asks for racial heritage and part of which asks for racial identity (if any). I further recommend that institutions state how data will be aggregated so that students will know what will happen to their data if they check more than one heritage. For example, an institution might ask, "To what racial and/or ethnic groups do your parents belong? (indicate as many as apply)," followed by a list of the six categories determined by OMB or by a more detailed list that includes specific ethnic groups and nationalities within the six major categories. The next question would ask students how they identified. For example, "Please indicate how you identify (indicate as many as apply)," followed by a list of monoracial categories, "bi- or multiracial," and "other: _____." A short description of data aggregation rules would precede or follow these two questions, explaining how multiple category responses will be used. A statement might read, "Multiple responses will be included fractionally in total counts. If you indicate two categories, data will be counted as .5 in one and .5 in the other," or "Multiple responses will be included as whole numbers in total counts. If you indicate two categories, you will be counted once in each category." Although fractional and whole assignment methods are considered standard and acceptable for data aggregation, neither is without significant drawbacks,[1] the most significant being that respondents lose the right to determine how they are counted. Given the strength of students' desire to self-identify, some means to account for self-determination in data aggregation should be incorporated, even if it is statistically inconvenient or outside the design of current student information system software. An ideal plan might include completely open-ended questions, with space for elaboration ("Well, it depends . . ."), though the feasibility of such an option seems highly questionable, to say nothing of the near impossibility of interpreting such data and comparing it intra- and interinstitutionally.

Perhaps more important than how we determine who counts for how much in what categories is what happens to students when they are on our campuses. The findings of this study support the creation and maintenance of public venues for claiming Multiracial Identity and for questioning racial categories. As I have argued elsewhere (Renn, 1998, 2000, 2003; Renn & Bilodeau, 2002), the presence of identity-based spaces on campus is critical for individuals' identity development and for community building across differences. In a study of identity politics on campus, Rhoads (1997) concluded, "Cultural identity is for many students a basic foundation for learning," and "Identity groups and identity politics should not necessarily be seen as the source of campus fragmentation" (p. 517). Time and again, the students I interviewed at Ivy, Big Ten, and Catholic, where there were either formal student organizations (Spectrum, Hapa) or an informal network on its way to becoming a formal student group (at Catholic), described the power of designated multiracial space. For some students, it was a cornerstone of their identity (e.g., Jonathon, Kate, Julia, Phillip, Kimlien, Summer, Jennifer), while for others it provided an important springboard into other activities (Eleanor, B. J.) or respite from the relentless pressure to conform to a monoracial norm (David, Dan).

What might this space look like outside of designated student organizations? The inclusion of a bi- and multiracial group at Ivy's preorientation program was one way to create institutional support for this space, as was the hiring of a multiracial student programmer on a par with the monoracial group programmers at the Third World Center. On campuses where the multicultural infrastructure is not so well developed or supported, student affairs professionals can take more simple steps such as sponsoring speakers on mixed race issues (other than just interracial dating, an issue that is somewhat about mixed race students, but really is more about their parents and people like them), including opportunities for mixed students to participate in cultural displays or performances (students at Ivy performed a polyvocal narrative about the experience of being multiracial), increasing campus media coverage of mixed issues, and supporting the visibility of mixed students already involved in campus leadership. As study participants indicated, it is not necessary to have an ongoing multiracial space; temporary public spaces where mixed identity could be discussed and experienced were powerful influences on identity, even in the absence of ongoing groups.

Findings from this study support existing literature on the development of students of color on predominantly white campuses in its calls for providing role models for students from a variety of backgrounds. Christina's faculty mentor, whom she suspected to be "mulatta, in all the problematic ways that term gets used," was a significant role model, as were Phillip's advisors who introduced him to the term *hapa* and to Filipino culture and history. Students repeatedly claimed that they could identify other mixed students by their appearances, but they rarely mentioned faculty or staff in this regard; given racial demographics, mixed race people are less likely to occur in older generations within the population, but demographics alone do not explain the dearth of mixed race role models among faculty and staff. Naomi Zack has claimed that mixed race academics must "write themselves into existence" in the academy, which is built on an assumption of monoraciality. Challenging that assumption may be easier in some ways for students than for faculty and administrators, who have themselves accepted the academy as a desirable work environment; supporting mixed faculty and staff in any efforts they might make to "come out" as multiracial would be an important step toward increasing the visibility of mixed people in higher education.

Whether or not mixed students choose to take advantage of public multiracial space and the visibility of other multiracial students, faculty, and staff, the presence of these resources and role models sends a message that in spite of the necessity to conform in many respects to the monoracial norm of the outside world, an institution values and supports its mixed race members. Such a message would go a long way to counterbalance the powerful messages students received from peer and institutional culture that being mixed was somehow "not normal" (David) or that they were somehow at fault for "unpurifying the races" (Eleanor). Together with obvious steps like ceasing to ask individuals to "check one box only," promoting these counterbalancing messages in institutional micro-, meso-, and exosystems could influence students' sense of the possibility and desirability of fluid multiracial identification.

Structural Diversity

Addressing structural diversity, including the number of students of color—and mixed race students in particular—on campus remains a challenge, the resolution of which could enhance developmental conditions for mixed race students. Although increasing the number of students of color on campus does not automatically increase the population of mixed race students, given current racial demographics in the United States, it seems sensible to conclude that as the number of students of color rises, so will the number of multiracial students. And with that increase likely will come increased opportunities for mixed students to encounter one another and form peer networks.

I have raised the issue of critical mass in determining the availability of explicitly mixed race spaces (Renn, 1998, 2000), and the findings from all phases of the study support the idea that without a critical mass of mixed students who encounter one another through formal or informal networks, it is unlikely that a formal multiracial space on campus will emerge. Students at Ivy and Big Ten had already created such spaces and had the student population to support them; enough mixed students at Catholic had connected that they were on the brink of forming a student group at the time I collected data there. Since then, the group has formed and a prominent biracial scholar has become the faculty advisor. Students at Liberal Arts said they would be interested in such a group, but until the focus group I conducted, they had not met other mixed students on campus. In addition to critical mass, the motivation to organize was an essential element in the creation of student-led space; students at Rural University seemed to have the critical mass but not the motivation necessary to create a mixed student organization.

It is important to remember that all study participants attended predominantly white institutions, so most of the time that students spent outside formal and informal groups of students of color (monoracial or multiracial) they were immersed in mainstream white student culture. The findings of my study echo in part the findings of any study of students of color on predominantly white campuses; they frequently felt like outsiders (Audrey: "I don't feel like it's my school."). Making connections with faculty, administrators, and other students of color, whether monoracial or multiracial, was a key to students' social and academic integration at these schools (see Tinto, 1993, for a discussion of the influence of academic and social integration on student retention). But even within communities of color, students said again and again how they felt like outsiders, lacking in sufficient cultural knowledge, authenticity, and legitimacy. So although it might be tempting to classify mixed race students' experiences only as those of outsiders on predominantly white campuses, to do so would be to ignore the very specific effects of being outside the assumed monoracial norm. For all of these reasons—increasing the number of mixed students, achieving a critical mass for student organizing, and for challenging the monoracial and predominantly white norm—increasing the number and diversity of students of color in higher education is an important step in improving opportunities for mixed race students to thrive.

Promoting Alternative Approaches to Race and Identity on Campus

At the same time as it is important to attend to the racial and ethnic composition of student, faculty, and administrative bodies, the findings of this study suggest that campuses could do much to deemphasize traditional conceptions of race, thereby providing students with the knowledge, skills, and attitudes to consider a wider range of racial identity patterns. I propose that faculty and administrators work to promote a social constructionist approach to race and racial identity in the curriculum, cocurriculum, and administrative infrastructures. Infusing campus culture with alternatives to the notion of fixed, rigid racial categories would introduce students to additional options for identity, whether or not they chose to take up those identities.

Participants often remarked on how opportunities to engage in academic work in the area of identity provided meaningful settings to think, read, hear, and talk about important issues related to identity. For example, Audrey, Dee Dee, Amy, and Phillip's experiences led them to examine their ideas about race, culture, and identity in academic microsystems; Jazz, Sina, Summer, and Jeff took up projects or courses made available to them by decisions at the exosystem level of faculty decisions about curricula and course content. These findings reinforce those of other researchers who urge educators to ground teaching and learning in students' experiences and lives (see, for example, American College Personnel Association, 1994; Astin, 1999; Baxter Magolda, 1999; Kuh, 1996; Terenzini, Pascarella, & Blimling, 1996). In the context of this study, the findings further suggest that the introduction of courses, texts, workshops, lectures, and informal learning experiences that deal directly with the mixed race experience or with other aspects of socially constructed identity could provide more students—of any racial heritage—opportunities to explore racial and other identities on campus. The increasing presence of mixed race students and discussion of the history and current prevalence of multiraciality expose the myth of "racial purity" on which social, economic, and political systems have operated in the United States.

Study findings further suggest that we have sold many undergraduates short in the widespread belief that postmodern theory is over their heads and that explicit discussion of the social construction of identities is less important than mandatory "diversity training" during new student orientation. Merely grounding learning in students' experiences is not enough; purposefully providing them with language, theory, and cognitive tools (as illustrated by several participants in this study) to understand better the complexity of race, race relations, and raciality may facilitate individual development and could enhance identity development across the spectrum of undergraduate diversity.

It is not enough, though, to confine these messages to the classroom; congruent messages from academic and peer microsystems could support an ethos of critical examination of cultural assumptions about race, gender, class, and sexuality. One campus in the study (Ivy) had particularly strong, congruent messages across the mesosystem that encouraged intellectual pursuits outside the formal curriculum. On that campus, for example, Dan's experience of an Orientation Week activity and Sina's observation of how campus groups interacted in the cocurriculum supported their in-class opportunities to explore the construction of racial identity, for example. Capitalizing on the developmentally instigative characteristics of students inclined to pursue cognitive complexity will reach some students (like those in this study who sought opportunities to pursue identity-related academic or cocurricular projects), but saturation of the environment with congruent messages may be necessary to reach those whose inclinations lead them elsewhere.

Promoting a Peer Culture That Supports Boundary Crossing and Multiple Identifications for Mixed Race Students

The ability to move freely between and among academic and social microsystems enhanced students' degree of exploration of multiple identity patterns, including the option not to identify along racial lines. Although the efficacy of attempts to alter student peer cultures is limited (see, for example, Dalton & Petrie, 1997), educators can take steps to enhance students' ability to move between microsystems. For example, at Liberal Arts, where students reported the greatest degree of freedom to move between settings, the residential system was designed to promote annual redistribution of all on-campus students among all halls through mixed class housing and a "no squatting" policy requiring every student to enter the housing lottery; a student living on campus for four years would share a residence hall with a substantially different 10 percent of the student population each year, encouraging new acquaintanceships and potential peer groupings. Distribution of students across required courses and activities (e.g., orientation, advising, etc.), creative use of physical spaces for the scheduling of courses and meetings, and attention to architectural and design decisions in public spaces can influence the mesosystem by causing microsystems to encounter one another physically as well as intellectually or emotionally.

In addition to supporting the design of environments that promote boundary crossing, the study suggests supporting a peer culture that allows maximum flexibility for identity exploration and multiple, shifting identifications for mixed race—and, indeed, all—students. I do not propose that educators attempt to become architects of student peer cultures (if, indeed, that is even possible), but I do suggest that educators seek access to and actively engage peer culture when they encounter it. Student affairs administrators have access to formal leadership structures of student organizations, as well as the ability to influence campus media not editorially but through active participation as contributors. Advisers and faculty (like the two at Big Ten who influenced Phillip's Pilipino and hapa identities) have one-on-one connections with students and can engage conversations about race, identity, and community. I do not advocate withdrawal of support for monoracial student groups or students of color who are immersed in exploration of their own monoracial heritage, but I do advocate active introduction of questions about the validity of "race," "monoraciality," and the often tacit criteria students enforce for membership in various campus communities, as well as open support for students and others who identify in and with more than one community on campus. Recognition from respected nonstudent advisers, leaders, and administrators that multiracial students with more than one identity pattern are not underdeveloped or confused, but at a healthy point of Situational Identity, could make a significant difference in some campus peer cultures.

There are no easy formulas for transforming higher education policy and practice better to reflect and meet the needs of an increasing number of mixed race students. It is impossible, of course, to prescribe a formula for higher education policy and practice that would create campus environments that fostered only positive outcomes for mixed race students, even if that were a desirable goal. Student development occurs as a result of both positive and negative experiences, feelings of inclusion and exclusion, and successful and unsuccessful attempts to identify in certain ways; to attempt to take the edge off the sometimes difficult processes of learning and development would be a disservice to students and might ultimately blunt their development. But this study suggests that attention to messages—both formal and informal—related to the fixedness or fluidity of race and racial identity in the institutional environment would be an important first step in addressing identity issues for multiracial students without necessarily attempting to eliminate developmental challenges they might encounter. A mixed race student might choose only one identity pattern, but knowing there were options—making an active identity choice—would seem a positive outcome for all students, of any racial heritage.

NATIONAL POLICIES

Beyond institutional policy and practices, matters of national policy affect mixed race students, from what could be considered the exosystem in an ecological systems analysis. That is, there are matters decided at the level of federal policy that affect multiracial students, but from environmental systems of which the students themselves are not part. For example, the 1997 revisions to OMB Directive 15 change how racial and ethnic data are collected as well as how those data must be reported to the Department of Education through the National Center for Education Statistics (NCES) Integrated Postsecondary Education Data System (IPEDS). Although changes were supposed to be in place by January 1, 2003, competing proposals from various federal agencies slowed the adoption process, and it is not yet clear what the outcome will be and when postsecondary institutions will have to comply with new standards.[2] When they do, however, they will be required to allow students to indicate more than one racial background on institutional forms, they will not be permitted to include a "multiracial" category in data for IPEDS reporting, and they will be instructed how to aggregate responses for individuals indicating more than one racial background.

Data collection and reporting might seem to be peripheral to the identities of mixed race students, but the findings of this study indicate that the ability to self-determine was important to students and that the process of filling out forms—being forced in the moment to claim an identity as circumscribed by the authors of the forms—made racial identity salient for students in higher education settings. In fall 2002, 62 percent of a random sample of two- and four-year institutions collected data in a five-race, one-ethnicity, "choose-only-one" format; other institutions provided additional categories, allowed respondents to choose more than one category, or both (Renn & Lunceford, 2002, p. 29). Whatever the case at an individual student's institution, he or she encounters this question and its opportunity to consider and reconsider racial and multiracial identity. Forces well outside the student's environment thus introduce a developmental prompt into the day-to-day world of life on campus, where filling out forms may occur at admissions, when applying for scholarships, taking standardized tests, completing research surveys, and so on. It is not clear what the ultimate outcome of federal policy on racial and ethnic data collection will be, but it is clear that decisions in this arena can influence mixed race students' identity processes.

SCHOLARSHIP AND THEORY

The experience of mixed race college students lies at the intersection of two main bodies of scholarship: studies of multiraciality and research on college student development. Studies like this one draw from both areas and, in turn, enrich knowledge and theory applicable in each arena. In this section I discuss possible directions for expanding research on mixed race college students in ways that would further enhance higher education practice, policy, and scholarship.

Employing Quantitative Research Methods in Large-scale Studies

There have been few large-scale studies of mixed race college students and there is much yet unknown about this very diverse population. Most work in the area of multiraciality has employed small, qualitative samples in limited geographic areas (e.g., Hall, 1992; Kerwin, Ponterotto, Jackson, & Harris, 1993; Kich, 1992; Root, 1990;). Rockquemore and Brunsma (2002) conducted the largest study of biracial college students to date (177 students), but they limited their sample to mixed black-white individuals. Other studies that have included multiracial undergraduates have done so incidentally, rather than as the focus of the study (e.g., Kilson, 2001; Wallace, 2001); some have included only college students as the population, but usually as a matter of convenience rather than for the purpose of examining the college setting (e.g., Mass, 1992; Standen, 1996). These studies have produced important information about the lives and identities of mixed race people of particular heritage combination, in specific geographic areas, or in particular contexts. My study, while drawing participants from diverse geographic regions and heritage backgrounds, is limited because of its sample size and research method. But the result is that little is known about mixed race college students that might be generalized in any meaningful way.

Large-scale studies currently conducted (e.g., Cooperative Institutional Research Project [CIRP], National Student of Student Engagement [NSSE], Consortium on Financing Higher Education [COFHE]) could allow students to indicate more than one racial heritage, creating a data set that interested researchers could analyze for information on the experiences of this population. Katalin Szelenyi (2002) has begun this work in the area of family income and multiple heritage respondents to the annual CIRP survey; her work reveals not only important information about the students surveyed but also how information about biracial students is masked in most analyses of these data and, indeed, complicates the data in ways previously unconsidered. Patterns of specific heritage mixes, differences by geographic region, family patterns, educational plans, and college satisfaction and outcomes could be analyzed for mixed race students from existing surveys.

It is time for a national study of mixed race students, their experiences, identities, and college outcomes. A study specific to the mixed experience, the ways students identify in different situations, and intersections of identity and environment would provide information valuable to researchers of multiraciality as well as to higher education policy makers attempting to determine criteria to bridge data from "old" choose-only-one categories to whatever "new" choose-as-many-as-apply data. Although Root (1992a) called for increased use of qualitative research approaches, research in the intervening decade has provided adequate information from which to craft a survey instrument for national implementation. Information gleaned from such data collection and analyses yield important insights into mixed students and how higher education is—or is not—meeting their needs for learning and development.

EXAMINING DEVELOPMENTAL THEORIES FOR
BIAS TOWARD UNILATERAL IDENTITY OUTCOMES

Many student development theories and theories that have been adopted for research on college students (e.g., Cass, 1979; Chickering & Reisser, 1993; Cross, 1995; Helms, 1995) posit identity development as a process leading to a unitary, integrated, and "synthesized" individual identity. Students who do not commit to an identity cannot reach what Marcia (1966) called the "Identity Achievement status" and are left in Identity Moratorium or Identity Diffusion. Even early models of biracial identity development posited unitary outcomes; Poston (1990) predicted Integration, wherein individuals would recognize and value all of their ethnic identities, and Kich (1992) predicted an endpoint of biracial/bicultural identity. Root's (1996a) introduction of four "border crossings" representing healthy outcomes of biracial identity formation marked a significant break from the notion that racial identity development must lead inexorably to the same outcome for all individuals. From her research and that of Kilson (2001), Wallace (2001), and Rockquemore and Brunsma (2002), as well as this study, it seems clear that Root's theory of multiple possibilities for healthy outcomes of identity is an important direction for identity research.

Scholars, students, and practitioners of student development theory should examine not only racial identity development theories but also other theories in the field for evidence of bias in favor of unilateral outcomes. An awareness that many theories considered foundational (e.g., Chickering, 1969; Erickson, 1968; Kohlberg, 1976; Perry, 1968) were based on predominantly white samples comprised primarily or only of college men prompted exploration of alternative and/or more inclusive theories (e.g., Atkinson, Morten, & Sue, 1993; Gilligan, 1977; Josselson, 1987; Tatum, 1995). But even these new theories rely on the notion that identity outcomes in the areas of race or gender identity look more or less the same across a given population. I do not challenge the utility of theories that attempt to predict outcomes across broad populations, but I do argue that just as many early identity theories failed to reflect the experiences of women and people of color, even the newer theories assume a somewhat linear progression and uniform outcomes. They do not account for the reality of identities that are "outside the boxes." Students who do not—and do not choose to—fit neatly into one identity category or another will not fit neatly into a theory that predicts a racial identity that tacitly takes *monoraciality* as the norm; neither, indeed, will students who identify outside the homo/heterosexual dichotomy and the gender binary fit neatly into theories predicated on static gender and sexual identities.

In a study of identity politics on campus, Robert Rhoads (1997) argued against theories that suggest that "identity pride" or "immersion" stages represent an unfinished level of identity development, but I take the argument one step further to question the value of stage or progressive theories that posit unitary identity outcomes. How might we make space in student development theory for students who will not ever end up in a unitary identity? How might we consider their development in ways that honor their experience and the multiple, shifting, contextually responsive identities they might hold? How, at the same time, might we work toward student development theories that are useful for exploring and understanding identities across a range of institutions and student characteristics? In short, how can we balance the need for specificity and context sensitivity with the need for reasonable levels of generalizability? The answers are not simple, but continuing to explore these questions is critical for the continued relevance of student development theories in a postsecondary education environment that will increasingly contain individuals who do not fit predetermined boxes and existing developmental trajectories.

EXPLORING ECOLOGICAL ANALYSES OF PEER CULTURE AND ITS INFLUENCES ON STUDENT LEARNING AND DEVELOPMENT

One promising approach to the challenge of balancing context-specific development and generalizable principles of identity formation lies in the ecology model. As I argued in chapter 2, it provides a heuristic for analyzing the influences of individual characteristics (Person), interactions with the various levels of the environment (Process and Content), and changes over Time. The ecology model provides a number of levels of analysis (individual, microsystems, mesosystem, exosystem, macrosystem, chronosystem), as well as process-related elements such as the modes of interaction between person and environment, as represented by developmentally instigative characteristics and features of the proximal settings.

At the level of the mesosystem, which is of particular interest to me because of the powerful role it played in mixed race students' identity choices, opportunities for research and theorizing abound. Examining the looseness or tightness of mesosystem couplings, the rigidity of boundaries around peer microsystems, and the congruity or incongruity of mesosystem messages related to race and identity are all potential means of approaching mesosystem effects on mixed identity. It may be the case that features or processes common to mesosystems on many campuses or institutional types influence identity in similar ways; a resulting theory would allow for variation in individual characteristics and outcomes while providing some generalizable propositions about the *processes*, if not the outcomes, of student development.

It is clear from existing research that peers have a powerful influence on student outcomes (Astin, 1977, 1984, 1993; Kuh, 1990; Kuh, Hu, & Vesper, 2000; Pascarella & Terenzini, 1991), but it is not well understood how these influences occur (Renn & Arnold, 2003; Kuh, 1995). Utilizing an ecology model as I propose provides an explicit location for the analysis of peer culture in the mesosystem. By integrating peer culture in a multi-level analysis of influences and outcomes, researchers could gain a holistic view of student development that, rather than muting all individual characteristics in an attempt to homogenize data for uniform analytic treatment, could take into account unique combinations of personal characteristics and multiple, nonlinear student identity outcomes. Such an approach could make more clear the processes of peer influence on individuals as well as the outcomes of this influence.

The three directions I propose for research and theory on mixed race students—conducting large-scale, quantitative studies of identity and identification, examining existing theories for bias toward unilateral identity outcomes, and using an ecology model to study peer culture influences and effects—could benefit not only this population but also others. Incorporating the postmodern idea that race and other identities are socially constructed does not mean abandoning all modernist research methods and student development theories; but it does mean that old assumptions about what it means to have or be a race cannot be allowed to go unchallenged in educational research, theory, policy, and practice. Study participants made clear that they understand race as a social construction; if undergraduates have the cognitive flexibility to understand "race isn't real" but that it has very real meaning and effects in society, then certainly scholars and educators can accommodate this idea in research and practice. Not to, I fear, sends the message that we do not know or care that a society premised on monoracial categories no longer rests quietly on its modernist, racialized, categorized foundations. The population has changed and will continue to; higher education scholars and educators can either adapt or fall behind.

CONCLUSION

Changes in higher education policy and practice and developments in scholarship and theory are important and imminent. But they did not and will not happen in time to influence the developmental ecologies of Mike, Amy, Dee Dee, Marisa, Kimlien, Phillip, Kate, and the other forty-nine students who participated in this study. For these students, campus life was comprised of sometimes welcoming, sometimes exclusionary microsystems and mesosystems that, for better and for worse, interacted to create rich developmental ecologies from which the five identity patterns emerged. Some students will likely remain in the identities they engaged during the time of the study, others will, as Jonathon suggested, take up their right to identify differently at different times in their lives. The complex ecology of campus life will be replaced by the complex ecology of work, adult partnerships, and family, transforming proximal environments as profoundly as they were transformed when students came to these six campuses.

It is not clear what the future holds for these fifty-six young adults, nor is it clear what direction multiracial identities and politics will take. What *is* clear is that the mixed race population is growing and will continue to grow rapidly in higher education. Mixed race students themselves know it and challenge educators and scholars to meet them in their multiple ways of identifying. Our preparedness for this challenge—in institutional practice, student support infrastructure, and theoretical flexibility—will be put to the test, a test we must pass in order to serve all of our students, regardless of their racial heritages.

appendix A

Revisions to the Standards for the Classification of Federal Data on Race and Ethnicity

Taken from the Office of Management and Budget Directive 15, available online at http://www.whitehouse.gov/OMB/fedreg/Ombdir15.html

STANDARDS FOR MAINTAINING, COLLECTING, AND PRESENTING FEDERAL DATA ON RACE AND ETHNICITY

This classification provides a minimum standard for maintaining, collecting, and presenting data on race and ethnicity for all Federal reporting purposes. The categories in this classification are social-political constructs and should not be interpreted as being scientific or anthropological in nature. They are not to be used as determinants of eligibility for participation in any Federal program. The standards have been developed to provide a common language for uniformity and comparability in the collection and use of data on race and ethnicity by Federal agencies.

The standards have five categories for data on race: American Indian or Alaska Native, Asian, Black or African American, Native Hawaiian or Other Pacific Islander, and White. There are two categories for data on ethnicity: "Hispanic or Latino" and "Not Hispanic or Latino."

CATEGORIES AND DEFINITIONS

The minimum categories for data on race and ethnicity for Federal statistics, program administrative reporting, and civil rights compliance reporting are defined as follows:

American Indian or Alaska Native. A person having origins in any of the original peoples of North and South America (including Central America), and who maintains tribal affiliation or community attachment.

Asian. A person having origins in any of the original peoples of the Far East, Southeast Asian, or the Indian subcontinent including, for example, Cambodia, China, India, Japan, Korea, Malaysia, Pakistan, the Philippine Islands, Thailand, and Vietnam.

Black or African American. A person having origins in any of the black racial groups of Africa. Terms such as "Haitian" or "Negro" can be used in addition to "Black or African American."

Hispanic or Latino. A person of Cuban, Mexican, Puerto Rican, Cuban [sic], South or Central American, or other Spanish culture or origin, regardless of race. The term, "Spanish origin," can be used in addition to "Hispanic or Latino."

Native Hawaiian or Other Pacific Islander. A person having origins in any of the original peoples of Hawaii, Guam, Samoa, or other Pacific Islands.

White. A person having origins in any of the original peoples of Europe, the Middle East, or North Africa.

Respondents shall be offered the option of selecting one or more racial designations. Recommended forms for the instruction accompanying the multiple response question are "Mark one or more" and "Select one or more.

appendix B

Summary of Study Participants

TABLE B.1
Alphabetical List of Participants, Institutions, Year in School, and Heritages

Pseudonym	School/year	Self-description and Ethnic Background (father/mother)
Alexandra	Catholic University, junior	multiracial; hispanic & Chinese/native american
Amy	Rural University, senior	mixed or no label; black/white
Ann	Big Ten University, junior	half black & half white; african american/white
Audrey	Liberal Arts College, sophomore	multiracial; Scottish, English/Irish, African, Chinese
Benjamin	Big Ten University, first year	Islander; Micronesian/English, Irish, Dutch
Beth	Rural University, senior; went to community college first	biracial, half hispanic and the other half is a mixture of a lot of things; half-Mexican/anglo & Austrian Jew
B. J.	Catholic University, first year	multiracial; african american/Filipino (plus white stepfather)
Bob	Big Ten University, first year	Mexican American; Mexican American (hispanic)/caucasian
Bridget	Big Ten University, sophomore	biracial; african american/Puerto Rican (raised by Puerto Rican grandmother)

261

Pseudonym	School/year	Self-description and Ethnic Background (father/mother)
Christina	Ivy University, senior	multiracial; white/Indian-Jamaican
Clarice	Big Ten University, junior	half Indian, half white; Indian (south asian)/white—Irish, German, English
Dan	Ivy University, sophomore	biracial asian american or biracial Chinese American; Italian/Chinese (raised with white stepmother)
Dave	Liberal Arts College, senior	multiracial; Iranian/American
David	Ivy University, senior	biracial or hapa yonsei; third generation French-Irish/third generation Japanese American
Dee Dee	Ivy University, senior	black; african american/South Asian
Delores	Big Ten University, first year	mixed; from Germany/black
Dwayne	Rural University, sophomore	black; african american/Canadian
Eleanor	Ivy University, junior	biracial, black; african american/Scottish
Elektra	Catholic University, senior	half asian or half; white/Chinese
Elizabeth	Liberal Arts College, first year	biracial; Japanese American/white
Ellen	Rural Community College, sophomore	multiracial; Mexican & black/native american & black
Erika	Liberal Arts College, first year	half American, half Japanese, or international; Japanese/American (meaning "white")
Florence	Big Ten University, first year	multicultural, "mutt"; American Indian, white, black/white, black, American Indian
Fred	Catholic University, senior	half Japanese; English, Irish, Scottish/second generation Japanese American
Jack	Rural Community College, second year	mixed, mulatto; black/white

Pseudonym	School/year	Self-description and Ethnic Background (father/mother)
Jazz	Liberal Arts College, sophomore	multicultural; Egyptian/white
Jeff	Ivy University, junior	hapa, biracial, or multiracial; second generation Japanese American/European American (French, German, Spanish)
Jennifer	Catholic University, senior	half white, half Filipino; Filipino/white
John	Liberal Arts College, sophomore	black; black/Puerto Rican
Jonathon	Ivy University, senior	multiracial, biracial, multiracial asian american, hapa, Amerasian, Eurasian, asian american, multiracial Japanese Jewish American, Japanese Jewish American, Japanese European American; Jewish/Japanese American
Juan	Rural University, sophomore	mixed or Chicano; Mexican/Anglo
Julia	Ivy University, sophomore	biracial; white/black
Kate	Ivy University, first year	biracial; Chinese/Peruvian
Kayla	Ivy University, junior	mixed race, mixed, or multiracial; Hungarian Jew/Hindu Indian
Kimlien	Big Ten University, first year	hapa or Vietnamese American; French American/Vietnamese, Chinese American
Kira	Ivy University, sophomore	biracial; white/Filipina
LuLu	Rural University, junior	mixed; Swedish (from Sweden)/Chinese (from China)
Luz	Ivy University, junior	biracial; white/Filipino
Marisa	Liberal Arts College, senior	Jamaican, multiracial, or black; Indian/Afro-Caribbean & white
Mark	Big Ten University, sophomore	Mexican American; Mexican/white

Pseudonym	School/year	Self-description and Ethnic Background (father/mother)
May	Rural University, first year	mixed; white (Russian)/Middle Eastern, Arabic
Mike	Rural University, first year	biracial, mixed, black; african american/hispanic or Puerto Rican
Mina	Rural Community College, first year	South Asian; south asian/Scottish, Dutch, English
Phil	Catholic University, first year	mixed, biracial, or half asian; German, Austrian, Hungarian/Chinese
Phillip	Big Ten University, sophomore	hapa; white/Pilipino
Princess	Big Ten University, senior	biracial; african american/white
Renee	Rural Community College, sophomore	mixed; white/african american
Rhonda	Rural Community College, third year	mixed or black; black/Italian
Samantha	Rural University, senior	biracial; white/black
Sapo	Liberal Arts College, sophomore	Mexican American; Mexican/Irish
Sina	Ivy University, junior	biracial; white/Samoan, of Chinese descent
Stacey	Ivy University, sophomore	multiracial ("Ameripino"); white/Filipina
Steve	Big Ten University, junior	mixed; black or african american/white or Caucasian
Summer	Catholic University, senior	half asian; Latvian Jewish/Korean
Tim	Rural Community College, first year	biracial; white/hispanic
Vincent	Catholic University, sophomore	multiple heritage or international; Swiss/Chinese

TABLE B.2
Summary of Participants by Heritages

Heritage	Participants
Two parents of color	Alexandra
	Beth
	B. J.
	Bridget
	Christina
	Dee Dee
	Ellen
	Florence
	John
	Kate
	Marisa
	Mike
One asian & one white parent	Clarice
	Dan
	David
	Elektra
	Elizabeth
	Erika
	Fred
	Jeff
	Jonathon
	Kayla
	Kimlien
	LuLu
	Mina
	Phil
	Summer
	Vincent
One black & one white parent	Amy
	Ann
	Delores
	Dwayne
	Eleanor
	Jack
	Jazz
	Julia
	Princess
	Renee
	Rhonda
	Samantha
	Steve

Heritage	Participants
One latino/a & one white parent	Bob
	Juan
	Mark
	Sapo
	Tim
One Pacific Islander & one white parent	Benjamin
	Jennifer
	Kira
	Luz
	Phillip
	Sina
	Stacey
One mixed & one white parent	Audrey
	Dave
	May

Interview and Focus Group Protocols

INDIVIDUAL INTERVIEW PROTOCOL

BACKGROUND INFORMATION:

1. Where did you go to high school?
2. In what ways was it similar to or different from your college? (prompt for: size, public/private, racial composition of student body)
3. How did you decide to come to _____?
4. How do you describe yourself? (prompt for: racial/ethnic identity)

THE COLLEGE EXPERIENCE:

5. Now think about yourself when you came to college. Has that description changed since then? If so, in what way(s)? If not, why not?
6. What do you think contributed to that change/reinforced that description?
7. Tell me about your friends and other peers here. How does your sense of identity play off of your relationships with them?
8. What kind of activities are you involved in on or off campus? In what ways do your activities reflect or contribute to your identity as multiracial?
9. In terms of academic work, what is your major? What kinds of classes have you taken? Have you ever done coursework, or an assignment, that dealt with your racial identity? What did you make of that?
10. Is there anything else you'd like to tell me about yourself or your experience here?

PROTOCOL FOR FOCUS GROUPS

1. Introduction

- Discuss purpose of the focus group session: to check my findings and to give participants a chance to interact with one another about the topic of being a multiracial college student
- Introduction of participants (name, year, anything else they'd like to add)

2. Summary of findings

- Describe progress of study to date (interviews completed, analysis, etc.)
- Invite questions about progress
- Hand out copies of data summary portrait for the school
- Ask participants to talk about their reactions to the portrait:
  —What strikes them as correct?
  —What seems incorrect? What would be more correct?
  —What's missing?
  —Was anything surprising?
  —Has something another participant said prompted a reaction from anyone?

3. Specific questions

- What seems to be missing from the big picture?
  —Are there other options for racial identity?
  —Does the theory about space and peer culture seem plausible? Does it fit their experience?
- Does anyone have any theories about why more women than men responded to publicity or invitations to participate in project?
- Does anyone have any theories about the preponderance of asian ethnicities in the sample?

4. What else should I know?

5. What other questions do you have for me or for each other?

Notes

CHAPTER TWO

1. It is important to note that not all literature used to support the practice of student affairs was intended as "student development" research; an interdisciplinary field, student affairs draws from a variety of disciplinary traditions, including sociology and psychology. Although a few theories were developed specifically to address the concerns of college students, many (like Cross, Helms, Cass, and the Bronfenbrenner I introduce in this chapter) have been incorporated into higher education theory and practice from other fields.

2. For a transhistorical description and analysis of student experiences, see Helen Lefkowitz Horowitz's *Campus Life* (1987) or Barbara Solomon's *In the Company of Education Women* (1985).

3. A notable exception is Marion Kilson's *Claiming Place: Biracial Young Adults of the Post-Civil Rights Era* (2001), which is one of the few scholarly treatments of biraciality to include a national sample: nineteen participants from the Northeast, sixteen from the Mid-Atlantic, seven from the Midwest, and ten from the West (p. 11). Kilson included young adults ages twenty-four through thirty-four, and eleven of the fifty-two were undergraduate or graduate students at the time of the study. Individuals—regardless of student status—from the Southeast and Southwest are rarely represented in studies of the multiracial experience.

4. Institutional names are pseudonyms selected for ease of identification of the schools in the text. In previous reports of this study (e.g., Renn, 1998, 2000, 2003) some institutional pseudonyms are different.

5. I decided to include two students from Liberal Arts College and one Rural University student who did not fit my usual definition of multiracial as having parents from more than one federally designated racial category. Dave, a Liberal Arts College senior grew up in suburban Massachusetts with his parents who were from Iran. His father was Iranian, and his mother, although she had been living in Iran, was white and an American citizen. He said he identified as multiracial in part because he did not fit into any of the other racial categories and because he experienced his life as very different culturally from his parents' lives. Furthermore, he believed that he looked "racially ambiguous" with his medium brown skin tone and tightly curled hair. He said that he often had to explain how he fit, or did not fit, into a racial category.

For these reasons, he strongly held the identity that he called "multiracial."

The other Liberal Arts student who did not fit the usual definition of multiracial was a sophomore, Jazz, who grew up in Egypt with her dark-skinned Egyptian father and her white mother. While her father as a Middle Easterner would not be categorized as "Black or African American" in the Office of Management and Budget directive (1997), she strongly believed that in the United States her family would be considered interracial and that she would be labeled "biracial." Like the young man with Iranian parents, she attributed much of her multiracial identity to her appearance, which did not, according to her, fit into any "standard race" in the United States. Similarly, May, a first-year student at Rural University, insisted that in the United States, her family would be considered interracial. Now attending Rural University on an athletic scholarship, May had immigrated with her family from Eastern Europe to Israel. The daughter of a light-skinned, Russian-speaking man and a dark-skinned, Arabic-speaking woman, May described being frequently mistaken for having been orphaned and adopted by whichever parent she was seen with alone in public.

Because these three students strongly identified as multiracial and, understanding the purpose of my research, requested to be included, I decided to include them. Their experiences are reflected both in the aggregated Liberal Arts College and Rural University data and in individual attributions in the text. I discuss the complications of international experience in contrast to life in the highly racialized United States at various points in the book, and the voices of these three students are an important part of the story of college students with multiple heritages.

6. OMB Directive 15 stipulated that by January 1, 2003, all federal agencies, including those that manage data relating to higher education, must do so. As of November 2003, the Integrated Postsecondary Education Data System, a project of the U.S. Department of Education's National Center for Education Statistics, had not announced final categories for racial and ethnic data collection and was recommending that institutions not make changes (see Renn & Lunceford, 2002 for an analysis of the delay in implementation).

CHAPTER THREE

1. I am deeply indebted to research assistant Christine Pereira for raising this important point and to my colleague Anna Ortiz for pressing me to think more deeply about it.

2. Names for students depicted by the five composite portraits are fictional. These portraits represent an amalgamation of student experiences and are not meant to represent any individual study participant.

3. It is important to note that the high percentage of students identifying in this pattern is likely due in part to the way I recruited participants. I discuss this factor in more detail in the research design section of chapter 2.

4. There is a stereotype that interracial marriages, faced with the additional pressures of societal discrimination, are more fragile than marriages of people of the same racial category. My data do not support this stereotype; parents of students in my study remained married at a disproportionate rate as compared to the general population,

where nearly one in two marriages ends in divorce (U.S. Census Bureau, 2001). In their interviews, several students raised the issue of the stereotyped fragility of interracial marriages, concerned that I not reinforce it through my research. I told them that a very high percentage of participants had parents who remained married (eighteen of twenty-four in Phase II of the study) and asked them why they thought that might be. Some of the explanations offered included: socioeconomic privilege associated with families that are able to send children to college and the reduced stress on marriages that accompanies that economic privilege; conscious decisions on the part of parents to work hard to stay in difficult relationships so as not to create additional stress for children who were already "different" from other kids; and decreased societal disapproval of interracial families. I suspect that the socioeconomic argument may be a strong contributing factor; over half of the students I interviewed attended independent institutions whose tuition bills might require a dual income. Children of divorced parents might not be able to afford such a school and might therefore be underrepresented among the student bodies from which my sample was drawn.

5. The idea that whites do not have a racialized identity is one to which I do not subscribe. The "color-blind" philosophy that dominated antiracist discourse of the 1970s assumed that assimilation to the (white, middle-class) norm was desirable. The "tolerance" and "welcoming diversity" mantras prevalent in the 1980s reinforced the notion that whiteness was the norm and that everyone else had "culture" that should be at least tolerated, if not welcomed and celebrated. The "pluralism" and "multiculturalism" movements of the late 1990s and early 2000s more clearly articulated the presence of white culture and concomitant white privilege, creating space for the interrogation of whiteness, white culture, and their construction. It is true, however, that students come to college with a range of exposure to these ideas, some attached to a color-blind ideal, others prepared to welcome other (nonwhite) cultures, and some with a clearly defined, progressive sense of white racial and ethnic identity (some students also come with a reactionary, intolerant sense of white racial and ethnic identity, but they are not the subject of this discussion). For an excellent discussion of white identity and multicultural competence, see Anna Ortiz and Robert Rhoads (2000) "Deconstructing whiteness as part of a multicultural educational framework: From theory to practice."

6. For a fuller discussion of the hazards of taking a deconstructionist stance on racial categorization, see Ferber, 1995; Renn, forthcoming; Zack 1995.

7. In describing her respondents, Kilson stated, "I have used the convention of having the father's racial identity precede that of the mother in Biracial labels. A person identified as European American/Asian, for example, has a European American father who was born in the United States and an Asian mother born in Asia" (Kilson, 2001, p. 9). She used hyphens between labels (e.g. African American-Native American) to indicate mixed heritage in parents.

8. Rockquemore and Brunsma (2002) indicated that the total percentage of respondents falling in their four identity categories does not come to one hundred "because we provided individuals with the option of writing their own response to our survey question on racial identity. Only 8 percent of respondents chose to write in something other than what was provided. Many of the write-in responses were subtle

variations of the options we provided and could have been collapsed back into the categories presented. . . . However, we chose not to do this and treated these cases as missing data" (in footnote 27 to chapter 3; p. 152).

CHAPTER FOUR

1. For over twenty-five years, politically active students of color at Ivy had taken the name *Third World* to describe their community. They did so to indicate political solidarity with people of color from developing and colonized nations. Periodically, students, faculty, and/or administrators raised the issue of changing the designation to something more common and less politically charged. At the time of the interview, the term *Third World* was still used in official organizational programs, functions, and structures (e.g., the Third World Center is a building for academic, social, and networking activities; entering students of color are invited to participate in the Third World Transition Program for three days prior to the start of the institutional orientation program for new students).

2. For an in-depth discussion of this phenomenon in relation to mixed race women, see Kerry Ann Rockquemore's (2002) gendered analysis of black/white biracial women's identities.

3. AHANA was the acronym used at Catholic University to denote African, Hispanic, Asian, and Native American. The community of politically and socially active students of color was known as the AHANA community or simply "the AHANAs." Resembling the Third World community at Ivy, AHANA students at Catholic had a strong and distinct student culture, sharply separated from the mainstream white student culture.

CHAPTER FIVE

1. It could be argued that Iranians are white. It can also be argued that they are significantly different from white Americans in culture and appearance and are not viewed as white in the United States. Dave himself said, "I went to a multi-cultural, minority conference. And one girl was saying to me, 'It's a little different being Iranian, because you're not recognized as a minority, people don't really know what you are.' But then in America, being middle eastern isn't counted as a 'real' minority, but we're not counted as being white, either. So it's sort of both." I decided to include Dave in the study because his experience, including the experience of not appearing stereotypically white, substantially resembled that of students who were mixed race according to the OMB racial categories.

CHAPTER SIX

1. As noted in the research design section of chapter 2, the high percentage of students identifying in this pattern is in part an artifact of how I recruited students for the study. Students who did not identify in this pattern would be less likely to respond to a recruiting flyer, email, or announcement seeking bi- and multiracial students.

2. I was also surprised that six of the students had lost a parent, one during early childhood, but the others late in high school or during college. The effect of these deaths on students' identities is not known, though some of them discussed lost opportunities to gain cultural and personal knowledge about the deceased parent and her or his extended family.

3. Phillip clarified his use of "Pilipino" (with a *P*) rather than "Filipino" (with an *F*). He learned the pronunciation from Doug, the FA faculty advisor. "And I say Pilipino with a P because the original language, Tagalog, didn't have an F sound, but it came from Spanish colonization, so Pilipinos in America are trying to empower themselves and go back to their roots by using the P instead of the F. Also, there's another thing where 'pili' means chosen and 'pino' means people, so with the P, it's like the chosen people. A lot of students who Doug has taught, we're using the P, we say Pilipino a lot more, just to empower ourselves in that way."

CHAPTER SEVEN

1. This practice will end in postsecondary education when institutions adopt new standards for collecting and reporting data on race and ethnicity in accordance with forthcoming guidance from the National Center for Education Statistics (NCES) Integrated Postsecondary Education Data System (IPEDS) director. As of fall 2002, 62 percent of a random sample of 127 institutions were still collecting data in the "mark one only" format specified by the Office of Management and Budget in 1977, and 38 percent had changed to a "choose all that apply" and/or expanded category format (Renn & Lunceford, 2002).

CHAPTER EIGHT

1. Having lived in Japan until she moved to the United States for boarding school, Erika tended to conflate "American" and "white." Her mother was a white American, and Erika experienced her own identity as "Japanese and American," meaning Japanese and *white* American.

CHAPTER NINE

1. The question of fractional versus whole assignment of multiple responses is complex and politically fraught. For a discussion of the advantages and disadvantages of various methods of whole and fractional assignment, see Farley, 2001. For a discussion of proposed methods for "bridging" from racial/ethnic data collected before the 1997 revision in OMB standards to data collected under the new standards, see Renn and Lunceford, 2002.

2. For an analysis of the process leading up to the August 2002 notification by NCES that institutions should make no changes until further notice, see Renn and Lunceford, 2002.

References

Alcoff, L. (1995). Mestizo identity. In N. Zack (Ed.), *American mixed race: The culture of microdiversity* (pp. 257–78). Lanham, MD: Rowman & Littlefield.

Allman, K. M. (1996). (Un)natural boundaries. In M. P. P. Root (Ed.), *The multiracial experience: Racial borders as the new frontier* (pp. 277–90). Thousand Oaks, CA: Sage.

American College Personnel Association. (1994). *The student learning imperative: Implications for student affairs.* Washington, DC: Author. Retrieved September 20, 2002, from http://www.acpa.nche.edu/sli/sli.htm.

Anzaldùa, G. (1987). *Borderlands/La frontera: The new mestiza.* San Francisco: Spinsters/Aunt Lute Foundation.

Arnold, K. D. (2000, April). The ecology of college student peer culture: A theoretical framework for research. Paper presented at the Annual Meeting of the American Educational Research Association. New Orleans, LA.

Astin, A. W. (1968). *The college environment.* Washington, DC: American Council on Education.

Astin, A. W. (1977) *Four critical years.* San Francisco: Jossey-Bass.

Astin, A. W. (1984). Student involvement: A developmental theory for higher education. *Journal of College Student Personnel, 25* (4), 297–308.

Astin, A. W. (1993a). An empirical typology of college students. *Journal of College Student Development, 34* (1), 36–46.

Astin, A. W. (1993b). *What matters in college: Four critical years revisited.* San Francisco: Jossey-Bass.

Astin, A. W. (1998). The changing American college student: Thirty-year trends, 1966–96. *Review of Higher Education 21* (2): 115–35.

Astin, A. W. (1999). Involvement in learning revisited: Lessons we have learned. *Journal of College Student Development, 40* (5), 587–98.

Atkinson, D. R., Morten, G., & Sue, D. W. (1979). *Counseling American minorities: A cross cultural perspective.* Dubuque, IA: Brown.

Atkinson, D. R., Morten, G., & Sue, D. W. (1993). *Counseling American Minorities: A Cross-Cultural Perspective* (4th ed.). Dubuque, IA: Brown & Benchmark.

Atkinson, R., & Flint, J. (2001, Summer). Accessing hidden and hard-to-reach populations: Snowball research strategies. *Social Research Update, 33*. Retrieved March 15, 2002, from http://www.soc.surrey.ac.uk/sru/SRU33.html

Azoulay, K. G. (1997). *Black, Jewish, and interracial: It's not the color of your skin, but the race of your kin, and other myths of identity*. Durham, NC: Duke University Press.

Banning, J. H., & Kaiser, L. (1974). An ecological perspective and model for campus design. *Personnel and Guidance Journal, 52*, 370–75.

Baron, D. (1998, April 3). How to be a person, not a number, on the U.S. Census. *The Chronicle of Higher Education*, p. B8.

Barrath, D. A. (1995). Race and racism. In N. Zack (Ed.), *American mixed race: The culture of microdiversity* (pp. 279–86). Lanham, MD: Rowman & Littlefield.

Baxter Magolda, M. B. (1999). Engaging students in active learning. In G. S. Blimling & E. J. Whitt (Eds.), *Good practice in student affairs: Principles to foster student learning* (pp. 21–44). San Francisco: Jossey-Bass.

Bloland, H. G. (1995, September/October). Postmodernism in higher education. *Journal of Higher Education, 66*, 5.

Bordieu, P. (1977). Cultural reproduction and social reproduction. In J. Karabel & A. H. Halsey (Eds.), *Power and ideology in education* (pp. 487–511). New York: Oxford University Press.

Boyatzis, R. E. (1998). *Transforming qualitative information: Thematic analysis and code development*. Thousand Oaks, CA: Sage.

Bradshaw, C. K. (1992). Beauty and the beast: On racial ambiguity. In M. P. P. Root (Ed.), *Racially mixed people in America* (pp. 77–90). Newbury Park, CA: Sage.

Bronfenbrenner, U. (1977). Toward an experimental ecology of human development. *American Psychologist, 32*, 513–31.

Bronfenbrenner, U. (1979). *The ecology of human development: Experiments by nature and design*. Cambridge: Harvard University Press.

Bronfenbrenner, U. (1989). Ecological systems theory. In R. Vasta (Ed.), *Six theories of development* (pp. 187–249). Greenwich, CT: JAI Press.

Bronfenbrenner, U. (1993). The ecology of cognitive development: Research models and fugitive findings. In R. H. Wozniak & K. W. Fischer, (Eds.), *Development in context: Acting and thinking in specific environments* (pp. 3–44). Hillsdale, NJ: Erlbaum.

Bronfenbrenner, U. (1995). Developmental ecology through space and time: A future perspective. In P. Moen, & G. H. Elder, Jr. (Eds.), *Examining lives in context: Perspectives on the ecology of human development* (pp. 619–47). Washington, DC: American Psychological Association.

Brown, P. M. (1990). Biracial identity and social marginality. *Child and adolescent social work, 7* (4), 319–37.

Brown, U. M. (1995). Black/white interracial young adults: Quest for racial identity. *American Journal of Orthopsychiatry, 65* (1), 125–30.

Camper, C. (Ed). (1994). *Miscegenation blues: Voices of mixed-race women*. Toronto, Canada: Sister Vision Press.

Cass, V. C. (1979). Homosexual identity formation: A theoretical model. *Journal of Homosexuality, 4* (3), 219–35.

Cauce, A. M., Hiraga, Y., Mason, C., Aguilar, T., Ordonez, N., & Gonzales, N. (1992). Between a rock and a hard place: Social adjustment of biracial youth. In M. P. P. Root (Ed.), *Racially mixed people in America* (pp. 207–22). Newbury Park, CA: Sage.

Cerulo, K. A. (1997). Identity construction: New issues, new directions. *Annual Review of Sociology, 23*, 385–409.

Chao, C. M. (1996) A bridge over troubled waters: Being Eurasion in the U. S. of A. In J. Adleman & G. Enguidanos-Clark (Eds.), *Racism in the lives of women: Testimony, theory, and guides to antiracist practice* (pp. 33–43). New York: Haworth Press.

Chickering, A. W. (1969). *Education and identity*. San Francisco: Jossey-Bass.

Chickering, A. W., & Associates. (1981). *The modern American college: Responding to the new realities of diverse students and a changing society*. San Francisco: Jossey-Bass.

Chickering, A. W., & Havighurst, R. J. (1981). The life cycle. In A. W. Chickering & Associates, *The modern American college: Responding to the new realities of diverse students and a changing society* (pp. 16–50). San Francisco: Jossey-Bass.

Chickering, A. W., & Reisser, L. (1993). *Education and identity* (2nd ed.). San Francisco: Jossey-Bass.

Clancy, J. (1995). Multiracial identity assertion in the sociopolitical context of primary education. In N. Zack (Ed.), *American mixed race: The culture of microdiversity* (pp. 211–20). Lanham, MD: Rowman & Littlefield.

Clark, B. R. & Trow, M. (1966). The organizational context. In T. M. Newcomb and E. K. Wilson (Eds.), *College peer groups: Problems and prospects for research* (pp. 17–70). Chicago: Aldine.

Coffey, A., & Atkinson, P. (1996). *Making sense of qualitative data: Complementary research strategies*. Thousand Oaks, CA: Sage.

Cornel, S., & Hartmann, D. (1998). *Ethnicity and race: Making identities in a changing world*. Thousand Oaks, CA: Pine Forge Press.

Cross, W. (1987). A two-factor theory of black identity formation: Implications for the study of identity development in minority children. In J. S. Phinney & M. J. Rotheram (Eds.), *Children's ethnic socialization: Pluralism and development* (pp. 117–33). Newbury Park, CA: Sage.

Cross, W. (1991). *Shades of black: Diversity in African American identity*. Philadelphia: Temple University Press.

Cross, W. E., Jr. (1995). The psychology of nigrescence: Revising the Cross model. In J. G. Ponterotto, J. M. Casas, L. A. Suzuki, & C. M. Alexander (Eds.), *Handbook of multicultural counseling* (pp. 93–122). Thousand Oaks, CA: Sage.

D'Augelli, A. R. (1994). Identity development and sexual orientation: Toward a model of lesbian, gay, and bisexual development. In E. J. Trickett, R. J. Watts, & D. Birman (Eds.), *Human diversity: Perspectives on people in context* (pp. 312–33). San Francisco: Jossey-Bass.

Dalton, J. C. & Petrie, A. M. (1997). The power of peer culture. *The Educational Record, 78* (3–4), 18–24.

Daniel, G. R. (1992). Beyond black and white: The new multiracial consciousness. In M. P. P. Root (Ed.), *Racially mixed people in America* (pp. 333–41). Newbury Park, CA: Sage.

Daniel, G. R. (1996). Black and white identity in the new millennium: Unsevering the ties that bind. In M. P. P. Root (Ed.), *The multiracial experience: Racial borders as the new frontier* (pp. 121–39). Thousand Oaks, CA: Sage.

Davis, F. J. (1991). *Who is black? One nation's definition.* University Park: Pennsylvania State University Press.

Erikson, E. (1968). *Identity, youth, and crisis.* New York: W.W. Norton.

Evans, N. J., Forney, D. S., & Guido-DiBrito, F. (1998). *Student development in college: Theory, research, and practice.* San Francisco: Jossey-Bass.

Farley, R. (2001). *Identifying with multiple races: A social movement that succeeded but failed?* PSC Research Report no. 01–491. Ann Arbor: Population Studies Center at the Institute for Social Research, University of Michigan. Retrieved October 17, 2002, from http://www.psc.isr.umich.edu/pubs/papers/rr01–491.pdf

Feldman, K. A., & Newcomb, T. M. (1969). *The impact of college on students.* San Francisco: Jossey-Bass.

Ferber, A. L (1995). Exploring the social construction of race. In N. Zack (Ed.), *American mixed race: The culture of microdiversity* (pp. 155–68). Lanham, MD: Rowman & Littlefield.

Field, L. D. (1996). Piecing together the puzzle: Self-concept and group identity in biracial black/white youth. In M. P. P. Root (Ed.), *The multiracial experience: Racial borders as the new frontier* (pp. 211–26). Thousand Oaks, CA: Sage.

Fowler, J. (1976). Stages of faith: The structured developmental approach. In T. C. Hennessey (Ed.), *Values and moral development* (pp. 173–211). New York: Paulist Press.

Funderberg, L. (1994). *Black, white, other: Biracial Americans talk about race and identity.* New York: William Morrow.

Gergen, K. J. (1991). *The saturated self: Dilemmas of identity in contemporary life.* New York: Basic Books.

Gibbs, J. T. (1989). Biracial adolescents. In J. T. Gibbs, L. M. Huang, & Associates (Eds.), *Children of color: Psychological interventions with minority youth* (pp. 322–50). San Francisco: Jossey-Bass.

Gibbs, J. T., & Hines, A. M. (1992). Negotiating ethnic identity: Issues for black-white biracial adolescents. In M. P. P. Root (Ed.), *Racially mixed people in America* (pp. 223–38). Newbury Park, CA: Sage.

Gilligan, C. (1977). In a different voice: Women's conceptions of self and morality. *Harvard Educational Review, 47,* 481–517.

Gilligan, C. (1981). Moral development. In C. W. Chickering & Associates, *The modern American college: Responding to the new realities of diverse students and a changing society* (pp. 139–57). San Francisco: Jossey-Bass.

Giroux, H. (1992). *Border crossings: Cultural workers and the politics of education.* New York: Routledge.

Glaser, B., & Strauss, A. L. (1967). *The discovery of grounded theory: Strategies for qualitative research.* Chicago: Aldine.

Goldberg, D. T. (1995). Made in the USA. In N. Zack (Ed.), *American mixed race: The culture of microdiversity* (pp. 237–56). Lanham, MD: Rowman & Littlefield.

Graham, S. R. (1996). The real world. In M. P. P. Root (Ed.), *The multiracial experience: Racial borders as the new frontier* (pp. 37–48). Thousand Oaks, CA: Sage.

Grove, K. J. (1991). Identity development in interracial Asian/white late adolescents: Must it be so problematic? *Journal of Youth and Adolescence, 20,* 617–28.

Hall, C. C. I. (1992). Please choose one: Ethnic identity choices for biracial individuals. In M. P. P. Root (Ed.), *Racially mixed people in America* (pp. 250–64). Newbury Park, CA: Sage.

Hall, C. C. I. (1996). 2001: A race odyssey. In M. P. P. Root (Ed.), *The multiracial experience: Racial borders as the new frontier* (pp. 395–410). Thousand Oaks, CA: Sage.

Heath, D. H. (1978). A model of becoming a liberally educated and mature student. In C. A. Parker (Ed.), *Encouraging development in college students* (pp. 189–212). Minneapolis: University of Minnesota Press.

Helms, J. E. (1990). *Black and white racial identity: Theory, research, and practice.* New York: Greenwood Press.

Helms, J. E. (1995). An update of Helms's white and people of color racial identity models. In J. G. Ponterotto, J. M. Casas, L. A. Suzuki, & C. M. Alexander (Eds.), *Handbook of multicultural counseling* (pp. 181–98). Thousand Oaks, CA: Sage.

Herschel, H. J. (1995). Therapeutic perspectives on biracial identity formation and internalized oppression. In N. Zack (Ed.), *American mixed race: The culture of microdiversity* (pp. 169–81). Lanham, MD: Rowman & Littlefield.

Herschel, H. J. (1997). The influence of gender and race status on self-esteem during childhood and adolescence. In N. Zack (Ed.), *Race/sex: Their sameness, difference, and interplay* (pp. 109–16). New York: Routledge.

Holland, J. L. (1966). *The psychology of vocational choice: A theory of personality types and model environments.* Waltham, MA: Blaisdell.

Horowitz, H. L. (1987). *Campus life: Undergraduate cultures from the end of the eighteenth century to the present.* New York: Knopf.

Hu, S., & St. John, E. P. (2001). Student persistence in a public higher education system: Understanding racial and ethnic differences. *Journal of Higher Education, 72* (3), 265–86.

Jones, L. (1994). *Bulletproof diva: Tales of race, sex and hair*. New York: Doubleday.

Jones, N. A., & Smith, A. S. (2001). *The two or more races population: 2000*. Census 2000 Brief. Washington, DC: U.S. Census Bureau.

Jones, S. R., & McEwen, M. K. (2000). A conceptual model of multiple dimensions of identity. *Journal of College Student Development, 41* (4), 405–14.

Josselson, R. (1987). *Finding herself: Pathways to identity development in women*. San Francisco: Jossey-Bass.

Katchadourian, H., & Boli, J. (1985). *Careerism and intellectualism among college students*. San Francisco: Jossey-Bass.

Kegan, R. (1982). *The evolving self: Problem and process in human development*. Cambridge: Harvard University Press.

Kegan, R. (1994). *In over our heads: The mental demands of modern life*. Cambridge: Harvard University Press.

Kerwin, C. (1991). Racial identity development in biracial children of black/white racial heritage. (Unpublished doctoral dissertation, Fordham University).

Kerwin, C., & Ponterotto, J. G. (1995). Biracial identity development: Theory and research. In J. G. Ponterotto, J. M. Casas, L. A. Suzuki, & C. M. Alexander (Eds.), *Handbook of multicultural counseling* (pp. 199–217). Thousand Oaks, CA: Sage.

Kerwin, C., Ponterotto, J. G., Jackson, B. L., & Harris, A. (1993). Racial identity in biracial children: A qualitative investigation. *Journal of Counseling Psychology, 40* (2), 221–31.

Kich, G. K. (1992). The developmental process of asserting a biracial, bicultural identity. In M. P. P. Root (Ed.), *Racially mixed people in America* (pp. 263–76). Thousand Oaks, CA: Sage.

Kich, G. K. (1996). In the margins of sex and race: Difference, marginality, and flexibility. In M. P. P. Root (Ed.), *The multiracial experience: Racial boundaries as the new frontier* (pp. 304–20). Newbury Park, CA: Sage.

Kilson, M. (2001). *Claiming place: Biracial young adults of the post–civil rights era*. Westport, CT: Bergin & Garvey.

King, P. M., & Kitchener, K. S. (1994). *Developing reflective judgment: Understanding and promoting intellectual growth and critical thinking in adolescents and adults*. San Francisco: Jossey-Bass.

King, R. C., & DaCosta, K. M. (1996). Changing face, changing race: The remaking of race in the Japanese American and African American communities. In M. P. P. Root (Ed.), *The multiracial experience: Racial borders as the new frontier* (pp. 227–44). Thousand Oaks, CA: Sage.

Kohlberg, L. (1976) Moral stages and moralization: The cognitive-developmental approach. In T. Lickona (Ed.), *Moral development and behavior: Theory, research and social issues*. New York: Holt, Rinehart, and Winston.

Kuh, G. D. (1990). Assessing student culture. In W. G. Tierney, (Ed.), *Assessing academic climates and cultures* (pp. 47–60). San Francisco: Jossey-Bass.

Kuh, G. D. (1995). Cultivating "high-stakes" student culture research. *Research in Higher Education, 36* (5), 563–76.

Kuh, G. D. (1996). Guiding principles for creating seamless learning environments for undergraduates. *Journal of College Student Development, 37* (2), 135–48.

Kuh, G. D., Hu, S., & Vesper, N. (2000). "They shall be known by what they do": An activities-based typology of college students. *Journal of College Student Development, 41* (2), 228–44.

Kuh, G. D., Schuh, J. H., & Whitt, E. J. (1991). *Involving colleges.* San Francisco: Jossey-Bass.

Lewin, K. (1935). *A dynamic theory of personality.* New York: McGraw-Hill.

Marcia, J. E. (1966). Development and validation of ego identity status. *Journal of Personality and Social Psychology, 3,* 551–58.

Marcia, J. E. (1980). Identity in adolescence. In J. Adelson (Ed.), *Handbook of adolescent psychology* (pp. 159–87). New York: Wiley.

Mass, A. I. (1992). Interracial Japanese Americans: The best of both worlds or the end of the Japanese American community? In M. P. P. Root (Ed.), *Racially mixed people in America* (pp. 265–79). Newbury Park, CA: Sage.

McDonough, P. M., Antonio, A. L., & Trent, J. W. (1997). Black students, black colleges: An African American college choice model. *Journal for a Just and Caring Education, 3,* (1), 9–36.

Miles, M. B., & Huberman, A. M. (1994). *Qualitative data analysis: An expanded sourcebook.* Thousand Oaks, CA: Sage.

Miller, R. L. (1992). The human ecology of multiracial identity. In M. P. P. Root (Ed.), *Racially mixed people in America* (pp. 24–36). Newbury Park, CA: Sage.

Minerbrook, S. (1996). *Divided to the vein: A journey into race and family.* New York: Harcourt Brace.

Moos, R. H. (1979). *Evaluating educational environments: Procedures, measures, findings, and policy implications.* San Francisco: Jossey-Bass.

Moraga, C. (1993). *The last generation.* Boston: South End Press.

Nakashima, C. L. (1992). An invisible monster: The creation and denial of mixed-race people in America. In M. P. P. Root (Ed.), *Racially mixed people in America* (pp. 162–78). Newbury Park, CA: Sage.

Nakashima, C. L. (1996). Voices from the movement: Approaches to multiraciality. In M. P. P. Root (Ed.), *The multiracial experience: Racial borders as the new frontier* (pp. 79–97). Thousand Oaks, CA: Sage.

National Center for Education Statistics. (2001). *Digest of education statistics, 2001.* Retrieved online December 15, 2002 from http://www.nces.ed.gov/pubs2002/digest2001/tables/dt207.asp

Newcomb, T. M. (1966). The general nature of peer group influence. In T. M. Newcomb & E. K. Wilson (Eds.), *College peer groups* (pp. 2–16). National Opinion Research Center Monographs in Social Research. Chicago: Aldine.

Office of Management and Budget. (1997). Revisions to the Standards for the Classification of Federal Data on race and ethnicity. Retrieved April 23, 2002 from http://www.whitehouse.gov/omb/fedreg/ombdir15.html

Ortiz, A. M., & Rhoads, R. A. (2000). Deconstructing whiteness as part of a multicultural educational framework: From theory to practice. *Journal of College Student Development, 41* (1), 81–93.

Pascarella, E. T., & Terenzini, P. T. (1991). *How college affects students.* San Francisco: Jossey-Bass.

Perry, W. G. (1981). Cognitive and ethical growth: The making of meaning. In A. W. Chickering & Associates, *The modern American college: Responding to the new realities of diverse students and a changing society* (pp. 76–116). San Francisco: Jossey-Bass.

Perry, W. G., Jr. (1968). *Forms of intellectual and ethical development in the college years: A scheme.* New York: Holt, Rinehart, & Winston.

Phinney, J. (1990). Ethnic identity in adolescents and adults: Review of research. *Psychological Bulletin, 108,* 499–514.

Pinderhughes, E. (1995). Biracial identity—Asset or handicap? In H. W. Harris, H. C. Blue, & E. E. H. Griffith (Eds.), *Racial and ethnic identity: Psychological development and creative expression* (pp. 73–93). New York: Routledge.

Poston, W. S. C. (1990). The biracial identity development model: A needed addition. *Journal of Counseling and Development, 69,* 152–55.

Reisser, L. (1995). Revisiting the seven vectors. *Journal of College Student Development, 36* (6), 505–11

Renn, K. A. (1997, March). *(De)construction work ahead: Bi/multiracial college students give meaning to race, identity and community.* Paper presented at the University of Pennsylvania Ethnography in Education Research Forum, Philadelphia, PA.

Renn, K. A. (1998). Claiming Space: The College Experience of Biracial and Multiracial Students on Predominantly White Campuses. Unpublished doctoral dissertation. Chestnut Hill, MA: Boston College.

Renn, K. A. (2000). Patterns of situational identity among biracial and multiracial college students. *The Review of Higher Education, 23,* 399–420.

Renn, K. A. (forthcoming). Tilting at windmills: The paradox and promise of researching mixed race, with strategies for scholars. In K. R. Wallace (Ed.), *Working with multiracial students: Critical perspectives on research and practice.* Greenwich, CT: Information Age Publishing.

Renn, K. A. (2003). Understanding the identities of mixed race college students through a developmental ecology lens. Accepted for publication in the *Journal of College Student Development, 44,* 383–403.

Renn, K. A., & Arnold, K. D. (2003). Reconceptualizing research on peer culture. *Journal of Higher Education, 74*, 261–91.

Renn, K. A., & Bilodeau, B. (2002, November). *Queer student leaders: A case study of leadership development and lesbian, gay, bisexual, and transgender student involvement.* Paper presented at the 27th meeting of the Association for the Study of Higher Education, Sacramento, CA.

Renn, K. A., & Lunceford, C. L. (2002, November). *Because the numbers matter: Transforming racial/ethnic reporting data to account for mixed race students in postsecondary education.* Paper presented at the 27th meeting of the Association for the Study of Higher Education, Sacramento, CA.

Rhoads, R. A. (1997). Interpreting identity politics: The educational challenge of contemporary student activism. *Journal of College Student Development, 38* (5), 508–19.

Rich, A. (1986). *Blood, bread, and poetry: Selected prose 1978–1985.* New York: Norton.

Rockquemore, K. A. (2002). Negotiating the color line: The gendered process of identity construction among Black/White biracial women. *Gender and Society, 16*, 485–503.

Rockquemore, K. A., & Brunsma, D. L. (2002). *Beyond black: Biracial identity in America.* Thousand Oaks, CA: Sage.

Root, M. P. P. (1990). Resolving "other" status: Identity development of biracial individuals. *Women and Therapy, 9* (1/2), 185–205.

Root, M. P. P. (1992a). Back to the drawing board: Methodological issues in research on multiracial people. In M. P. P. Root (Ed.), *Racially mixed people in America* (pp. 181–89). Newbury Park, CA: Sage.

Root, M. P. P. (1992b). Within, between, and beyond race. In M. P. P. Root (Ed.), *Racially mixed people in America* (pp. 3–11). Newbury Park, CA: Sage.

Root, M. P. P. (1995). The multiracial contribution to the psychological browning of America. In N. Zack (Ed.), *American mixed race: The culture of microdiversity* (pp. 231–36). Lanham, MD: Rowman & Littlefield.

Root, M. P. P. (1996a). A bill of rights for racially mixed people. In M. P. P. Root (Ed.), *The multiracial experience: Racial borders as the new frontier* (pp. 3–14). Thousand Oaks, CA: Sage.

Root, M. P. P. (1996b). The multiracial experience: Racial borders as a significant frontier in race relations. In M. P. P. Root (Ed.), *The multiracial experience: Racial borders as the new frontier* (pp. xiii–xxviii). Thousand Oaks, CA: Sage.

Root, M. P. P. (1997). Mixed race women. In N. Zack (Ed.), *Race/sex: Their sameness, difference, and interplay* (pp. 157–72). New York: Routledge.

Sanford, N. (1960). *Self and society.* New York: Atherton Press.

Sebring, D. (1985). Considerations in counseling interracial children. *Journal of non-White Concerns in Personnel and Guidance, 13*, 3–9.

Seidman, I. E. (1991). *Interviewing as qualitative research: A guide for researchers in education and the social sciences*. New York: Teachers College Press.

Shrage, L. (1995). Ethnic transgressions: Confessions of an assimilated Jew. In N. Zack (Ed.), *American mixed race: The culture of microdiversity* (pp. 287–96). Lanham, MD: Rowman & Littlefield.

Sodowsky, G. R., Kwan, K. K., & Pannu, R. (1995). Ethnic identity in Asians in the United States. In J. G. Ponterotto, J. M. Casas, L. A. Suzuki, & C. M. Alexander (Eds.), *Handbook of multicultural counseling* (pp. 123–54). Thousand Oaks, CA: Sage.

Solomon, B. M. (1985). *In the company of educated women*. New Haven: Yale University Press.

Spickard, P. R. (1989). *Mixed blood: Intermarriage and ethnic identity in twentieth-century America*. Madison: University of Wisconsin Press.

Spickard, P. R. (1992). The illogic of American racial categories. In M. P. P. Root (Ed.), *Racially mixed people in America* (pp. 12–23). Newbury Park, CA: Sage.

Standen, B. C. C. (1996). Without a template: The biracial Korean/white experience. In M. P. P. Root (Ed.), *The multiracial experience: Racial borders as the new frontier* (pp. 245–59). Thousand Oaks, CA: Sage.

Stephan, C. W. (1992). Mixed-heritage individuals: Ethnic identity and trait characteristics. In M. P. P. Root (Ed.), *Racially mixed people in America* (pp. 50–63). Newbury Park, CA: Sage.

Stonequist, E. V. (1937). *The marginal man: A study in personality and culture conflict*. New York: Russell & Russell.

Strange, C. C., & Banning, J. H. (2001). *Educating by design: Creating campus learning environments that work*. San Francisco : Jossey-Bass.

Strauss, A., & Corbin, J. (1994). Grounded theory methodology: An overview. In N. K. Denzin & Y. S. Lincoln (Eds.), *Handbook of qualitative research* (pp. 273–85). Thousand Oaks, CA: Sage.

Streeter, C. A. (1996). Ambiguous bodies: Locating black/white women in cultural representations. In M. P. P. Root (Ed.), *The multiracial experience: Racial borders as the new frontier* (pp. 305–20). Thousand Oaks, CA: Sage.

Stuart, I. R., & Abt, L. E. (1973). *Interracial marriage: Expectations and realities*. New York: Grossman.

Szelenyi, K. (2002). Multiple race data in higher education research: Implications for the racial categorization of biracial college students. Paper presented at the Association for the Study of Higher Education, Sacramento, CA.

Tatum, B. D. (1995). *"Why are all the black kids sitting together in the cafeteria?" and other conversations about race*. New York: Basic Books.

Terenzini, P. T., Cabrera, A. F., Colbeck, C. L., Bjorklund, S. A., & Parente, J. M. (2001). Racial and ethnic diversity in the classroom: Does it promote student learning? *Journal of Higher Education, 72*, 509–31.

Terenzini, P. T., Pascarella, E. T., & Blimling, G. S. (1996). Students' out-of-class experiences and their influence on learning and cognitive development: A literature review. *Journal of College Student Development, 37,* 149–62.

Thomas, R., & Chickering, A. W. (1984). Education and identity revisited. *Journal of College Student Personnel, 25* (5), 392–99.

Thornton, M. C., & Wason, S. (1995). Intermarriage. In D. Levinson, (Ed.), *Encyclopedia of marriage and the family* (396–402). New York: Macmillan.

Tierney, W. G. (1993). *Building communities of difference.* Westport, CT: Bergin & Garvey.

Tinto, V. (1993). *Leaving college: Rethinking the causes and cures of student attrition.* Chicago: University of Chicago Press.

Tizard, B., & Phoenix, A. (1993). *Black, white or mixed race? Race and racism in the lives of young people of mixed parentage.* London: Routledge.

Twine, F. W. (1996). Heterosexual alliances: The romantic management of racial identity. In M. P. P. Root (Ed.), *The multiracial experience: Racial borders as the new frontier* (pp. 291–304). Thousand Oaks, CA: Sage.

U.S. Census Bureau. (2001). *Mapping Census 2000: The geography of diversity.* Retrieved March 15, 2002, from http://factfinder.census.gov

U.S. Census Bureau. (2002). *Interracial married couples: 1980 to present.* Retrieved online December 15, 2002, from http://www.census.gov/population/socdemo/hh-fam/tabMS-3.txt

Wachs, T. D. (1992). *The nature of nurture.* Individual Differences and Development Series, Volume 3. Newbury Park, CA: Sage.

Wallace, K. R. (2001). *Relative/outsider: The art and politics of identity among mixed heritage students.* Westport, CT: Ablex.

Weidman, J. C. (1989). Undergraduate socialization: A conceptual approach. In J. C. Smart (Ed.), *Higher education: Handbook of theory and research, Volume 5* (pp. 289–322) New York: Agathon.

Weisman, J. (1996). An "other" way of life: The employment of alterity in the interracial individual. In M. P. P. Root (Ed.), *The multiracial experience: Racial borders as the new frontier* (pp. 152–66). Thousand Oaks, CA: Sage.

Williams, G. H. (1995). *Life on the color line: The true story of a white boy who discovered he was black.* New York: Penguin Books.

Williams, T. K. (1996). Race as process: Reassessing the "What are you?" encounters of biracial individuals. In M. P. P. Root (Ed.), *The multiracial experience: Racial borders as the new frontier* (pp. 191–210). Thousand Oaks, CA: Sage.

Williams, T. K., Nakashima, C. L., Kich, G. K., & Daniel, G. R. (1996). Being different together in a university classroom: Multiracial identity as transgressive education. In M. P. P. Root (Ed.), *The multiracial experience: Racial borders as the new frontier* (pp. 359–79). Thousand Oaks, CA: Sage.

Williamson, J. (1995). *New people: Miscegenation and mulattoes in the United States.* Baton Rouge: Louisiana State University Press.

Yemma, J. (1997, May 11). Race debate simmers over who is what. *The Boston Globe*, pp. 1, A30.

Youn, T. I. K., Arnold, K. D., & Salkever, K. (1998). *Baccalaureate origins and career attainments of American Rhodes Scholars.* Paper presented at the meeting of the Association for the Study of Higher Education, Miami, FL.

Zack, N. (1993). *Race and mixed race.* Philadelphia: Temple University Press.

Zack, N. (1995). Life after race. In N. Zack (Ed.), *American mixed race: The culture of microdiversity* (pp. 297–307). Lanham, MD: Rowman & Littlefield.

Index

SUNY series: Frontiers in Education
Philip G. Altbach, Editor

List of Titles

Community Colleges as Cultural Texts: Qualitative Explorations of Organizational and Student Culture—Kathleen M. Shaw, James R. Valadez, and Robert A. Rhoads (eds.)

Educational Knowledge: Changing Relationships between the State, Civil Society, and the Educational Community—Thomas S. Popkewitz (ed.)

Transnational Competence: Rethinking the U.S.-Japan Educational Relationship—John N. Hawkins and William K. Cummings (eds.)

Women Administrators in Higher Education: Historical and Contemporary Perspectives—Jana Nidiffer and Carolyn Terry Bashaw (eds.)

Faculty Work in Schools of Education: Rethinking Roles and Rewards for the Twenty-first Century—William G. Tierney (ed.)

The Quest for Equity in Higher Education: Towards New Paradigms in an Evolving Affirmative Action Era—Beverly Lindsay and Manuel J. Justiz (eds.)

The Racial Crisis in American Higher Education (Revised Edition): Continuing Challenges for the Twenty-first Century—William A. Smith, Philip G. Altbach, and Kofi Lomotey (eds.)

Increasing Access to College: Extending Possibilities for All Students—William G. Tierney and Linda Serra Hagedorn (eds.)

Burning Down the House: Politics, Governance, and Affirmative Action at the University of California—Brian Pusser

Mixed Race Students in College: The Ecology of Race, Identity, and Community on Campus—Kristen A. Renn

From High School to College: Evaluating Access—William G. Tierney, Zoë B. Corwin, and Julia E. Colyar (eds.)

9626803R00175

Made in the USA
San Bernardino, CA
21 March 2014